CONSERVATISM INC.

D1569057

JAMES KIRKPATRICK

CONSERVATISM —— INC. ——

THE BATTLE
for the
AMERICAN RIGHT

ARKTOS
LONDON 2019

ISBN	978-1-912975-55-6 (Softcover)
	978-1-912975-56-3 (Ebook)
EDITING & LAYOUT	John Bruce Leonard
COVER	Tor Westman

⊕ Arktos.com   f fb.com/Arktos   🐦 @arktosmedia   ⓞ arktosmedia

TABLE OF CONTENTS

PREFACE

Peter Brimelow

The Beat poet Allan Ginsberg famously wrote in Howl (1956):

> I saw the best minds of my generation destroyed by madness,
>> starving hysterical naked,
> dragging themselves through the negro streets at dawn looking
>> for an angry fix…

Of course, this was ridiculous rubbish. The counter-culture that Ginsberg personified was in fact eagerly embraced by America's intellectual Establishment and he himself was inundated with honors by the time he reached middle age.

In contrast, however, I actually have seen a generation destroyed, or at least beaten to the ground — not by "madness," but because it told the truth.

It's not my generation: I am, alas, a Boomer. (I never liked them. I think my twin brother and I are the only Boomers who never smoked marijuana.)

And it is, in fact, two generations — I've seen so many individuals from both Generation X (mid-1960s-early 1980s) and Millennials (early 1980s-early 2000s) marginalized, silenced, their careers, even in completely non-political areas where their professional performance had never been impugned, nevertheless destroyed because they dared to question the Politically Correct Narrative — above all on race and, my particular concern as Editor of VDARE.com, on immigration.

This is a Reign Of Terror far more serious, and much longer lasting, than the much-denounced phenomenon of "McCarthyism." Senator Joseph McCarthy gave his famous Wheeling WVA speech about

Communist subversion in 1950: he was censured by the Senate, generally regarded as the end of his career, in 1954.

Furthermore, McCarthy was right about Communist subversion.

In contrast, this Reign Of Terror has been rising for decades; I believe that it dates to the late 1960s and the Ruling Class's imperative need to repress mounting evidence that the egalitarian assumptions of the 1964 Civil Rights Act were disastrously wrong. And it has dramatically intensified, especially via corporate Cultural Marxist censorship of the internet, in reaction to President Donald J. Trump's upset election in November 2016.

Moreover, unlike Ginsberg and his groupies, the victims of this new Terror are not perverts, druggies and Communists. They are, generally, family-oriented tax-paying patriots. America's auto-immune system has turned on itself.

James Kirkpatrick, whose work is celebrated in this volume, is widely regarded, by severe judges, as the most brilliant political writer of his (Millennial) generation. You have never seen him interviewed on network or even cable television, profiled in the prestige press, invited to address a college commencement (a significant but unspoken slush fund for the Left), or receiving a MacArthur Award. In every respect, he is the opposite of Conservatism Inc.'s Ben Shapiro or, needless to say, the Main Stream Media's Alexandra Ocasio-Cortes. Once a rising figure in the Beltway Right, he has for some years now lived in prudent obscurity (see Reign Of Terror, above). Nevertheless, to the extent that the civilization of the West survives, and even revives, it is his name that will be remembered.

Most of the articles in this volume first appeared in VDARE.com, which I edit. From an editor's point of view, Kirkpatrick is a godsend. His intense pieces seem to be written in a sort of Dionysiac frenzy, taking remarkably little time from commission to filing, arriving essentially letter perfect. His only flaw: a tendency to despair, which is (as he should know) prohibited by Christian theology. But in his case, and in the case of his generation, it's understandable… if, from my battle-scarred Boomer perspective, premature.

Reading this volume, I find myself deeply moved by Kirkpatrick's account, original to this volume, of his personal experience of Trump's November 8, 2016 victory:

> Casually endangering my own life and the lives of around me, I kept lurking on /pol/, posting on *VDARE*'s Twitter account, and refreshing the vote counts while speeding around heavy northern-Virginia traffic. Of all nights, I was somehow able to secure a parking spot near the hotel. Already, there was a crowd both inside and outside the [Trump] hotel. ...
>
> To be on the "far right" when young is to doom yourself to being a Cassandra. You know, and you accept, that your prophecies will go unheeded. ...
>
> Thus, there was a sense of unreality at the moment of victory. It was the culmination of that magical, literally magical feeling that had been building over the past year, that certain laws no longer applied, that a new era had begun. Novus ordo seclorum. The resistance from within the conservative movement had been so fierce, and the hysteria from the leftists so unlimited, that it was likewise easy to imagine that "we" had just taken power, in the same sense as if we had marched on Rome or seized the Winter Palace. Maybe I'd be running an office in the Department of Homeland Security under Kris Kobach. Maybe he'd shut down the Antifa networks nationwide. Maybe Peter Brimelow would give the keystone address at CPAC next year! Anything seemed possible.

Kirkpatrick, in his gloomy way, contrasts this moment to the Trump Administration's subsequently unfulfilled (as yet) promise. But it reminds me of another poem, G. K. Chesterton's The Donkey:

> Fools! For I also had my hour;
> One far fierce hour and sweet:
> There was a shout about my ears,
> And palms before my feet.

It needs only to be added that the donkey's hour, however isolated as it may have appeared, was in fact just a precursor to the rise of the greatest civilization in the history of the world.

INTRODUCTION

Against Conservatism Inc.

THE BATTLE FOR THE AMERICAN RIGHT

Except for the pieces unique to this text, these columns were written in the heat of action. They sometimes refer to controversies that have faded away, people who have lost importance, movements that have already flickered out. And yet a theme organically emerges from each part of this work, so that the whole reads like a novel, building slowly to a climax — one that has yet to arrive. The story of the American Right since the 2012 election is the struggle by patriots to redefine the Republican Party as a nationalist party. This requires expelling the parasitic organism that I call "Conservatism Inc." or the "Beltway Right," a conglomeration of nonprofits, media outlets, and membership organizations dedicated to its own survival and profits, not to political victory. The outcome of this struggle is, as of this writing, still in doubt. But what is certain is that the very existence of the historic American nation hinges on the outcome.

The Beltway Rights exists to provide grassroots conservatives with reasons why they are not allowed to pursue productive political action. It is a movement that forever talks about "principles" and "values," both of which are ill-defined and creep ever leftward as the Left's Long March continues. The one eternal principle seems to be that "our values prohibit us from defending our interests."

Within only a few generations, America has been deconstructed culturally, religiously, institutionally, and demographically. Vast swathes of territory and entire cities can be called "American" only in the loosest possible sense. And yet, throughout this entire process, the conservative movement confidently proclaims that America remains a "center-right" nation and that the heirs of William F. Buckley have somehow thwarted the march of history. The truth is far darker. The conservative movement did not stop the revolution. Indeed, it now exists to consolidate and legitimize the leftist victories of the past.

Conservatism Inc.'s complacency conceals the reality that the historic American nation exists under something close to an occupation. Cultural Marxists control the commanding heights of the economy, the media, and what under the Trump Administration has been called the "Deep State" of the permanent bureaucracy. I confess to some embarrassment in writing these words; invoking "Cultural Marxists" and speaking wildly about shadowy foes ensconced in high places reeks of the worst sort of right-wing clickbait. Yet everyone in the country not only knows this reality but has internalized the patterns of behavior appropriate to living under a police state.

Everyone knows that there are certain topics never to be discussed, certain figures never to be criticized, certain people that must be avoided lest you share their terrible fate. Every "movement conservative," no matter how respectable, exists every moment looking over his shoulder. And even a casual glance at the newspaper reveals another random person whose life was destroyed in an instant for making the wrong joke, saying the wrong thing, or holding the wrong opinion. As the standards for what is acceptable seem to change every day, we are in some ways even worse off than those who live under an openly authoritarian political system, because we don't even know what we are and are not allowed to criticize.

Progressives are increasingly defined by their commitment to this program of never-ending social engineering. Of course, there is nothing inherently "conservative" about immigration patriotism. This country would be far better off if Congress had followed the immigration policy recommendations of the late Barbara Jordan, the progressive Georgia Congresswoman who was the first black female to deliver the keynote address to the Democratic National Convention. Yet contemporary progressives understand that their path to permanent electoral supremacy lies in replacing American citizens with a more pliable Third World population.

This is the process that Peter Brimelow, quoting Bertolt Brecht, terms "electing a new people."[1]

It is not possible to ameliorate income inequality, environmental destruction, crumbling infrastructure, low wages, crime, education, health care, or a host of other problems without being an immigration patriot. Yet if progressives have abandoned their traditional concern for the American worker, the leadership of the American conservative movement seems unaware that American workers even exist. Rather than defending the nation, all too many professional conservatives are committed to defending The Economy, an amorphous entity that we are seemingly bound to blindly serve. The conservative movement has the relationship between the nation and the economy fundamentally backwards. The economy exists to serve the nation, not the nation the economy.

Yet no intellectual can make such a case and expect to thrive within the Beltway Right. Subsidized by the cheap labor lobby, trapped in the outdated rhetoric of the Cold War, Conservatism Inc. is not only unable to meet the challenges of the new century, it is unable to even identify what those challenges are. Thus, it is not surprising that they never saw Donald Trump coming. His appeal to the "forgotten man," his promises to protect blue-collar workers and protect American industry, his cry to "Make America Great Again," all of this is as anathema to the shills and hacks of the Beltway Right as were the campaigns of Pat Buchanan, whose legacy was triumphantly redeemed by candidate Trump in 2016.

Yet upon taking office, President Trump in many ways has governed like a typical product of the conservative movement. As of this writing, fall 2018, the economy is booming. Unemployment is at historic lows, especially (as President Trump never ceases to point out) for blacks and Hispanics. The stock market is soaring, consumer confidence is high, and by every measure businesses large and small are eager to make new investments. However, President Trump has largely failed to consolidate the new political coalition his campaign seemingly promised. The Rust Belt is slipping back

---

[1]   From Brecht's 1953 play *Die Lösung*: https://en.wikipedia.org/wiki/Die_L%C3%B6sung.

into Democratic hands, once safe states like Texas and Georgia are looking to go blue, and overt socialism is rising in the once staid Democratic party, fueling an insurgency of eager progressive activists.

The solution for American rightists who want to save their country is to look beyond Donald Trump and see where this movement really came from. As the pieces in this collection make clear, Donald Trump did not emerge out of nowhere. Immigration patriotism, economic populism, and the political formulation I term "National Conservatism" has been percolating on the American Right for almost a decade now. Donald Trump was the first to capture its energy, but even he seems not to have fully realized what he had tapped into. As demographics continue to shift, the political center collapses in both Europe and America, and immigration grows increasingly important with each election cycle, the future of the American Right will depend on brave activists, candidates, and writers willing to break with the taboos of Conservatism Inc. and champion the new National Conservatism that has already proven its ability to create a winning national coalition. Indeed, a candidate even more capable than Donald Trump is likely to emerge in the future and fulfill the promise of 2016.

That is, of course, if the American conservative movement doesn't prevent it. Perhaps the greatest disappointment from the perspective of 2018 is how little the American conservative movement seems to have learned from recent years. Even now, the hucksters and frauds are plotting their comeback, ready to recycle the old shibboleths from the George W. Bush era. Yet no matter what their wishes, President Donald Trump, the political wrecking ball, has changed things permanently. History has restarted and there is no going back. To know where we are going, we have to know where we've been. And this collection is the best guide I can give you to understanding the roots of the new American nationalism.

Thank for you reading, and I'll see you in the trenches.

James Kirkpatrick

PART ONE

THINGS FALL APART

CHAPTER ONE

The Nature of Conservatism Inc.

Those of us who worked in it called it "the movement." Yet it's an open question whether the "conservative movement" is really a movement at all.

Every political, social, and cultural movement in history has been characterized by one organizational truth. This truth is that the leadership is more committed than the followers. Yet this doesn't apply to the conservative movement. Uniquely in history, the conservative movement is led by those less dedicated and committed than the rank and file.

I can name dozens of "movement conservatives" who have given everything to the cause — not just sacrificing time, money, or opportunities, but destroying their own individual futures in the name of the greater good. Young activists will be smeared by the liberal media or catch a beating at protests. Men and women with full time jobs will invest their own money in fledgling conservative organizations, sometimes falling into debt as a consequence. Activists with nothing behind them will investigate leftists, start their own media outlets, and send story after to story to conservative publications, vainly hoping to turn back the relentless progressive tide. And yet, when one surveys the multi-million dollar foundations that litter northern Virginia, they are with few exceptions led by men and women who have never sacrificed anything.

Indeed, they are led by people whose chief qualification is a petty cunning that allows them to eliminate rivals. More than any political grouping, American conservatives are notorious for abandoning their own wounded, almost eagerly throwing their own comrades under the bus at the behest of a mainstream media hit piece or a single phone call by the Southern Poverty Law Center. Unlike progressives, conservatives are always enthusiastic about denouncing the most stalwart and energetic activists on their own side. This is the preferred method for removing competitors within their own organizations or securing a spot as the token "conservative" on a liberal media network. Not surprisingly, many dedicated conservatives eventually quit the movement in disgust, having been betrayed or utterly used up by those they trusted.

I recall one incident when some fellow conservatives and I went to an anarchist convention in disguise. The denizens at the convention smelled terrible, cursed freely, and advocated policies that were monstrously evil. And yet there was an undeniable spirit of comradeship and sacrifice, with people raising money to support fellow activists who had been imprisoned or had suffered financial hardship. Nothing could be more foreign to the fratricidal spirit often found among conservatives. As one young activist put it to me wistfully, "I wish our movement operated this way." (Not long afterward, she quit.)

The weakness and self-centeredness of so many conservative "leaders" is partially explained by the movement's artificial nature. The conservative movement, in its present form, was cobbled together after the Second World War in order to create a coherent opposition to the Soviet Union. In the triumphalist narrative familiar to every conservative, William F. Buckley assembled a cast of intellectuals at *National Review*, loosely united them around Frank Meyer's "fusionism"[1] of social conservatives and free market supporters, and "purged" the unrespectable elements of the movement. After the disastrous defeat of Barry Goldwater in 1964, the movement eventually captured the Republican Party and ultimately succeeded with the election of Ronald Reagan, who brought victory in the Cold War. The moral, as taught to movement conservatives, is the need to be "respectable" and hold to Reagan's traditional tripartite creed defined by free market economics/limited government, a "strong" foreign policy, and social conservatism.

---

1   Edwards, Lee. "The Conservative Consensus: Frank Meyer, Barry Goldwater, and the Politics of Fusionism." January 22, 2007. Accessed March 28, 2019. https://www.heritage.org/political-process/report/the-conservative-consensus-frank-meyer-barry-goldwater-and-the-politics.

Yet this "creed" isn't ideologically coherent. There is no reason that socially libertine Wall Street bankers and fundamentalist Southern evangelicals should be in the same movement without the glue of anti-Communism to hold it together. The conservative coalition was a tactical construction. Its purpose ended with the Cold War. Yet "movement conservatives" seem determined to simply relive the Reagan Administration eternally, trying to substitute "Islamo-fascism" or Putin's Russia as the new existential foe that will hold the movement together.

One wants to accuse conservatives of failing to get with the times. Yet to call American conservatives backward-looking and reactionary is to give them far too much credit. Opposition to civil rights laws or support for the Confederate flag are firing offenses within the Beltway Right, though both were core conservative causes at one time. The same movement conservatives that talk about the eternal "principles" of their theories simply trail behind the leftist vanguard in practice. Indeed, the movement's "principles," which are really just slogans, seem increasingly unconnected to the concrete realities of politics in the 21st century.

Consider the movement's approach to mass immigration. The current wave of non-white immigration to North American and Europe is one of the most historically significant developments in world history. If left unchecked, it could spell the literal end of Western Civilization. Even those who consider this an alarmist prediction should at least concede that admitting unlimited numbers of foreigners into a civilization is a historically unprecedented gamble. It is profoundly unconservative in the most basic sense. And conservatives, out of sheer self-interest, should be worried about it, considering that their electoral base is almost entirely composed of white voters.

Yet "movement conservatives" seem to regard this process both as inevitable and unstoppable. Moreover, the solution proposed by conservative intellectuals is to share "our ideas" with the newcomers and "convert" them. The overwhelming levels of support for leftist parties displayed by blacks and Hispanics in the United States, not to mention the monolithic leftist control over the media, suggests this is a questionable proposition.

Indeed, one might say that anyone who advances such a theory doesn't really believe in his "principles" at all.

Yet this fundamentally misreads the psychology of the American conservative movement and the mindset of its members. The key assumption of American conservatism is that defeat is not possible. As a corollary, conservatives believe that they are somehow still in control of America and that the United States remains a "center-right" nation, even while the Cultural Marxist left dominates almost every media and cultural institution. In contrast, modern leftists style themselves as a "resistance" under siege from a far-right government, even though progressives enjoy the all but monolithic support of media and corporate elites. The Left possesses the concrete reality of power but cloaks itself as a victim. In contrast, the apparatchiks of the Beltway Right, with their business cards, foppish demeanor, and disdain for activism, act as if they are part of an aristocratic ruling class, even though they are all but powerless.

While "conservatism," classically understood, is a pessimistic temperament, the Beltway Right is optimistic, forward-looking, almost naïve. "American exceptionalism" means that limited government and the Constitution are destined to triumph in the end. When there are defeats, they are retconned into victories. Thus, Martin Luther King Jr., the philandering democratic socialist whose efforts to end segregation were initially opposed by William F. Buckley,[2] becomes a Republican hero and a true conservative. The advance of global neoliberalism, which has undermined national loyalties, traditional religious faith, and cultural identities, is celebrated as a liberating force. Even as conservatives are routed from battle to battle, they retain a curious complacency. After all, today's left-wing radical becomes tomorrow's conservative hero.

What the conservative movement actually *does*, besides providing employment for various hangers-on, is lobby for the interests of its donors. Thus, despite the popularity of immigration restrictionism among the

---

2 Buckley, William. "Why The South Must Prevail," *National Review.* https://adamgomez.files.wordpress.com/2012/03/whythesouthmustprevail-1957.pdf.

Republican base, almost every conservative conference features corporate lobbyists arguing for more immigration as part of a "pro-growth" agenda. Despite the importance of the white working-class vote in the Rust Belt to future Republican victories, "free trade" is a staple of the Beltway Right. Despite the reliance of many elderly Republican voters on programs such as Medicare, "entitlement cuts" are part of the conservative platform, even though they are vastly unpopular among the general public. And while American "nationalism" is a dirty word among conservatives, there is not one Beltway Right conference that doesn't feature overwrought tributes to Israel, "our greatest ally," whose own ethno-nationalism is evidently to be praised.

Our principles, conservatives seem to be telling us, prevent us from fighting for our interests. The assumption of victory is key to how the movement functions. "Fighting," after all, presupposes both the possibility of defeat and the existence of an enemy. In contrast, the conservative movement's assumption of victory means that there really is no enemy, at least not on the Left. Thus, politicians like Mitt Romney and Marco Rubio are tolerant of antifa, but sound the alarm about the racial insensitivity of President Trump. Moreover, if politics can be defined as the pursuit of power, movement conservatives aren't even really involved in politics, since they are trying to persuade the world with their universal "principles," not trying to acquire power to defeat enemies.

All of this resembles not so much a political movement as a religious organization. Victory comes not through political mobilization, but through recitations of the true conservative creed—"limited government, free markets, a strong national defense, our Judeo-Christian values." The regular conservative "purges" of the unrespectable right are the excommunications, the withholding of jobs, media access, and funding akin to career damnation. And while there is no serious effort to defeat the Left, movement conservatives have a highly developed political sense when it comes to climbing the career ladder within Conservatism Inc. As in organized religion, personal eccentricities and metaphysical speculations flourish within the Beltway Right. You'll meet everything from market anarchists to reactionary monarchists; one person I met even claimed to be a "Christian Objectivist." Yet all of these postures are essentially meaningless, for so long as they work within the official conservative movement and regard themselves as a part of the Beltway Right, they further an agenda no different than anything produced by the Chamber of Commerce. The pretensions and ideological obsessions of movement conservatives only have meaning when it comes to forming factions competing for jobs and positions within the Beltway Right.

What is the Beltway Right? It is a parasite that endangers the life of its host, the historic American nation. Rather than serving as a vanguard to further the interests of European-America, it exploits the grievances and frustrations of a dying people to fuel policies that actually further that dispossession. For the nation to live, the Beltway Right must be radically reformed, or, more likely, broken.

"All their patriotic words were empty," Joseph Sobran eventually realized about his conservative colleagues. "It was all a game, or a way of making of living." Like the fraternity from *Animal House*, its only purpose is a "long history of existence." Ultimately, a new American Right must be created, less dependent on multi-million dollar foundations, more rooted in the challenges facing the historic American nation. These challenges include increasingly overt anti-white sentiment, the inability to support a family on a single income, collapsing public infrastructure, terrorism, cultural alienation, and above all, the cascading catastrophes engendered by mass Third World immigration. More than that, the asinine combination of goofy naïvete and extreme personal cynicism that characterizes the American conservative movement must be abandoned.

Instead, a spirit of selfless idealism must be married to a mature political philosophy that draws its inspiration from James Burnham, Sam Francis, and other key thinkers that came out of the American conservative movement but transcended it. The existential issue of the next century is identity, the key challenge is resisting the Death of the West, and the template to follow is the Donald Trump campaign of 2016, which proved that National Conservatism *can win*.

This is the mission of our generation. The inevitability of victory cannot be assumed. The danger of extinction is real. And at long last, it is time for a movement that actually moves.

CHAPTER TWO

Romney, the White Working Class, and the Limits of "Economism"

The GOP presidential contender should not have lost.

Take the forecasting model from the University of Colorado. In contrast to many other polls, it stresses state-level economic data. It has accurately predicted the winner of every Presidential election since it was first developed in 1980. In the 2012 election, it projected over 330 electoral votes for the Republican challenger.[1]

There's also unemployment. Only Franklin D. Roosevelt was able to win e-election with unemployment this high.[2] Republicans repeatedly argued that the jobs crisis alone should have guaranteed President Obama's defeat.

Finally, it's a truism that if an incumbent cannot crack a 50% favorable rating in the polls close to an election, he's sunk. In poll after poll, even in the battleground states, Obama failed to obtain a favorable majority.[3]

What actually happened: the decades-long effort to elect a new people

---

1   Caughey, Peter, and David Kelly. "Updated Election Forecasting Model Still Points to Romney Win, University of Colorado Study Says." University of Colorado. October 4, 2012. Accessed May 17, 2018. https://www.colorado.edu/today/2012/10/04/updated-election-forecasting-model-still-points-romney-win-university-colorado-study-says.

2   King, John. "John King: To Win, Obama Must Make History Again — CNNPolitics." CNN. September 04, 2012. Accessed May 17, 2018. https://www.cnn.com/2012/09/03/politics/king-dnc-preview/index.html.

3   "As Obama Can't Even Come Close to 50% in Polls, His Electoral Future Withers." Libertarian Neocon (blog), October 29, 2012. Accessed May 22, 2018. http://libertarian-neocon.blogspot.com/2012/10/as-obama-cant-even-come-close-to-50-in.html.

is finally coming to fruition. The old rules no longer apply. Barack Obama could afford to lose a few swing states, whereas Romney had no room for error. Even his Southern flank was weak, with Florida and Virginia going to Obama this round, just as they did in 2008. Nor could a full-scale surrender on immigration issues save the GOP. Hispanics, especially recent immigrants, are simply more liberal.

Note also that the Democrats practice their own form of "inreach" to their white supporters, especially university students and single women. Leftist social issues like gay marriage and abortion may not be winners nationwide, but Obama's strong stand on them motivate the high-income, highly-informed, and highly-motivated white liberals in the major cities. Even the Democrats' supposedly white working-class hero Joe Biden is saying that "transgender rights" (?!) are now the "civil rights issue of our time."[4] This alliance between a minority of socially liberal whites and overwhelmingly Leftist ethnic minorities makes the electoral math for Republicans increasingly difficult.

In contrast, Romney's vision was "economism" — trying to defeat the president solely with wonkery about taxes and unemployment (but not of course mentioning an anti-unemployment immigration moratorium). Romney did not even run the implicit white campaign of George W. Bush in 2004, when the war rallied patriotic white voters — he ran an *implicit* implicit white campaign. He could have forced Obama onto the defensive on a host of issues, including (of course) immigration, anti-white racial preferences, trade, and social concerns. But he was cautious, characteristically, to the point of cowardice. The fact that he still won a solid majority of the white vote shows the deep disgust that average Americans have with the Obama regime.

Unfortunately, the new post-America has reached the point that it no longer matters who is the better economic manager.

Take Nevada, for instance. While ostensibly a swing state, it went

---

4   "Biden: Transgender Discrimination Is 'Civil Rights Issue of Our Time.'" *Newsmax.* October 30, 2012. Accessed May 17, 2018. https://www.newsmax.com/Newsfront/biden-transgender-discrimnation/2012/10/30/id/462145/.

Democratic despite having the worst economy in the country. The housing crisis, fueled by mass immigration and Bush's mortgage Hispandering, has devastated the state. Unemployment is well over 11%, and has actually increased considerably from the time when Barack Obama took office.[5]

But the state's high concentration of Hispanics combined with blacks means that a large percentage of the population simply lies beyond economic appeals. In fact, Hispanic voters in Nevada nearly flipped a Senate seat to the Democrats, despite the fact that their candidate was under investigation for corruption and wasn't even expected to be competitive.[6]

A story from Illinois's 2nd Congressional District illustrates what is happening to the country as a whole. Incumbent Jesse Jackson Jr. went on medical leave starting in June for a variety of "health issues." This didn't stop him from hitting the bars with his friends, although he didn't hold a single campaign event or public appearance.[7] His wife stood by him, despite his past adultery (with a blonde bikini model), which is now public knowledge.8 This might have something to do with the several thousand dollars a month his campaign pays her "consulting firm."[9] Jackson is also the subject of an ongoing federal probe into his questionable finances.

But there was absolutely no chance that Republicans could make this

5   Ordonez, Franco. "Obama, Helped by Latino Vote, Tries to Cling to Nevada." Miami Herald. October 29, 2012. Accessed May 17, 2018. http://www.miamiherald.com/latest-news/article1944101.html.

6   Ibid.

7   Skiba, Katherine. "Jackson Declares Victory." The Chicago Tribune. November 07, 2012. Accessed May 17, 2018. http://articles.chicagotribune.com/2012-11-07/news/chi-jackson-declares-victory-20121106_1_republican-brian-woodworth-sandi-jackson-jesse-jackson.

8   "Jesse Jackson Jr.'s Wife Talks About His Affair." CBS News. September 26, 2010. Accessed May 22, 2018. https://www.cbsnews.com/news/jesse-jackson-jrs-wife-talks-about-his-affair/.

9   Ahern, Mary Ann. "Jesse Jackson Jr. Isn't Campaigning, But He's Still Spending." NBC 7 San Diego. October 19, 2012. Accessed May 22, 2018. https://www.nbcsandiego.com/news/national-international/Jesse-Jackson-Jr-Isnt-Campaigning-But-Hes-Still-Spending--174931371.html.

race even close. With 63% of the vote, Jackson won an absolute majority in a three-way race, despite doing no campaigning.[10]

This might have something to do with the fact that Republican candidate Brian Woodworth, a white lawyer trying to represent a majority black, urban county, wanted to win voters by telling them that the "Government needs to get off the backs of businesses." Even more exciting, he challenged not just the laws of political reality, but mathematics itself by claiming, "I am not looking to protect the '1%'; I will be working to provide more opportunity for every American to become part of the '1%.'"[11]

This economism doesn't seem to be doing much good, even though unemployment in both Illinois and Chicago is worse than in the country as a whole.[12]

Black and Hispanic identity politics make increasingly large areas of the country essentially immune to elections. As in South Africa's one-party state, it doesn't matter what the economy is doing or what policies are pursued—after the nominations, everyone knows who is going to win the election. Regardless of how many people are out of work in Stockton, California or Detroit, Michigan, Republicans are not going to win on a platform of tax cuts for the rich and pious platitudes about a Constitution written by hated white males.

In swing districts and swing counties, minority voters can tip the balance to a liberal minority, with each new immigrant or refugee expressing his tribal loyalties at the ballot box essentially disenfranchising Americans trying to make an informed choice.

---

10 Skiba, Katherine. "Jackson Declares Victory." The Chicago Tribune. November 07, 2012. Accessed May 17, 2018. http://articles.chicagotribune.com/2012-11-07/news/chi-jackson-declares-victory-20121106_1_republican-brian-woodworth-sandi-jackson-jesse-jackson.

11 "Issues." Woodworth for Congress. Accessed May 17, 2018. http://webarchive.loc.gov/all/20121003182642/http://www.woodworthforcongress.com/issues.

12 Frillman, Carrie. "Chicago Unemployment Rates Drop in September." Patch. November 01, 2012. Accessed May 22, 2018. https://patch.com/illinois/northcenter-roscoevillage/chicago-unemployment-rates-drop-in-september-9c98046d.

The Republican Party has to make a fateful choice if it isn't to become extinct. The Democrats have written off the white working class. They have nothing to offer those left behind by mass immigration, outsourcing, racial preferences, and continuous cultural warfare. The GOP could gain a new lease on life and increase their share of white vote with a populist appeal to American workers. It could potentially form a new alliance to save not just the Party, but the country.

But Romney/Ryan offered the white working class nothing. And, unfortunately, Conservatism Inc. is already at work condemning "New Economic Nationalism" and invoking the specter of Patrick J. Buchanan. Conservatism Inc., and its neoconservative controllers, would rather lose than associate with the likes of him. Conservative Inc.'s reigning ideology and the aspirations of the Republican Party to win national elections are, ultimately, irreconcilable.

On its current course, the Republican Party will probably continue its doomed effort to pursue minority voters, urged on by self-interested consultants, brain-dead movement "intellectuals," and liberals eager to see it commit suicide.

But the results from Ohio carry a message that goes beyond the election and the fate of the man from Bain Capital.

For the white working class and the Republican Party, it is "Join — or Die."

CHAPTER THREE

RIP NELSON MANDELA

AND THE DREAM OF A FIRST-WORLD SOUTH AFRICA

With the death of Nelson Mandela, a tidal wave of schmaltz and sentimental dreck is about to descend on our already beleaguered Republic. Part of this will include the inevitable Conservatism Inc. efforts to pretend that they were actually on Nelson Mandela's side all along; such are already rolling in from the likes of Ted Cruz, Marco Rubio, and John Boehner.

In fact, of course, conservatives at the time, including the now-sainted Ronald Reagan, were suspicious of Mandela and his African National Congress (ANC). In 1987 Margaret Thatcher said, "The ANC is a typical terrorist organisation. ... Anyone who thinks it is going to run the government in South Africa is living in cloud-cuckoo land."[1] We can look forward to a host of exclamation-point-laden articles at the likes of *Gawker* and *The Huffington Post* pointing out the Beltway Right's prior opposition to Mandela, to which Conservatism Inc. will respond by feigning ignorance.

The irony is that the American Right was largely correct about Mandela. Though he denied it at the time, we now know that Mandela was in fact a member of the Communist Party and his ANC was funded by a grab bag of Socialist Bloc countries, including the Soviet Union itself. Mandela received training in guerrilla warfare and was imprisoned not because of opposition to apartheid, but because of his plan to unleash a bloody insurgency on South Africa. Even when offered release if he renounced violence, he refused.

Even in power, even after he became a global icon, Mandela was a

---

1   Bevins, Anthony. "Nelson Mandela: From 'Terrorist' to Tea with the Queen.' *The Independent*. July 08, 1996. Accessed May 17, 2018. https://www.independent.co.uk/news/world/from-terrorist-to-tea-with-the-queen-1327902.html.

reliable voice for anti-American charges and harsh criticism of the American leaders who kissed up to him.

Mandela is now benefiting from the "soft bigotry of low expectations" when it comes to black Africa. Unlike Robert Mugabe or other "post-colonial" African leaders, Mandela did not immediately unleash a reign of terror on his political opponents. He even refrained from eating his enemies, unlike, say, Idi Amin. Instead, Mandela simply squeezed the white population of South Africa and feigned polite concern about the opening stages of Afrikaner genocide.

The result is that the Afrikaners were destroyed as a people but a sufficient number of them were kept alive to pay the taxes for Mandela's one party state. However, as the social norms of a former First World country are lost, the quality of life in South Africa is decreasing and those whites who can flee the country largely do. The Boer farmers forced to stay behind because of the concentration of their wealth in the land are brutally slaughtered, to the blithe indifference of the global media.

The legacy of Nelson Mandela is slow-motion white genocide and the ruin of a once great country. However, he didn't kill all his opponents. Implicit in the rejoicing of the Main Stream Media at his legacy is the idea that South African whites deserve to be murdered, but Mandela magnanimously refrained. This should provide a useful lesson for Western whites who are being reduced to minorities in their own historic homelands.

In "post-Apartheid" South Africa, all one has to do to be a civil rights hero is not be too enthusiastic in calling for the murder of whites. If one does kill them, the media won't praise you… but they won't condemn you either.

We all must face death, so RIP to Nelson Mandela. He certainly is not the worst leader Africa has produced.

But what no one else will say is: RIP to the Boer farmers being murdered every day, to the Afrikaners attacked in the streets, to the poor blacks savaged by ANC thugs and police… and finally, rest in peace, the dream of a First World South Africa.

CHAPTER FOUR

Tom Clancy's American Dream

Tom Clancy's death means that *Command Authority*, released on December 3, will be the last book from the man who largely invented the military techno-thriller. Clancy generated a seemingly endless stream of material about heroic spies and soldiers making the world safe for democracy with futuristic weaponry and old-fashioned American ingenuity. Around the country, aging conservative men read stories about the adventures of Jack Ryan while their sons curse out other teenagers on Xbox 360 playing *Tom Clancy's Splinter Cell*.

To older Americans, Clancy is best known as the author of the Jack Ryan series of books. The inspiration for this character had to have come from Clancy himself. Raised a bookish Roman Catholic, Tom Clancy volunteered to be an Army officer, but was rejected for service because of poor eyesight. Instead, he became an insurance salesman. Well into middle age, he wrote *The Hunt for Red October*, introducing the world to his alter ego.

Ryan was a super version of Clancy himself, with all his actual traits magnified. Jack Ryan is a faithful Catholic, a Marine officer, a financial expert who makes millions on Wall Street, and eventually an analyst from the CIA who leaves his desk to kick Communist ass in the field.

As Clancy may have seen himself in Ryan, so Americans saw what they wanted to see in the heroic CIA analyst. No less an authority than Ronald Reagan praised *The Hunt for Red October*.[1] In future adventures, Ryan would rise to become National Security Adviser, Vice President, and

---

1   Lekachman, Robert. "Virtuous Men and Perfect Weapons." *The New York Times*, July 27, 1986. Accessed May 22, 2018. https://www.nytimes.com/1986/07/27/books/virtuous-men-and-perfect-weapons.html.

eventually President of the United States. In these books, he would represent a kind of pro-military Reaganite conservatism, where patriots get the job done against America's enemies, with liberals occasionally getting in their way.

Still, even though Jack Ryan fights against a President's illegal war in *Clear and Present Danger*, there was a militaristic aggression in Ryan's books that appeals to a certain kind of conservative. In *Without Remorse*, John Clark murders criminals in American streets and even executes a Senate aide and anti-war activist who betrayed American POWs. President Ryan starts "The Campus," an off-the-books intelligence agency that has 100 blank signed Presidential Pardons so they can execute the people who need to be executed. When the "United Islamic Republic" hits America with a terrorist attack, President Ryan shuts down transportation in the entire country, even though he has no authority to do so. When he blows up the opposing head of state with a missile, he makes sure it is aired to the entire world as part of his Presidential address.

Reporters are whiny eggheads who don't understand what needs to be done to protect the country; foreigners are always plotting against American interests. Even Ryan's political opponent, the nefarious and immoral "Ed Kealty," seems to bear more than a passing resemblance to the late Ted Kennedy. Interestingly, in Clancy's fictional universe, Russia is a key ally of the United States (it even joins NATO), while China is a dangerous foe. Ryan recognizes the independence of Taiwan. The enemies are Communists, Arab terrorists, and even radical environmentalists. President Ryan even gives us a flat tax.

However, just like Glenn Beck or other "movement" conservatives, Ryan holds to a kind of raceless civil religion of Americanism where the overwhelming majority of Americans of all races are patriots loyal to Freedom, Flag, and Founding Fathers.

There are still, however, white racists lurking in the shadows… In *Executive Orders*, racist militia members plot against President Ryan, but are stopped before launching their attack. Ryan's best friend in many of the books (and later his Vice-President) is Robby Jackson, a black

Vice-Admiral, who later becomes President in his own right (the first black President in Clancy's alternative reality)... before being assassinated by a member of the Ku Klux Klan. Incidentally, this is what allows the evil liberal Ed Kealty to become President. Ryan then fantasizes about killing the assassin. This may also be inspired by Clancy's personal life, as his second wife (who remained with him until his death), was Alexandra Marie Llewellyn, daughter of J. Bruce Llewellyn, one of the first black owners of a Coca-Cola bottling plant.

The problem of course is that even the raceless "Jack Ryan conservatism" is dependent on white privilege and racist cultural assumptions. Why, after all, should the non-white America identify with the history, heroes, heritage, and institutions of a country created by WASP slaveholders? Why not instead transfer loyalty to a global sense of anti-racism or liberal values?

In one of the films based on the Jack Ryan stories, one of his antagonists mocks him, saying, "You are such a Boy Scout!" Today, of course, the Boy Scouts are not a paragon of morality and straight-laced living. More poignantly, when Ryan finally brings Captain Marko Ramius to America, Ramius quotes the words of Christopher Columbus, "The sea will grant each man new hope, the sleep brings dreams of home." Ryan smiles and says, "Welcome to the New World, sir." Certainly, one could never positively identify The Admiral of the Ocean Sea with America now, in the age of Indigenous People's Day and mandated mourning that Europeans made it to America.

Rather than a symbol of the old America, Clancy's legacy lives on in two ways. First, there is a new generation of techno-thrillers written by authors like Brad Thor. These continue to perpetuate an image of America serving as a "Global Force for Good" in a dangerous world.

Secondly, and more importantly, Clancy lives on in the wave of video games and cultural appropriation of military lingo in pop culture, especially through his *Splinter Cell* series. Even as the military becomes ever more remote from the lives of most Americans, millions (of all political persuasions) sit on the couch to blast away and play soldier from the comfort of their own home. As *Call of Duty: Black Ops* puts it, "There's a soldier in all of us."

As America's legions bomb all around the globe and her soldiers and Marines continue to die in the field for seemingly unknown purposes, American culture has grown more militaristic (just look at our police). However, this militarism is divorced from a sense of national identity, culture, or even pride. It is militarism for militarism's sake. You can even fantasize about being an "operative" in your new "Brad Thor Alpha Jacket." In both the new techno-thrillers and the fantasies of *Generation Kill*, American power is strangely disconnected from anything resembling an actually existing American nation. Instead, we're just a big collection of Diversity living in the same place, united by terrifying weapons.

In *The Hunt for Red October*, a Soviet officer speaks hopefully about the possibilities of living in Montana, where he can raise rabbits, get an American wife to cook them for him, and drive around the country with "no papers" in a "pickup truck." He also hopes he can live in Arizona in the winter.

It's probably better Captain 2nd Rank Vasily Borodin is killed before he makes it to America. The Department of Agriculture's armed response team would raid his farm and demand paperwork for the rabbits; his American wife would divorce him after attending a Gender Studies class; he'd be inspected by the TSA while driving around the country; and if he rediscovered Orthodoxy in Montana, the Southern Poverty Law Center ($PLC), or the Army, would file a report on him as a homophobic religious extremist. If he fled to Arizona, he'd be murdered on his ranch by illegals — unless he defended himself, in which case the $PLC would confiscate his farm.

Tom Clancy's books hearken back to the Indian summer of the historic American nation in the 1980s, when patriots imagined they were battling godless Communists in a fight for the free world. But they also point to the new grim reality — that the American government is warring against the American nation, that our technologically advanced military is defending an empty shell, and that maybe we lost the Cold War after all.

CHAPTER FIVE

Defining America Down

JOSE ANTONIO VARGAS AND WHAT'S AT STAKE IN THE LATEST AMNESTY/IMMIGRATION SURGE WAR

The great Amnesty/Immigration Surge battle of 2013 is about to begin. What's at stake is not simply policies or regulations. Congress is in effect about to determine what it means to be "American."

If this year's treason has a multicultural mascot, it's illegal alien Jose Antonio Vargas. As a coveted diversity "twofer," both non-white and gay, Vargas (a Filipino, not a Mexican, as Steve Sailer has pointed out — but hey, what can you do?[1]) is a hero to his friends and colleagues in the Main Stream Media (MSM), many of whom actively assisted in his law-breaking.

Note: Vargas is not called a hero because he served America in war, or rendered some public service. Objectively speaking, it's doubtful that the real problem facing the United States is a critical lack of homosexual journalists who think America is "racist."

No, Vargas is a hero to Obama's America precisely *because* he despises it — and wants to remake it.

Vargas's law-breaking has been both blatant and public. In 2011, the *New York Times* published a lengthy description of his illegal activities.[2] MSM reaction was ecstatic. Since then, Vargas has spoken before television

---

1   Sailer, Steve. "The Hunt For The Great Bright Illegal." *VDARE.* July 04, 2011. Accessed May 21, 2018. https://www.vdare.com/posts/the-hunt-for-the-great-bright-illegal.

2   Vargas, Jose Antonio. "My Life as an Undocumented Immigrant." *The New York Times.* June 22, 2011. Accessed May 21, 2018. https://www.nytimes.com/2011/06/26/magazine/my-life-as-an-undocumented-immigrant.html.

cameras, college campuses, and even Congress. *Time* magazine has even put him on its cover.

And, needless to say, there has been no attempt to enforce "strategic deportation" against this astonishingly arrogant criminal.

In a typically overwrought and verbose article, Vargas even attempts to answer the obvious question of why he hasn't been deported. After a few thousand words of moralistic hectoring, he recounts that he personally contacted Immigration and Customs Enforcement to ask what ICE planned to do with him. Astonishingly, even though Vargas's illegal status had been quite literally broadcast across the entire country, ICE said they had no record of his existence, *even as an ICE agent spoke on the phone with him about his criminal status.*[3]

As Vargas himself asserts, the "game changer" in the immigration debate has been the "coming out" of illegals around the country.[4] Of course, such a tactic is only possible precisely because of the federal government's treasonous indulgence of illegals. It is this treasonous indulgence that allows what the Israelis would call "criminal infiltrators" to complain, in America, about "oppression."

This is not to say that the Obama Administration does not practice strategic deportation. The Regime has been notably energetic in seeking to deport the Romeikes, a German family who claimed asylum in the United States. The family's crime: being evangelical Christians who practice homeschooling, which is illegal in their native country. The Obama Administration believes that homeschooling is not a "right," and the German government's threats to seize the children apparently do not constitute repression.

Michael Farris of the Home School Legal Defense Association, which is representing the family, contrasted Obama pursuing amnesty for tens of millions of illegals while the Romeike family is to be deported, protesting "It just doesn't make any sense."[5]

---

3   Vargas, Jose Antonio. "Not Legal Not Leaving." Time, June 25, 2012. Accessed May 21, 2012. http://time.com/2987974/jose-vargas-detained-time-cover-story/.

4   Ibid.

5   Gabbay, Tiffany. "Obama Admin. Trying to Deport German Evangelical Family

But of course, it makes perfect sense. What Sam Francis called "anarcho-tyranny" is a perfectly consistent policy. The traditional American nation is specifically targeted for dispossession, and the law is simply redefined to assist in whatever furthers this goal.[6]

As of now, the law is still on the side of immigration patriots. In theory, a patriot President or governor (such as Jan Brewer) could easily reverse these anti-American policies.

But if amnesty is granted to tens of millions of illegals, it will be much harder to backtrack. If amnesty passes, the government will be permanently and actively aligned with the likes of Jose Antonio Vargas, who seek to make America into just another Third World dumping ground.

Vargas is actually quite forthright in his ideological defense of this process. As shown by his unfortunately (but predictably) successful lobbying to force AP journalists to stop using the term "illegal immigrants," the heart of Vargas's case is that illegals are "human beings."[7] Vargas's challenge to the country he seeks to subvert is to "Define American" — asking what American identity really means.

Vargas's definition: anyone who "works hard" and "isn't a burden."[8] Needless to say, as aliens are enjoying the vast largesse of the debt-financed American welfare state, this definition (if he actually meant it) would exclude many millions of the criminals to whom Vargas and the Obama Regime seek to give citizenship.

However, in a deeper sense, what Vargas means is that anyone who "works" and participates in the economy is an American. As he put it:

Seeking Asylum Over Homeschooling." The Blaze. March 15, 2013. Accessed May 21, 2018. https://www.theblaze.com/news/2013/03/15/obama-admin-trying-to-deport-german-evangelical-family-seeking-assylum-over-homeschooling.

6   Francis, Sam. T. "Anarcho-Tyranny, U.S.A." Chronicles, July 1994, 14-19. Accessed May 22, 2018. http://www.unz.com/print/Chronicles-1994jul-00014.

7   Malkin, Michelle. "The Open-Borders 'Journalists' Who Banned 'Illegal Immigrant.'" MichelleMalkin.com. April 03, 2013. Accessed May 22, 2018. http://michellemalkin.com/2013/04/03/the-open-borders-journalists-who-banned-illegal-immigrant/.

8   Vargas, Jose Antonio. "Jose Antonio Vargas." Define American. Accessed May 21, 2018. https://defineamerican.com/stories/view/josesstory/.

"We are working with you, going to school with you, paying taxes with you, worrying about our bills with you... when will you realize that we are one of you?"[9]

Of course, actual Americans know that our national identity is not an economic input. "American" refers to a specific cultural context and to institutions created by a specific people from a specific background. This was essentially defined for us by Samuel Huntington's seminal book *Who Are We?* which identified "Anglo-Protestant culture and political values" as key determinants of American identity — the default culture that each new wave of immigrants must assimilate *to* in order to be "Americans."[10]

The problem is that conservatives lack the vocabulary (and the courage) to define American identity in common-sense cultural terms. Even Ann Coulter, whose masterful address redeemed the 2013 Conservative Political Action Conference, seems to believe that Americans have an obligation to be replaced by foreigners who are "better than us" in terms of economic output.[11]

Current mass immigration will indeed damage the economy, the cause of limited government, the existence of the conservative movement, etc. But all of this misses the point.

Americans are a *people*. And the national government is designed to be the political expression of that people — in the interests of "ourselves and our posterity."

But instead, all too many conservatives now think the nation is designed to serve the economy, rather than the other way around. It's no surprise that quasi-Americans like Marco Rubio clearly believe American

9   Vargas, Jose Antonio. "Not Legal Not Leaving." Time, June 25, 2012. Accessed May 21, 2012. http://time.com/2987974/jose-vargas-detained-time-cover-story/.

10 Francis, Sam T. "Immigration vs. 'Anglo-Protestant' America – Which Side Are The Neocons On?" *VDARE.* February 26, 2004. Accessed May 21, 2018. https://www.vdare.com/articles/immigration-vs-anglo-protestant-america-which-side-are-the-neocons-on.

11 Poor, Jeff. "Coulter, Norquist Spar over Immigration Reform." *The Daily Caller.* April 14, 2013. Accessed May 21, 2018. http://dailycaller.com/2013/04/13/coulter-norquist-spar-over-immigration-reform/.

citizenship is a product, to be purchased for less than the cost of a high quality PC.

The result is that "Define American" is actually a cunning trap by Vargas and his supporters.

Ordinary Americans know instinctively that they are losing their country. However, because their self-appointed leaders can only speak in economic terms, they are sucked into an argument about economic wonkery rather than developing a movement to ensure national salvation. This leaves the field to Vargas and his compatriots to redefine what America actually means.

Conservative Inc. thinks that they can simply get "beyond" immigration, and get back to profitable corporate logrolling. Consequently, questions of identity are never truly settled. Vargas gloated in his Congressional testimony that "diversity is destiny" — but whose?[12] If America is simply defined as "diversity," then it only exists as a geographical expression, as Metternich once said of Italy. Rather than gratitude, illegals look at America with contempt. Perhaps they should. It is hard to respect a country that doesn't even respect itself.

But then, millions of real Americans do still believe in their country. And they are ready for the fight.

If amnesty is defeated, it means that America still exists as a real nation waiting for patriotic leadership to deliver it.

If amnesty passes, it means that the polity formerly known as the "United States of America" is on the verge of definitive deconstruction.

As shown by the contrasting treatment of the Christian Romeike family and the pervert Jose Antonio Vargas, the newly enshrined "Permanent Cultural Marxist Majority" will aggressively punish those who can assimilate to the core American culture. And, increasingly, there will be no appeal possible through electoral means.

At this point, the historic American nation must consider itself

12 "VIDEO: Jose Antonio Vargas Testifies in Congress." Latino Rebels. February 13, 2013. Accessed May 21, 2018. http://www.latinorebels.com/2013/02/13/video-jose-antonio-vargas-testifies-in-congress/.

occupied by a hostile power — as surely as if it had been invaded (which, of course, it has).

That is what's at stake.

We've been here before, and we've won before. But they only have to win once. And if they do, then America isn't "America," but just another Third World country.

Patriots will be forced to ask: "What next?"

Let's hope it doesn't come to that.

CHAPTER SIX

THE FERGUSON RIOTS

PAR FOR THE COURSE
IN THE "BLACK COMMUNITY"

It's just another day in one of America's black neighborhoods.

Democratic governor Jay Nixon of Missouri finally sent in the National Guard, without consulting with the Obama Administration.1 But, in a characteristic liberal vacillation, he has dropped the curfew.[2]

The Ferguson riots have now lasted longer than the 1965 Watts riot, but the Main Stream Media is still doing its best to defend the rioters and blame nonexistent "police brutality" — leading to hilarious situations like a *Huffington Post* reporter mistaking foam earplugs for rubber bullets.[3] But none of this is particularly unusual — the simmering violence, rampant lawlessness, and collapse of civic order is just par for the course in black neighborhoods all around the country. Take it from me, I've lived in them.

And, like anyone who has actually lived in a black neighborhood, I

---

1   "Report: Nixon Did Not Give White House 'Heads Up' He Was Calling In National Guard." CBS St. Louis. August 18, 2014. Accessed May 17, 2018. https://stlouis.cbslocal.com/2014/08/18/report-nixon-did-not-give-white-house-heads-up-he-was-calling-in-national-guard/.

2   Alcindor, Yamiche. "Chaos Erupts Again in Ferguson." *USA Today*. August 19, 2014. Accessed May 17, 2018. https://www.usatoday.com/story/news/nation/2014/08/18/ferguson-national-guard-michael-brown-jay-nixon/14219621/.

3   Z., Lori. "'Speechless!' You Won't Believe What Huffpo Journo Arrested in Ferguson Thought Were Rubber Bullets [photo]." *Twitchy*. August 17, 2014. Accessed May 17, 2018. https://twitchy.com/loriz-3139/2014/08/17/speechless-you-wont-believe-what-huffpo-journo-arrested-in-ferguson-thought-were-rubber-bullets-photo/.

can testify that the expectation of physical safety, respect for public and private property, or basic standards of social decorum are simply absent from vast swathes of what used to be our country.

In a real sense, these areas have simply dropped off the map of Western Civilization.

The events leading up to the shooting of Michael Brown show why these riots are not unusual, but a simple flare-up of a constant low-level intifada.

Liberal students kvetch about "micro-aggressions" or petty verbal violations of political correctness, but life in a black neighborhood is a never-ending series of real aggressions, as residents constantly push the boundaries to see what they can get away with. When those violated respond with force, blacks adopt the posture of helpless victims and are eagerly assisted by a media willing to push an anti-white narrative.

Life in the ghetto is Fourth Generation Warfare in miniature.

The fatal confrontation between Brown and the police was reportedly sparked by an officer telling Michael Brown and Dorian Johnson to get out of the road and stop blocking traffic.[4] This may seem petty, but it is a constant in black neighborhoods. Hence "sidewalks" were identified by satirist Paul Kersey as one of those things "black people don't like."[5]

Driving in a black neighborhood means having to avoid young African-Americans walking in the middle of the road, who curse or kick at cars when told to get out of the way. An inconvenience — except when their expression of territoriality predictably leads to accidents. As in the case of Steve Utash in Detroit, the "community's" response to these accidents is to beat the driver almost to death and steal his wallet.[6]

---

4   Lee, Trymaine, and Michele Richinick. "Police: Michael Brown Stopped Because He Blocked Traffic." MSNBC. August 19, 2014. Accessed May 17, 2018. http://www.msnbc.com/msnbc/ferguson-police-name-michael-brown.

5   Kersey, Paul. "#67. Sidewalks." Stuff Black People Don't Like. May 14, 2010. Accessed May 17, 2018. https://stuffblackpeopledontlike.blogspot.com/2010/05/67-sidewalks.html.

6   "White Man Beaten By Mob In Detroit After Hitting Boy With Truck: Was It A Hate Crime?" CBS Detroit. April 04, 2014. Accessed May 17, 2018. http://detroit.cbslocal.

Michael Brown had also participated earlier in the day in another common ritual in black neighborhoods — petty crime at the convenience stores. These stores are usually run by immigrants who quickly learn to arm themselves with pistols or bats. The result: racial tension between immigrants and the community they are "exploiting." Shopkeepers are faced with a constant choice between cracking down on petty crime and risking violence, or allowing theft and suffering ruin.

A Pakistani shopkeeper in a neighborhood I used to live in allowed a certain African-American gentleman to steal a small amount of snacks for some time. The shopkeeper finally detained him and threatened to call the police. When the shopkeeper was threatened with violence, he produced a bat. (In this case, *the other black customers* urged the thief to back down on the grounds that the shopkeeper had been reasonable by allowing previous thefts.)

This sort of cost-benefit analysis is simply the price of doing business in a properly "diverse" neighborhood.

And it is precisely what happened in Ferguson. "Gentle giant" Michael Brown used his enormous frame to intimidate a much smaller shopkeeper into letting him walk away with stolen cigars. Not surprisingly, given the above cost-benefit analysis, the store's owners did not call the police — a customer did, a distinction the terrified owners are exploiting to show their "commitment to the community." However, the residents of Ferguson are still burning down and looting other convenience stores, and spray-painting "Snitches get stitches" on the charred remains.[7]

This expression of solidarity with criminals is typical of these neighborhoods. They display a tribal sense of unity against outsiders *even when the community itself is victimized by crime.*

For example, the recent drive-by shooting of a woman in Ferguson has

---

com/2014/04/04/white-man-beaten-by-mob-in-detroit-after-hitting-boy-with-truck-was-it-a-hate-crime/.

7   Madden, Roche. "'Snitches Get Stitches' Message Spray Painted on Burned-out QuikTrip." Fox2 St. Louis. August 11, 2014. Accessed May 17, 2018. http://fox2now.com/2014/08/11/quiktrip-sprayed-with-graffiti-set-on-fire-during-overnight-looting-near-ferguson/.

attracted almost no attention and certainly no outrage from indifferent Ferguson residents (or, for that matter, from the national MSM).[8]

Michael Brown, an "aspiring rapper," seems to share this social code, at least judging from what we can delicately call his artistic output.

His songs, if I can be forgiven the term, refer to the usual trifecta of petty sexual boasting, glorifying in murder and crime, and drug use. For example, the late Mr. Brown refers to himself as a "real killa" who says, "I Only Like White Men On My Money" (i.e., portraits of George Washington and Benjamin Franklin) and laughs about the sound of bodies hitting the ground. He boasts about how, in his town, "when the sun goes down, you in trouble now."[9] Not surprisingly, autopsy results also reveal that Brown had drugs in his system when he was shot.[10]

Of course, this doesn't absolutely prove his moral depravity any more than whites listening to metal songs about war prove they are bloodthirsty lunatics. But there's this difference: violence in the black community is framed in a context of black "resistance." Therefore, the leadership of protests by openly violent, racist and anti-Semitic figures like the New Black Panthers Malik Shabazz, or black businesses confidently displaying signs indicating black ownership to avoid looting, is not unusual or offensive. In contrast, any such signs of white tribalism would be greeted with moral outrage, not least from other whites.

Not surprisingly, a solid majority of blacks believe Darren Wilson, the officer who shot Michael Brown, is guilty of murder, compared to less

8   Arkin, Daniel. "Woman Shot in Head in Missouri Town Roiled by Michael Brown Protests." NBC News. August 13, 2014. Accessed May 22, 2018. https://www.nbcnews.com/storyline/michael-brown-shooting/woman-shot-head-missouri-town-roiled-michael-brown-protests-n179286.

9   Hansen, Matt, and Kurtis Lee. "Michael Brown's Raps: Money, Sex, Drugs — and a Vulnerable side.' Los Angeles Times. August 17, 2014. Accessed May 17, 2018. http://graphics.latimes.com/towergraphic-michael-browns-raps/.

10 Wax-Thibodeaux, Emily, Wesley Lowery, and Mark Berman. "County Investigation: Michael Brown Was Shot from the Front, Had Marijuana in His System." *The Washington Post.* August 18, 2014. Accessed May 17, 2018. http://www.washingtonpost.com/news/post-nation/wp/2014/08/18/county-investigation-michael-brown-was-shot-from-the-front-had-marijuana-in-his-system/.

than a quarter of whites and other minorities. Over 40% of blacks also believe the rioting is "legitimate."[11]

This celebration of aggression coupled with ostentatious proclamations of victimization and demands for federal intervention is also typical. As Alexander Hart recounted during the "Epic Beard Man" incident, when an old white man defended himself against a black attacker, a black woman gleefully urged her racial kinsman to attack the white man, wailed and moaned when the tide turned, urged the erstwhile attacker to press charges — and then obliviously *videotaped herself* stealing property as retribution.[12]

Similarly, Michael Brown's mother has already called for the death penalty for Officer Darren Wilson — which seems to be the only real goal of the protests.[13]

The "protests" in Ferguson, when not involving looting and throwing Molotov cocktails, simply consist of young black males running at police bellowing obscenities and slurs and making threats — as even *National Review* conceded in their recent article on the matter, "Ferguson Protest to Cop: 'F*** You, N*****."[14] The obvious intent: to provoke a police reaction — which can then be interpreted by reporters and activists as "brutality", furthering an artificially created narrative with no connection to the facts on the ground.[15]

11 "A Tale of Two Cities? Blacks, Whites Sharply Disagree About Ferguson." Rasmussen Reports. August 18, 2014. Accessed May 17, 2018. http://www.rasmussenreports. com/public_content/lifestyle/general_lifestyle/august_2014/a_tale_of_two_cities_ blacks_whites_sharply_disagree_about_ferguson.

12 Hart, Alexander. "Epic Beard Man, The MSM, And Citizen Reportage." *VDARE*. February 23, 2010. Accessed May 17, 2018. https://www.vdare.com/articles/epic-beard-man-the-msm-and-citizen-reportage.

13 Bissell, Grant, Brandie Piper, and Elizabeth Matthews. "Police Use Tear Gas to Disperse St. Louis Looters." *USA Today*. August 11, 2014. Accessed May 22, 2018. https://www.usatoday.com/story/news/nation/2014/08/10/st-louis-teen-police-shooting/13856377/.

14 Lovelace, Ryan. "Ferguson Protester to Cop: 'F*** You, N*****.'" National Review. August 18, 2014. Accessed May 17, 2018. https://www.nationalreview.com/corner/ferguson-protester-cop-f-you-n-ryan-lovelace/.

15 "With 'Big Mike' Scheme Team Assembled — We'll Show You The Similarities of

But this pattern of either being at your throat or at your feet is typical of the organized black "community." It's why entering a black neighborhood requires situational awareness simply to avoid attack. It's why non-black residents constantly must ask themselves what petty violence and indignities they are willing to accept, knowing that their government won't help them if they resist. It's why whites are so desperate to avoid living in the midst of diversity—and why Ferguson's white population has dropped from 75% to less than 30% within 20 years.[16]

And it's why the militarization of the police to patrol these areas is inevitable.

When explaining "anarcho-tyranny," Sam Francis quoted Edmund Burke, "Society cannot exist unless a controlling power upon will and appetite be placed somewhere, and the less of it there is within, the more of it there must be without."[17]

But there is no "controlling power upon will and appetite" within America's black neighborhoods.

And the more activists, reporters, and academics cry about the "black community," the more evident it is that a functional "black community" doesn't even exist.

Ferguson, Missouri 2014 and Sanford, Florida 2012..." The Last Refuge. August 18, 2014. Accessed May 17, 2018. https://theconservativetreehouse.com/2014/08/18/with-big-mike-scheme-team-assembled-well-show-you-the-similarities-of-ferguson-missouri-2014-and-sanford-florida-2012/#more-87572.

16   Sailer, Steve. "White Flight Is Evil, But So Are Whites Not Fleeing." VDARE. August 16, 2014. Accessed May 17, 2018. https://www.vdare.com/posts/white-flight-is-evil-but-so-are-whites-not-fleeing.

17   Francis, Sam T. "Anarcho-Tyranny—Where Multiculturalism Leads." VDARE. December 30, 2004. Accessed May 17, 2018. https://www.vdare.com/articles/anarcho-tyranny-where-multiculturalism-leads.

CHAPTER SEVEN

Ferguson Fiasco Exposes Ruling Class's Relentless ANTI-WHITE AGENDA

Although *VDARE* patiently explained this summer that "The Answer To Race Riots Is Ruthless Coercion. What Is America Waiting For?"[1] Missouri Governor Jay Nixon ignored us and refused to deploy the National Guard. As a result, after a grand jury declined yesterday to indict police officer Darren Wilson in the shooting death of Michael Brown, Ferguson is now ablaze with violence, arson, and undocumented shopping.

But the real story isn't the collapse of yet another racial hoax — it's the perseverance of a Main-Stream-Media-created narrative about "white racism," even in the face of all evidence to the contrary.

No educated observer can still maintain that Michael Brown, hands held high in the air, was executed by Officer Darren Wilson. The grand jury declined not only to bring a charge of murder, but even a lesser charge like involuntary manslaughter.

According to St. Louis County Prosecuting Attorney Robert McCulloch (a Democrat): "Even the image of Brown's surrender may have been a fiction" as several witnesses (all black) claimed Brown ran towards the officer.[2]

---

1 Brimelow, Peter. "The Answer To Race Riots Is Ruthless Coercion. What Is America Waiting For?" *VDARE*. August 16, 2014. Accessed May 17, 2018. https://www.vdare.com/articles/the-answer-to-race-riots-is-ruthless-coercion-what-is-america-waiting-for.

2 Harlan, Chico, Wesley Lowery, and Kimberly Kindy. "Ferguson Police Officer Won't Be Charged in Fatal Shooting." *The Washington Post*. November 25, 2014.

Autopsy evidence also showed that Brown was not shot in the back. Michael Brown's "blood or DNA was found on the inside of the driver's door, the upper left thigh of Officer Wilson's pant leg, the front collar of Wilson's shirt, and on his weapon." And several eyewitnesses who initially said Brown surrendered "adjusted" their claims or admitted they weren't even there and were recounting stories secondhand.[3]

Officer Wilson's riveting testimony has also been released and, as would be expected, matches the evidence. Wilson says that he was in fear for his life from the hulking robbery suspect, who charged him and punched him twice in the face. The young officer had also never used his weapon before.[4]

In fairness, one critical detail reported by many conservative and MSM sources last August was that Office Darren Wilson suffered a severe orbital fracture. The pictures show (as I suspected) that this was not the case and that the initial report from Gateway Pundit was not true.[5]

It is nevertheless true that Officer Wilson was physically struck in the face by Michael Brown. Evidence and testimony suggests Brown struggled for Wilson's gun. And the narrative that was originally presented — that Gentle Giant Michael Brown was accosted and executed by a police officer for no reason — is simply a lie and has been known to be a lie for some time.

Brown turned out to be a criminal and a thug, given to the constant

---

Accessed May 17, 2018. https://www.washingtonpost.com/politics/grand-jury-reaches-decision-in-case-of-ferguson-officer/2014/11/24/de48e7e4-71d7-11e4-893f-86bd390a3340_story.html.

3   "Ferguson Grand Jury Declines To Indict In Michael Brown Case." CBS New York. November 24, 2014. Accessed May 17, 2018. http://newyork.cbslocal.com/2014/11/24/ferguson-grand-jury-declines-to-indict-in-michael-brown-case/.

4   Clarke, Rachel, and Mariano Castillo. "Darren Wilson's Grand Jury Testimony Released." CNN. November 26, 2014. Accessed May 17, 2018. https://www.cnn.com/2014/11/25/justice/ferguson-grand-jury-documents/index.html.

5   Hoft, Jim. "UPDATE: Officer Darren Wilson Suffered Severe Facial Contusions After Severe Beating During Mike Brown Attack." The Gateway Pundit. November 25, 2014. Accessed May 17, 2018. http://www.thegatewaypundit.com/2014/08/breaking-report-po-darren-wilson-suffered-orbital-blowout-fracture-to-eye-socket-during-encounter-with-mike-brown/.

aggression that's par for the course in black "communities." From Officer Wilson's testimony, it seems the last words of the Gentle Giant were, "You are too much of a pussy to shoot me." And there is no case anywhere in the country where someone could expect to *punch a police officer* and *grapple for his weapon* and not expect to be shot. If anything, Wilson has shown remarkable restraint.

Nonetheless, incredibly, a new narrative is taking shape: that Wilson was not injured severely enough to justify shooting Brown. The quasi-literates at *Jezebel* taunted Officer Wilson's purplish bruise as a "razor-burn."[6]

Presumably, he should have let the 290lb Gentle Giant pummel him a few more times and then give Brown his pistol to make it fair.

Indeed, even though everything the MSM told us about the case for months has turned out to be wrong, most of the coverage in the aftermath has the underlying premise that there has been a great travesty of justice and people are right to be outraged. Protests in other cities were given a largely positive spin. The *New York Daily News* even had a front page that read "Killer Cop Goes Free," before it was apparently changed.[7]

But most MSM outlets used more subtle methods, like focusing on the grief of Michael Brown's mother Lesley McSpadden. McSpadden has previously called for Darren Wilson to receive the death penalty and expressed "disappointment the killer of our child will not face the consequences."[8] Of course, they didn't mention that McSpadden is also being investigated for alleged involvement in a group beating of people selling

---

6 Rose, Rebecca "Burt". "Here Are Images the Grand Jury Saw of Darren Wilson's Injuries." Jezebel. November 25, 2014. Accessed May 17, 2018. https://jezebel.com/here-are-images-the-grand-jury-saw-of-darren-wilsons-in-1662998952/all.

7 Kirk, Michele. "See Why NY Daily News Changed Its 'KILLER COP GOES FREE' Riot-inciting Cover." Biz Pac Review. November 25, 2014. Accessed May 17, 2018. https://www.bizpacreview.com/2014/11/25/see-why-ny-daily-news-changed-its-killer-cop-goes-free-riot-inciting-cover-161256.

8 Alcindor, Yamiche. "Brown's Mother Screams, Sobs over Grand Jury Decision." *USA Today*. November 25, 2014. Accessed May 17, 2018. https://www.usatoday.com/story/news/nation/2014/11/24/michael-brown-mother-lesley-mcspadden-reacts-to-grand-jury-decision/70065102/.

Michael Brown T-shirts. McSpadden may be in more legal trouble right
now than Wilson.[9]

President Obama's response was disgraceful. He took the opportunity
to wax poetic about "a deep distrust [that] exists between law enforcement
and communities of color." He also ominously warned police to "show
care and restraint in managing peaceful protests that may occur."[10] Amus-
ingly, as the President was speaking, CNN showed a split screen with the
President on the left and chaos on the right.

Building off of Obama's determination to link what is a local law enforcement matter to a larger crusade for racial vengeance, the MSM is
already scrambling to consolidate a new party line. Wilson's release is,
according to reporters, just part of a greater pattern of systemic disrespect
against blacks. Race hustler Jamelle Bouie intones, "[A]ctual justice for
Michael Brown — a world in which young men like Michael Brown can't
be gunned down without consequences — won't come from the criminal
justice system."[11]

Well, then where will it come from?

The clear implication is that it will come from the streets. The neutered St. Louis Police are celebrating that no lives were lost last night, but
as with the LA Riots, April 29 – May 4, 1992, there's no reason to expect
that the violence will be limited to a single night. And the violence in
Ferguson seemed almost tailor-made to confirm the worst expectations,
with flag burnings, the destruction of businesses, and plenty of gunshots,

9   Weinreich, Marc. "Michael Brown's Mother May Face Felony Armed Robbery
     Charges: Report." New York Daily News. November 07, 2014. Accessed May 17, 2018.
     http://www.nydailynews.com/news/national/michael-brown-mom-face-felony-
     armed-robbery-charges-article-1.2001373.

10   Berman, Matt. "Obama Speaks on the Ferguson Decision." National Journal.
     November 24, 2014. Accessed May 17, 2018. https://www.nationaljournal.com/
     s/34927.

11   Bouie, Jamelle. "Why Darren Wilson Was Never Going to Be Indicted for Killing
     Michael Brown." Slate Magazine. November 25, 2014. Accessed May 17, 2018.
     https://www.slate.com/articles/news_and_politics/politics/2014/11/darren_wilson_
     was_never_going_to_be_indicted_for_killing_michael_brown_our.html.

and Americans around the country learning on Twitter about each new building that went up in flame.

Thus, the exoneration of Darren Wilson, the revelation of critical evidence, and the conclusion of the legal process has had *absolutely no effect on the MSM's narrative* of an innocent black "child" gunned down by a white cop. Prosecutor Bob McCulloch's press conference even featured a kind of shaming of the MSM for constantly feeding speculation — which has led to a mini-hate campaign against McCulloch by reporters reacting to his *lèse-majesté*.[12]

Paradoxically, social networking and mass media are actually leading to a dramatic restriction of the public debate. The internet enables citizens to break the MSM monopoly and expose facts that otherwise would not be known, but power, money, and access are still what determines what most people read and believe. People who know the truth are afraid to speak up for fear of social media flash mobs. Therefore, the media's utter refusal to back down from their Michael Brown fairy tale, all evidence to the contrary, is actually proving effective. We can expect more protests in Ferguson tomorrow, as well as in other cities around the country.

Darren Wilson, like George Zimmerman, will be a hunted man for the rest of his life. He did his job — and the ruling powers of his country will never forgive him.

The real damage may come to our legal system. Just as the acid of tribalism ate away immigration law, we may be witnessing the beginning of the end of the presumption of innocence in these kinds of crimes. Other prosecutors may not have the fortitude of Bob McCulloch to let justice be done, although the heavens (or at least the Little Caesar's pizzerias) fall. Police officers may continue to get some protection because of their powerful unions, but ordinary white citizens will be readily sacrificed for social peace.

The real message of Ferguson: we are seeing multiculturalism itself go

---

12 Horowitz, Alana. "Ferguson Prosecutor Gives Bizarre Press Conference." The Huffington Post. December 05, 2014. Accessed May 22, 2018. https://www.huffingtonpost.com/2014/11/24/bob-mcculloch-ferguson_n_6215986.html.

up in flames. A polity where the Chief Executive has to address the people over a local law enforcement matter is fatally unstable.

There are plenty more Fergusons out there, tinderboxes ready to be lit the next time a white cop confronts a black criminal. As the Ruling Class has empowered a permanent anti-white narrative seemingly impervious to facts, this is only the beginning of the violence.

Until the historic American nation can develop a collective identity of its own, there will be more sacrificial victims to the cult of diversity — and the next one might not be so lucky as Officer Darren Wilson.

CHAPTER EIGHT

STRONG TRIBE VS. WEAK NATION

ROTHERHAM RAPE SCANDAL SHOWS THE
TRUE FACE OF POLITICAL CORRECTNESS

Like all primitive religions, multiculturalism demands human sacrifice, especially of children:

> The sexual abuse of about 1,400 children at the hands of Asian [Pakistani] men went unreported for 16 years because staff feared they would be seen as racist, a report said today.
>
> Children as young as 11 were trafficked, beaten, and raped by large numbers of men between 1997 and 2013 in Rotherham, South Yorkshire, the council commissioned review into child protection revealed.
>
> And shockingly, more than a third of the cases were already known to agencies.
>
> But according to the report's author: 'several staff described their nervousness about identifying the ethnic origins of perpetrators for fear of being thought racist.'[1]

Keep this case in mind when you read about someone in the media screaming about "rape culture" at a fraternity, or how Republican politicians "hate women," or about the need to police speech in order to avoid "triggering" people.

The systematic rape of hundreds of children in one town will draw no

---

1 De Graaf, Mia. "Revealed: How Fear of Being Seen as Racist Stopped Social Workers Saving up to 1,400 Children from Sexual Exploitation at the Hands of Asian Men in Just ONE TOWN." *Daily Mail.* August 26, 2014. Accessed May 17, 2018. http://www.dailymail.co.uk/news/article-2734694/It-hard-appalling-nature-abuse-child-victims-suffered-1-400-children-sexually-exploited-just-one-town-16-year-period-report-reveals.html#ixzz3BYn6pWwV.

outrage from the Main Stream Media nor anger from reporters eager to express solidarity with looters and criminals. There will be no marches or expressions of solidarity from feminists.

In an age that prizes "equality" above all other taboos, some victims are more equal than others.

In late January, women's rights campaigners in the United Kingdom hailed new guidance for police officers that would require men to prove that they did not rape a woman if they are accused, thus blandly reversing centuries of English legal tradition in the name of feminism.[2]

Only a few days later, a damning government report showed that the systematic rape and sexual abuse of thousands of underage English girls in the town of Rotherham was actively enabled by the local government, which did not want to be accused of being racist. Thus, we see the function of the state during the Death of the West — not to uphold any objective standard of law or morality, but to enforce the multicultural pecking order.

The "Report of Inspection of Rotherham Metropolitan Borough Council"[3] is damning. Nor does it fail to ascribe blame to the local political leadership. The entire local government of Rotherham is described as "not fit for purpose." The Labour leadership of the local council has resigned, and five officials from the British government are to run the town.[4]

2   Rayner, Gordon. "Men Must Prove a Woman Said 'Yes' under Tough New Rape Rules." The Telegraph. January 28, 2015. Accessed May 17, 2018. https://www.telegraph. co.uk/news/uknews/law-and-order/11375667/Men-must-prove-a-woman-said-Yes-under-tough-new-rape-rules.html.

3   Casey, Louise. "Report of Inspection of Rotherham Metropolitan Borough Council." Department for Communities and Local Government. Accessed May 17, 2018. https://assets.publishing.service.gov.uk/government/uploads/system/uploads/ attachment_data/file/401125/46966_Report_of_Inspection_of_Rotherham_WEB. pdf.

4   Thornton, Lucy, and Jack Blanchard. "Rotherham Council Taken over by Government as Bosses Quit following Child Abuse Scandal." Mirror. February 05, 2015. Accessed May 17, 2018. https://www.mirror.co.uk/news/uk-news/rotherham-council-taken-over-government-5107505.

And the report does not pussyfoot around when it comes to who was responsible for years of systematic and comprehensive sexual assault: "Children were sexually exploited by men who came largely from the Pakistani Heritage Community." In describing the repeated testimony of witnesses that the perpetrators of sexual assault were Pakistani, the report acknowledges the reluctance to be politically incorrect, but insists that "This was a matter of fact."

More than that, the report acknowledges that it was the very desire to avoid seeming racist that enabled years of systematic abuse. This politically correct cowardice expressed itself in three major ways.

First, the local government actively suppressed any discussion because council members were afraid it "would cause a problem" if it was officially recognized that the perpetrators of sexual assault were "predominantly Asian [i.e., Muslim Pakistani] men."

Secondly, local government responsibility over Pakistanis was essentially outsourced to "Pakistani heritage Councillors" because "white Councillors… weren't sure or didn't want to deal with the issues around the Pakistani heritage community."

Lastly, the "political leadership of Rotherham faced little opposition in a solidly Labour town," allowing the creation of an "embedded and dominant" political culture. As a result, the great boogeymen feared by the Rotherham city government were not Pakistanis or investigators from London, but the British National Party (BNP) and the English Defense League (EDL). Senior members of the town's political establishment are described in the report as being "terrified of the BNP."

What we have then is a closed political class that actively knew of the problem but thought the greater evil came from the possibility that white fathers and mothers whose daughters were raped might get upset and support the Right.

Therefore, the town's police and political establishments closed ranks to prevent information from leaking out. As the report puts it: "Child abuse and exploitation happens all over the country, but Rotherham is different in that it was repeatedly told by its own youth service what was happening and it chose, not only to not act, but to close that service down."

When reports of what was happening did make it to the press, the local government tried to dismiss them because, in the words of one Councilor, "The accusations in the press appeared to be biased, political accusations from a newspaper — Murdoch press, with little evidence. They had felt that *The Times* was picking on a Labour [local government] authority."

Now, the facts are out. And on the one hand, the Rotherham report shows government acting decisively against official wrongdoing. The local leadership has suffered real political consequences, the central government is essentially taking over and the affair has received notable coverage in both the United Kingdom and the United States.

Yet the entire affair is still a masterpiece of modern banality. The investigation was ordered by the current "Secretary of State for Communities and Local Government," a Conservative Party functionary with the too-good-to-make-it-up name of "Eric Pickles." (Disarmingly, Pickles is a flag enthusiast who encourages the flying of English county flags and the English national flag, the Cross of St George.)[5]

The actual author is one Louise Casey, the "Director General, Troubled Families," a bureaucratic post that lies at the pinnacle of a career spent working under both Tories and Labour on various commissions and task forces. Incredibly, Casey spends a good bit of the report condemning the "Far Right" for trying to take advantage of the situation and even positing their existence as part of the explanation of the actions of the Rotherham government. Casey moans:

> By failing to take action against the Pakistani heritage male perpetrators of CSE [child sexual exploitation] in the borough, the Council has inadvertently fuelled the far right and allowed racial tensions to grow. It has done a great disservice to the Pakistani heritage community and the good people of Rotherham as a result.

---

5   "Eric Pickles." Wikipedia. May 03, 2018. Accessed May 17, 2018. https://en.wikipedia.org/wiki/Eric_Pickles#Flags.

In other words, to paraphrase the notorious USA General George Casey Jr. (who I don't think is a relation) in the wake of the Fort Hood shootings: as much as the systematic sexual assault of thousands of young girls is a tragedy, it would be a shame if Rotherham's diversity became a casualty as well.[6]

Louise Casey laments that the Rotherham government, by trying to be politically correct, has enabled a massive crime that "perversely" will allow "the far right to try and exploit the situation."

Yet it was the "far right" — and only the "far right" — in the form of the British National Party, that had actually tried to put a stop to what was going on. And for their trouble, the government of the United Kingdom put the leaders of the British National Party on trial, the Leftist "anti-fascist" groups protested against attempts to stop the mass rape of young girls, and the Main Stream Media actively buried its own reporting. Even when the scandal finally broke, the fact that it was the "Murdoch papers" publicizing the crimes was enough to make the Rotherham city government try to bury it by attacking the source.

The pattern continues. When UKIP leader Nigel Farage visited Rotherham a few days ago, the same Leftist protesters that were conspicuously absent while their town's daughters were being molested and raped turned up to showily protest the "racism" of UKIP. Sarah Champion, the Labour Party's sitting MP in Rotherham, says that Nigel Farage is trying to "gain office" from the child abuse scandal, which is "the lowest thing I've seen in politics."[7]

And there can be no doubt she means it — even though she has been quoted elsewhere as saying:

> I think there could be up to a million victims of exploitation nationwide,

6   Berger, Joseph. "Army Chief Concerned for Muslim Troops." *The New York Times.* November 08, 2009. Accessed May 21, 2018. https://www.nytimes.com/2009/11/09/us/politics/09casey.html.

7   Prince, Rosa. "Nigel Farage Abandons Walkabout in Rotherham as Protesters Blockade Him in Ukip Office." *The Telegraph.* February 06, 2015. Accessed May 17, 2018. https://www.telegraph.co.uk/news/politics/nigel-farage/11395260/Nigel-Farage-abandons-walkabout-in-Rotherham-as-protesters-blockade-him.html.

including right now. Girls in the process of being groomed. … [W]e know at least four big cases each with a couple of thousand each in smallest towns.[8]

As with mass immigration, the massive rape of English girls by Pakistanis in a typical city in Northern England is simply the cost of doing business by the political establishment. While they are no doubt unhappy it took place, the Labour Party, the British press and for that matter many British people do not seem to have the kind of righteous indignation about Rotherham that they have against "the far right."

Why? The reason is also, "perversely," contained in Louise Casey's report. As one local government official put it:

> [My] experience of council as it was and is — Asian men very powerful, and the white British are very mindful of racism and frightened of racism allegations so there is no robust challenge. They had massive influence in the town. For example, I know all the backgrounds to the Asian Councillors… but don't know anything about white Members. Not about race only but the power and influence — the family links in those communities are still very strong. Definitely an issue of race.

In any other age, the scandal of Rotherham would have led to revolution. It would certainly justify one. But if it's just a crime committed by one group of atomistic individuals committed against another group of random atomistic individuals — as the British establishment and media are now trying to claim — then it has no greater importance.

The problem for Britain is that it is replacing its own people with Third Worlders who have tribal values. Those values are proving their evolutionary superiority over the consumerist individualism that our political leaders seem so determined to celebrate.

The residents of Rotherham are learning what the entire West will soon understand — a strong tribe will defeat a weak nation.

---

8   Thornton, Lucy. "Child Sex Abuse Gangs Could Have Assaulted ONE MILLION Youngsters in the UK." Mirror. February 05, 2015. Accessed May 17, 2018. https://www.mirror.co.uk/news/uk-news/child-sex-abuse-gangs-could-5114029.

CHAPTER NINE

BARBARA BOXER

CASE STUDY OF DEMOCRATIC DECLINE IN IMMIGRATION PATRIOTISM

Democratic California Senator Barbara Boxer is retiring, and immigration patriots can only say good riddance. Yet there was a time when Barbara Boxer actually spoke about topics like border security and sealing the border with Mexico.[1] Less than two decades ago, Boxer voted for S.1664 (Immigration Control and Financial Responsibility Act of 1996), which, as described by the immigration restrictionists at NumbersUSA, contained

> dozens of provisions aimed at reducing illegal immigration. It authorized major increases in the border patrol forces. But it also had many provisions aimed at making life more miserable for illegal aliens who manage to get into the country, half of whom arrive with legal visas but then illegally overstay. Until passage of the bill, a person could be apprehended as an illegal alien, be deported and then turn around and come back to the U.S. on a legal student, tourist, worker or relative visa. After the bill, an illegal alien was barred from any kind of legal entry for 10 years.[2]

Boxer also voted against the Abraham Amendment that same year, which would have scrapped a voluntary workplace verification program.[3]

---

1   Castillo, Elias. "Homegrown Pressures for Reform." Social Contract, Spring 1995. Accessed May 20, 2018. http://www.thesocialcontract.com/artman2/publish/tsc0503/article_432.shtml.

2   "Senator Barbara Boxer Voting Record." NumbersUSA. Accessed May 20, 2018. https://www.numbersusa.com/content/my/congress/49/votingrecord#tabset-5.

3   Ibid.

Even when accusing Gov. Pete Wilson of "hatred" for using the immigration issue back in 1993, Boxer attacked Wilson *from the right* for being a proponent of "cheap labor" who was flip-flopping on the issue. She also called for the National Guard to be sent to the border. At the same time, Boxer's fellow Senator Diane Feinstein was advocating a $1 "toll" to cut down on border crossings.[4] Meanwhile, now Senate Minority Leader Harry Reid was pointing out that "no sane country" would give the children of illegal aliens birthright citizenship.[5]

By 2006, Boxer was snorting disdainfully that people who wanted English as the official language of the country were "insecure." As Steve Sailer then observed:

> Much of what passes for "debate" over immigration and the national question consists of this kind of posturing intended to suggest that the speaker is so rich, powerful, talented, and all-around superior that he or she can afford to be utterly insouciant about any conceivable side-effect of immigration.[6]

By 2010, Boxer was spitting out generic pap about immigration, like, "The way to get the economy going again is to go with comprehensive immigration reform."[7]

---

4   Morian, Dan, and Dianne Klein. "Democrats' Ad Attacks Wilson on Immigration : Politics: Party Leaders Say They Are Responding to the Governor's Tough Talk Last Week on Policies regarding Illegals. The TV Spot Says He Has Done a Flip-flop on the Issue since His Senate Days." Los Angeles Times, August 18, 1993. Accessed May 20, 2018. http://articles.latimes.com/1993-08-18/news/mn-25007_1_illegal-immigrants.

5   Fulford, James. "Video: Harry Reid Versus Birthright Citizenship (1993): 'No Sane Country' Would Give Citizenship To Children Of Illegals." *VDARE*. July 17, 2013. Accessed May 20, 2018. https://www.vdare.com/posts/harry-reid-versus-birthright-citizenship-1993-no-sane-country-would-give-citizenship-to-childr.

6   Sailer, Steve. "Sen. Barbara Boxer Wants You To Know She's Not Insecure, Unlike All You Losers Out There." *VDARE*. May 30, 2006. Accessed May 20, 2018. https://www.vdare.com/posts/sen-barbara-boxer-wants-you-to-know-shes-not-insecure-unlike-all-you-losers-out-there.

7   Condon, Stephanie. "Carly Fiorina Supports DREAM Act, but Says She's Against 'Amnesty.'" CBS News. September 02, 2010. Accessed May 20, 2018. https://www.cbsnews.com/news/carly-fiorina-supports-dream-act-but-says-shes-against-amnesty/.

What changed? After the courts blocked Prop 187, it was clear that California politics would be dominated by a new coalition between a growing Hispanic underclass and a socially liberal elite that benefited from cheap labor and Balkanized politics. "Cheap labor" became a feature, not a bug, within Democratic politics. Boxer and other leading Democrats simply transferred their loyalty from American workers to their plutocratic friends and subsidized multicultural allies.

Again, our political leaders actively *benefit* from social dysfunction and importing new problems.

Nowadays, opposition to mass immigration is smeared as "extremist" or "far right." *VDARE* is always charged with being a "hate site" or "white nationalist." But opposing what is obviously a harmful policy for all Americans of whatever race isn't extreme or hateful. Just ask any of these leading Democrats. Before they sold their soul to the cheap labor lobby, of course.

CHAPTER TEN

Leftist Blogger Andrew Sullivan Calls It Quits

THOSE WHO COME AFTER HIM ARE WORSE

Citing stress and the nonstop pressure of blogging, Andrew Sullivan of *The Dish* stepped down today and will no longer be posting constantly, though he claims his career as a writer is not over.

One of the earliest and most influential bloggers, Sullivan wrote, "Things cannot go on for ever. I learned this in my younger days: it isn't how long you live that matters. What matters is what you do when you're alive. And, man, is this place alive."[1]

Sullivan, his occasional man-of-the-Right pretensions notwithstanding, was never a real "conservative." He was a fervent — almost fanatical — Obama supporter who would end his hagiographic posts about the President with "Know Hope." (My own reaction when the President speaks sounds the same, but is spelled quite differently.)

He was borderline hysterical on the subject of Sarah Palin and consistently denounced opponents of mass Third World immigration as "ugly."[2] Obviously, Sullivan despises *VDARE*, our readers, and the historic American nation that we champion.

Yet Sullivan was not without courage, nor without occasional insight. Sullivan bravely discussed *The Bell Curve* when he was editor of *The New Republic*, a record he consistently defended up until the present against

---

1   Sullivan, Andrew. "A Note To My Readers." *The Dish*. January 28, 2015. Accessed May 20, 2018. http://dish.andrewsullivan.com/2015/01/28/a-note-to-my-readers/.

2   Sullivan, Andrew. "'Public Health Nativism.'" *The Dish*. July 16, 2014. Accessed May 20, 2018. http://dish.andrewsullivan.com/2014/07/16/public-health-nativism/.

withering criticism.[3] Sullivan is a homosexual who championed gay marriage for decades (on the grounds that it would make homosexuals more
bourgeois and conservative), but was disgusted at the new gay identity
politics of hounding dissenters out of careers and polite society. Sullivan
could be infuriating, flippant, and emotional, but could often surprise
even the most critical reader. And that kept people coming back.

Am I being too sympathetic to Sullivan? Perhaps. But when you look
at some of the reactions to his sabbatical — e.g., "The Internet loses yet
another crucial grumpy and confused white male voice."[4] — it's hard not
to think that the rent seekers who comprise the contemporary online Left
are far more predictable, malevolent, and willfully ignorant about the
things that matter.

3   Sullivan, Andrew. "TNR RIP." *The Dish*. December 05, 2014. Accessed May 20, 2018.
     http://dish.andrewsullivan.com/2014/12/05/tnr-rip/.

4   Walsh, Tracy. "The Media World Reacts To Andrew Sullivan's Departure From
     Blogging." Talking Points Memo. January 28, 2015. Accessed May 20, 2018. http://
     talkingpointsmemo.com/livewire/reactions-andrew-sullivan-quits-blogging.

CHAPTER ELEVEN

OFFENDED BY AMERICA

OBAMA'S "HODGEPODGE" ISN'T EVEN A COUNTRY

Democratic House Minority Leader Nancy Pelosi didn't just display the typical liberal hypocrisy when she preened about wanting to take home all the adorable *bambinos* besieging our Southern border. Her comment that "We are all Americans — North and South in this hemisphere"[1] may sound odd to Middle Americans but is already established practice at colleges and universities.

Any graduate student who's been forced to sit through "Chicano/a Studies" or a "Cultural Communications" class can tell you stories about how the affirmative action students will protest if someone refers to the United States as "America." Instead, they will lecture, "America is a continent, not a country." American must refer to themselves as "U.S.-Americans" lest they be thought politically incorrect.

Professional parasite Jose Antonio Vargas's site Define American features articles on the subject.[2] Again, not only do immigrants not assimilate, they are not even willing to accept the name of the country without taking offense.

---

1 Key, Pam. "Pelosi on the Border: We Have to Use This 'Crisis' as an 'Opportunity.'" *Breitbart*. June 28, 2014. Accessed May 17, 2018. http://www.breitbart.com/video/2014/06/28/pelosi-on-the-border-we-have-to-use-this-crisis-as-an-opportunity/.

2 Thomas, David. "A Geography Lesson: America Is a Continent, Not a Country." Define America. November 15, 2011. Accessed May 17, 2011. https://defineamerican.com/story/post/442/a-geography-lesson-america-is-a-continent-not-a-country/. Note: Interestingly, this post was deleted sometime in the summer or fall of 2016. It is archived here: https://web.archive.org/defineamerican.com/story/post/442/a-geography-lesson-america-is-a-continent-not-a-country/.

The rationale of course is that calling the USA "America" legitimizes the white settlement on the Northern American continent and the creation of the country, instead of treating it as an unfortunate invasion of what should be a "brown continent." As the Leftist *Z Magazine* put it:

> It is Manifest Destiny that calls this nation "America," thus denying any serious existence to over 550 million human beings who stretch across 7,785,000 square miles. For Latinos/as here and abroad, calling this country "America" is offensive. Perhaps unintentional, but offensive. We should all ask ourselves: do we really want to approve that racist, imperialist worldview by using the empire's name for itself?[3]

This kind of thinking serves as a groundwork for the legal deconstruction of citizenship the government now embraces. For example, the Obama Administration has decided that birthright citizenship, the lowest-common-denominator definition of citizenship, is too restrictive. You can now be a citizen of the United States even if you have never actually set foot in the United States or even if your parents have never set foot in the United States:

> President Barack Obama's administration has decided to let the surrogate birth industry sell U.S. citizenship — and access to the U.S. welfare system — to foreign parents who never even set foot in the United States.
>
> The fertility clinics will be able to pocket the profits, after granting access to American education, health, welfare and retirement services to the foreign children and the foreign parents.
>
> The giveaway is accomplished by a surprise change in regulations, which redefined the term "mother" to include women who contract to carry other women's embryos to birth.[4]

---

3   Martinez, Elizabeth Betita. "Don't Call This Country 'America.'" Z Magazine. July/August 2008. Accessed May 17, 2018. http://www.learntoquestion.com/resources/database/archives/003366.html.

4   Munro, Neil. "Obama Administration Allows Fertility Clinics To Sell US Citizenship." *The Daily Caller.* October 29, 2014. Accessed May 17, 2018. http://dailycaller.com/2014/10/28/obama-administration-allows-fertility-clinics-to-sell-us-citizenship/.

What does this mean?

> The change means that a woman who is a U.S. citizen can be hired by a re-
> productive medical clinic to become pregnant overseas and to give birth in
> China, Saudi Arabia, or anywhere else, and then effectively hand a U.S. pass-
> port to the baby.
>
> That's a huge benefit to the child, because it makes him or her a U.S citi-
> zen, even if he or she never breathes American air, or lives among Americans,
> knows English or shares any American cultural norms or ideas with their
> natural-born American citizens.
>
> It is also a huge benefit for the parents, because they too can get citizen-
> ship once their child becomes an adult. That citizenship allows them — and
> their other children — to move to the United States in time for them to access
> Obamacare or Medicare benefits in their retirement.[5]

One of the criticisms that could be made of birthright citizenship is that
it reduces the concept of the nation to a purely geographic expression. Instead of a community with common interests, the country becomes a spot
of dirt with a random collection of deracinated individuals living on it,
trying to cheat each other out of money and accepting welfare payments.

However, even that has become too charitable. "America" is being reduced before our eyes to something *less* than a geographic expression.
Obama is turning it into something like an absurdist piece of performance
art, a Dadaist farce that perpetuates itself with no end in sight.

It is difficult to see that as incidental, or as what a libertarian would
dub an "unintended consequence." Consider the President's response to
Ezra Klein's question about the problem of political polarization, especially when it comes to racial issues:

> I don't worry about that, because I don't think that's going to last. I worry
> very much about the immediate consequences of mistrust between police and
> minority communities. I think there are things we can do to train our police
> force and make sure that everybody is being treated fairly. And the task force
> that I assigned after the Ferguson and New York cases is intended to produce
> very specific tools for us to deal with it.

5   Ibid.

But over the long term, I'm pretty optimistic, and the reason is because this country just becomes more and more of a hodgepodge of folks. Again, this is an example where things seem very polarized at the national level and media spotlight, but you go into communities — you know, one of the great things about being president is you travel through the entire country, and you go to Tennessee and it turns out that you've got this huge Kurdish community. And you go to some little town in Iowa and you see some Hasidic Jewish community, and then you see a bunch of interracial black and white couples running around with their kids. And this is in these little farm communities, and you've got Latinos in the classroom when you visit the schools there. So people are getting more and more comfortable with the diversity of this country, much more sophisticated about both the cultural differences but more importantly, the basic commonality that we have. And, you know, the key is to make sure that our politics and our politicians are tapping into that better set of impulses rather than our baser fears.

And my gut tells me, and I've seen it in my own career and you see it generally, a politician who plays on those fears in America, I don't think is going to over time get a lot of traction. Even, you know, it's not a perfect analogy, but if you think about how rapidly the whole issue of the LGBT community and discrimination against gays and lesbians has shifted. The Republican party, even the most conservative, they have much less ability, I think, to express discriminatory views than they did even ten years ago. And that's a source of optimism. It makes me hopeful.[6]

As Neil Munro noted in *The Daily Caller*, Obama is predicting that immigration "would overwhelm conservative causes."[7]

However, it goes beyond that. Obama spends much of the rest of the interview bemoaning things like income inequality or the lack of interest in the common good. But those are *features* of mass immigration and a diverse society, not bugs in its correct working. Diversity leads to a

6   Klein, Ezra. "Obama on American Politics and Economy: The Vox Conversation." Vox. January 23, 2015. Accessed May 17, 2018. https://www.vox.com/a/barack-obama-interview-vox-conversation/obama-domestic-policy-transcript.

7   Munro, Neil. "Obama 'Hopeful' Immigration Will Drown Conservatism." *The Daily Caller.* February 10, 2015. Accessed May 17, 2018. http://dailycaller.com/2015/02/09/obama-hints-immigration-will-drown-conservatism/.

society of increased social distrust. It's not surprising that the highest societal value is "get yours."

In his analysis, Obama is essentially agreeing with the analysis of the late Sam Francis.

Mass immigration transforms a country into just a "hodgepodge of folks" who essentially have nothing in common with each other except that they live under the same government. The constant tension and dysfunction creates its own justification for never-ending government intervention and various "community organizers," "community leaders," and other rent seekers. Perhaps it is best that the denizens inhabiting such a chaotic conglomeration are offended by the word "America." The multicultural disaster being created doesn't deserve the name of the great nation that preceded it.

CHAPTER TWELVE

The Lesson of Charlie Hebdo

FRANCE, AND THE WEST, MUST CHOOSE IDENTITY OR EXTINCTION

The Islamic terrorist attack on the French satirical magazine *Charlie Hebdo* is as devastating as it was predictable. Twelve people are dead at the hands of "French" Muslims. But while the politicians posture and the Main Stream Media tries to shift the blame away from Islam, a larger struggle is taking root. Europeans are not going to be allowed to ignore the National Question. They are going to have to choose whether to embrace their identity and confront Islam or submit. Opting out is no longer an option.

Charlie Hebdo is best known internationally as a provocative journal that occasionally published cartoons of the Prophet Muhammad. Only a short time before the attack, *Charlie Hebdo* tweeted out a joke about the Islamic State with "Caliph" al-Baghdadi wishing everyone a Happy New Year.

However, the publication is hardly conservative and directed just as much fire at Judaism and Christianity. Just last month, the magazine published a vulgar image portraying the birth of Christ that could serve as an entry in its own right in *VDARE*'s War on Christmas Competition.[1] The cartoon still serves as the magazine's avatar on Twitter.

Several of the cartoonists who were killed were reportedly called out by name as the gunmen entered the magazine's offices. One of the names was editor Stéphane Charbonnier, who was "reportedly a supporter of the

---

1 Read, Max. "What Is Charlie Hebdo? The Cartoons That Made the French Paper Infamous." *Gawker.* January 7, 2015. Accessed May 17, 2018. http://gawker.com/what-is-charlie-hebdo-and-why-a-mostly-complete-histo-1677959168.

French Communist Party and his cartoons often featured Maurice et Pa-tapon, an anti-capitalist cat and dog."[2] In fact, the magazine's latest cover featured a vicious caricature of Michel Houellebecq, mocking the author for his newly released book prophesying the Islamic conquest of France.[3]

But equal opportunity willingness to offend didn't save Charbonnier or anyone else. Nor did the police protection that *Charlie Hebdo* enjoyed seem to even inconvenience the highly disciplined attackers: the unarmed officers were forced to retreat.[4] The terrorists' execution-style killing of a wounded French policeman begging for his life provided the defining image for the day. It should shame any self-satisfied protesters from ever using the despicable slogan "Hands Up, Don't Shoot."

Yet even as Leftist cartoonists and satirists were butchered in their of-fices, the MSM hastened to change the subject to the real danger — the anti-immigration policies of the *French National Front.*

Tony Barber at the *Financial Times* took the opportunity of the attacks to caution that "some common sense would be useful at publications such as *Charlie Hebdo*, and Denmark's *Jyllands-Posten*, which purport to strike a blow for freedom when they provoke Muslims." The danger, of course, is the "siren songs of the far right" represented by "Marine Le Pen and her far-right National Front."[5]

Richard Seymour veered into the territory of self-caricature by telling

2   "Called For By Name: Dead Cartoonists Identified." Sky News. January 07, 2015. Accessed May 17, 2018. https://news.sky.com/story/called-for-by-name-dead-cartoonists-identified-10376487.

3   Sailer, Steve. "Charlie Hebdo Shooting: Anti-Islam Writer Houellebecq Parodied on Cover of Magazine Slaughtered by Terrorists." *VDARE.* January 07, 2015. Accessed May 17, 2018. https://www.vdare.com/posts/charlie-hebdo-shooting-anti-islam-writer-houellebecq-parodied-on-cover-of-magazine-slaughtered-by-terrorists.

4   Rothman, Noah. "Unarmed French Police Literally Retreated in the Face of Islamist Attackers." Hot Air. January 07, 2015. Accessed May 17, 2018. https://hotair.com/archives/2015/01/07/unarmed-french-police-literally-retreated-in-the-face-of-islamist-attackers/.

5   Barber, Tony. "The Gunmen in Paris Attacked More than a Muslim-baiting Magazine." Financial Times. January 7, 2015. Accessed May 17, 2018. https://www.ft.com/content/9f90f482-9672-11e4-a40b-00144feabdc0#axzz3OBSP6tvd.

people that anyone who values the anti-Islamic caricatures of *Charle Hebdo* needs to be "reading Edward Said's *Orientalism*, as well as some basic introductory texts on Islamophobia, and then come back to the conversation." The fact that he wrote this in an American journal entitled *Jacobin* gives his words a special poignancy.

Progressives, writes Seymour,

> shouldn't line up with the inevitable statist backlash against Muslims, or the ideological charge to defend a fetishized, racialized "secularism," or concede to the blackmail which forces us into solidarity with a racist institution.[6]

And William Saletan at Slate mourns:

> France's far-right National Front was already on the rise. This attack could help it take over the country. Maybe … the dystopia on the French horizon … [is] a state run by the anti-immigrant right.[7]

Therefore, even as the bodies are not yet cold, the MSM lectures us that terrorism and murders in the streets must always be regarded with cool objectivity and rationality. At the same time, the possible democratic election of a political party that may limit immigration is met with wild denunciations and nightmarish prophecies of "dystopia."

Patriots shouldn't expect murderous attacks on journalists and cartoonists to awaken the MSM to the threat of Islamic terrorism. After all, it's Europeans who are the existential enemy. Instead, there will be a redoubling of efforts to demand that Europeans abolish their sovereignty and identity.

Thus, Yascha Mounk sneers at the German marches against Islam because

> their chants of "We are the People" betray how exclusionary their conception

6 Seymour, Richard. "On Charlie Hebdo." *Jacobin*. January 7, 2015. Accessed May 17, 2018. https://www.jacobinmag.com/2015/01/charlie-hebdo-islamophobia/.

7 Saletan, William. "Islamic Terrorists Aren't Avenging the Caricature of Their Faith. Actually, They Are the Caricature." *Slate*. January 07, 2015. Accessed May 17, 2018. https://www.slate.com/articles/news_and_politics/foreigners/2015/01/the_charlie_hebdo_terrorists_didn_t_avenge_islam_they_became_the_caricature.html.

of nationhood really is. Appropriating the most famous slogan of the 1989 protests that helped to bring down the Berlin Wall for their own purposes, they are signaling that they will never consider Muslims as true Germans...

[I]n rallying to the defense of our values, we must, as ever, remember what those values actually are: a set of rules and institutions that allows everyone who subscribes to them to live together peacefully — whether they be a devout Muslim or a blasphemous cartoonist.[8]

This is nothing less than a call for Europeans to abolish their own countries as meaningful entities and embrace "proposition nations" united by vague "rules" and "institutions."

The problem is that the Europeans have already tried this. From the multicultural model of Scandinavia to the assimilationist policies of France (where even keeping statistics on race is banned), Third World immigration is failing all over Europe. France is an especially troubling test case because the Republic's policies are as civic-national and color-blind as anything that could be dreamed up by a Beltway Right foundation.

And yet nonetheless, France finds itself embroiled in a kind of permanent low level insurgency in its own cities. In fact, there's no evidence that Muslims *want* to live under liberal rules and institutions: polls show that Muslims in Europe radically disagree with the cultural norms that Europeans take for granted.[9]

Therefore, even speaking about "living together peacefully" is misleading. Even if European governments could prevent the occasional terrorist attacks and "random" acts of violence from its newly imported underclass, sheer numbers will allow Muslims in Europe to impose a new political and cultural order on the Continent — regardless of the wishes

8   Mounk, Yascha. "Europe Is Both Too Islamophobic and Too Timid in Facing the Roots of Islamic Fundamentalism." Slate. January 07, 2015. Accessed May 17, 2018. https://www.slate.com/articles/news_and_politics/foreigners/2015/01/europe_s_ confused_debate_about_islam_and_terrorism_europeans_are_both_too.html.

9   Voeten, Erik. "How Widespread Is Islamic Fundamentalism in Western Europe?" *The Washington Post*. December 13, 2013. Accessed May 22, 2018. https://www. washingtonpost.com/news/monkey-cage/wp/2013/12/13/how-widespread-is-islamic-fundamentalism-in-western-europe/.

of the indigenous inhabitants. Whether this is done through violence or through the ballot box is ultimately irrelevant.

And as the attack on *Charlie Hebdo* shows, even those citizens who define their way of life as satire, irony, and cynical detachment will not be exempted from the demand that they submit to the new order.

The choice confronting Europe is brutal in its simplicity — does it want to be Islamic or not? Simply remaining deracinated consumers will not be an option much longer.

The West cannot be defined simply by the rejection of Islam or as a collection of legal norms. It is a culture created by a specific people and it will be destroyed if that people is dispossessed. Europeans have the self-evident right to secure their homelands for themselves, without regard to the claims others make upon it.

In the end, *Charlie Hebdo* isn't about whether the French have the right to practice satire. It's about whether France has the right to stay French.

CHAPTER THIRTEEN

Arab Immigrants Aren't Just Terrorists, They're An Islamic Underclass

As we've seen in other cases, at least one of the bombers in the November 2015 Paris attacks (that left 130 dead and 413 injured) wasn't exactly devout:

> Paris bomber Ibrahim Abdeslam smoked cannabis every day while he stayed at home listening to Arabic hip hop and claiming unemployment benefits, his former wife has said.
>
> Ibrahim, 31, blew himself up outside the Comptoir Voltaire Café on Friday, injuring three people and killing himself.
>
> His former wife, Niama, has revealed that during their two year marriage, from 2006 to 2008, her husband smoked three or four joints a day and stayed at home watching DVDs or listening to music, according to the MailOnline.[1]

One of the most common talking points right now is that Islamic terrorists aren't really Islamic or aren't "true Muslims." This variant of the "no true Scotsman" fallacy is used to lecture Westerners about why expressing skepticism concerning the wisdom of importing millions of Muslims is practically a hate crime.

But there is a larger issue. What the West is importing isn't some

---

1 "Paris Bomber Brahim Abdeslam 'Smoked Cannabis Every Day' but 'Had No Gripe with the West', Says Former Wife." *The Telegraph.* November 17, 2015. Accessed May 17, 2018. https://www.telegraph.co.uk/news/worldnews/europe/france/12002062/Paris-bomber-Ibrahim-Abdeslam-smoked-cannabis-every-day-but-had-no-gripe-with-the-West-says-former-wife.html.

kind of Saudi Arabia in its midst. It's importing a permanent underclass plagued by the same kind of social dysfunctions we see among many non-white minorities in the United States.

In Sweden for example, violent crime is soaring:

> Forty years ago, 421 rapes were reported to the police in Sweden annually. By 2010, according to a BBC report, police recorded the highest number of offences — about 63 per 100,000 inhabitants — of any force in Europe. That was the second highest in the world — surpassed only by Lesotho in southern Africa.
>
> In 2014, according to the Gatestone Institute, a respected American think tank, the number of rapes had risen to 6,620, an increase of 1,472 per cent since 1975.
>
> In August, a double murder in an Ikea store in Vasteras, a small city in central Sweden, sent shockwaves through the nation. The victims were ethnic Swedes, 55-year-old Carola Herlin and her 28-year-old son, Emil. Their attacker was a 36-year-old Eritrean migrant who confessed to the random killings, apparently carried out with knives seized from the store's kitchenware department.[2]

How many of these criminals are Muslims? Probably a majority are nominal Muslims who may even go to the mosque once in a while. But truly devout? There's no way to be sure, but probably a small number. However, in terms of their catastrophic impact on Swedish society, they are almost as harmful as an ISIS sympathizer who spends his days brooding on the injustices of the Crusader West.

This is the permanent underclass of the new Europe. "Islam makes the problem of the immigrant underclass even worse because, like in American prisons, it provides an ideological justification that explains the socioeconomic failure of non-whites as the result of "discrimination" and "religious oppression." Occasionally, some degenerate will turn his life around

2   Reid, Sue. "Torn Apart by an Open Door for Migrants: Sweden Is Seen as Europe's Most Liberal Nation, but Violent Crime Is Soaring and the Far Right Is on the March." *Daily Mail.* November 13, 2015. Accessed May 17, 2018. http://www.dailymail.co.uk/news/article-3317978/Torn-apart-open-door-migrants-Sweden-seen-Europe-s-liberal-nation-violent-crime-soaring-Far-Right-march-reports-SUE-REID.html.

by becoming a more devout Muslim, like Ibrahim Abdeslam did. And as the denizens of this underclass are now sufficiently numerous they cannot be tracked, the minority of terrorists now have the "sea" they can swim in, as Mao famously said of guerrillas.

As for the members of this underclass, we have to hope that they remain parasites, instead of becoming murderers. But they never actually provide a benefit to Europe. Assume Ibrahim Abdeslam had never become a terrorist. Instead, pretend he stayed at home doing drugs all day and mooching off Europeans like he did before. Would the Republic still have benefited in any way from his presence?

More to the point, why is it so important for Europeans to import millions more parasites just like him?

CHAPTER FOURTEEN

The "Great Replacement" Is Killing the EU Long Live A Europe Of Nations!

It looks like the country that will end the European Union is not Greece, but Germany. Chancellor Angela Merkel has been enjoying plenty of positive press for her efforts to welcome hundreds of thousands of "refugees" to Germany and force them on other European countries. Yet the European Union is straining under the burden, and several governments are already in open opposition to Merkel's plan to accept nation breaking numbers of Muslim immigrants. Only months after the Greek financial crisis pushed the European Union to the brink, the issue that is coming to define Continental politics is not economics, but demographics.

The breaking point may come sooner than anyone expects, as Merkel is trapped by her own rhetoric. The Main Stream Media, gleeful at the prospect of non-European Europe, is hailing Merkel as a "hero" who is leading the way by showing "compassion" to refugees.[1] But the problem with defining immigration policies in these simplistic terms is that it suddenly becomes immoral to speak of *any* upper limit on immigration.

And sure enough, underneath the hosannas to "Mama Merkel" by migrants and their MSM cheerleaders, one can hear the faint signals that Merkel is trying to find a way out.

Even as Merkel says that Germany's willingness to accept Third Worlders paints "a picture of Germany which can make us proud of our

---

1   LeBor, Adam. "Angela Merkel: Europe's Conscience in the Face of a Refugee Crisis." Newsweek. April 17, 2016. Accessed May 18, 2018. http://www.newsweek.com/2015/09/18/angela-merkel-europe-refugee-crisis-conscience-369053.html.

country," she's also pleading for the "European Union to pull its weight" and trying to impose "quota system" for different countries. Of course, as Merkel is also admitting the "breathtaking" flow of invaders will "occupy and change" a once-successful European country, other nations are beginning to openly wonder why they should go along with Merkel's conception of the European Union as a demographic suicide pact.[2]

The leaders of the Czech Republic and Slovakia have openly rejected quotas, defying France, Germany, and the leadership of the European Union. Poland is reluctantly accepting more migrants, but is protesting that it is already struggling with refugees from the conflict in Ukraine. *The Wall Street Journal*, inadvertently revealing what is actually motivating many of these "refugees," notes "Poland is scant with welfare benefits compared with many nations in Europe, a factor that discourages mass immigration."[3] The *Journal*, at least on its editorial page, would never admit that such a rationale is behind Third World immigration to America as well.

And then there's Hungary. President Viktor Orbán highlighted the obvious problem with Merkel's plan when he wondered aloud how a quota system would function in Schengen Area countries where passport and immigration controls have been abolished. "Has anyone thought this through?" he asked rhetorically.[4]

The obvious answer is "no." How can you, when common sense objections to the wisdom of admitting hundreds of thousands of dependents lead to accusations that you are responsible for the deaths of children?

2   "Migrant Crisis: Influx Will Change Germany, Says Merkel." BBC. September 07, 2015. Accessed May 18, 2018. http://www.bbc.com/news/world-europe-34173720.

3   Sobczyk, Martin M. "Poland Says It Will Accept More Refugees Than Previously Promised." *The Wall Street Journal.* August 31, 2015. Accessed May 18, 2018. https://www.wsj.com/articles/poland-says-it-will-accept-more-refugees-than-previously-promised-1441054277.

4   "Stream of Refugees through Austria Slows as Hungary PM Slams EU Quotas." Fox News. September 7, 2015. Accessed May 18, 2018. http://www.foxnews.com/world/2015/09/06/refugees-flow-west-on-hungarian-trains-13000-reach-austria.html.

Yet the answer to why Germany is so fanatically committed to pushing refugees on Europe may lie in geopolitics rather than morality. There is a contradiction at the heart of the European Union's (read: Germany's) approach to the refugee crisis. On the one hand, refugees represent an economic burden to those core nations who will end up accepting most of the migrants, which is why France and Germany are so insistent on other countries taking some. On the other hand, refugees are also a useful way to extend the European Union's control over some of its more independent-minded members, especially Hungary and other Eastern European nations.

After all, if the European Union can establish "refugee quotas" for its member states, those states have effectively lost control not only of their borders, but of any ability to defend their cultural identity. Indeed, Hungary's Orbán has explicitly recognized this, saying that what is at stake is the "survival or disappearance of European values and nations, or their transformation beyond recognition."[5]

If you are trying to extend the power of the European Union, however, this is a good thing for two reasons.

First, in a purely legal sense, you have centralized authority and gained more power by undermining independent nation-states.

Secondly, if Europe becomes simply a common market encompassing an ethnically, racially, and religiously mixed population, you no longer have to worry about any populist or nationalist movements screwing up your plans.

Just as immigration helped thwart the independence movement in Quebec,[6] so will a huge immigrant population make it difficult for any country to possess the requisite social capital to strike out on its own.

This is also the explanation for why Merkel's compassion was notably

5   Mariann, Őry, and Jancsó Orsolya. "Orbán: Europe Is at Stake." *Magyar Hirlap.* July 25, 2015. Accessed May 18, 2018. http://magyarhirlap.hu/cikk/31400/Orban_ Europe_is_at_Stake.

6   Fulford, James. "Swept Away — North Of The Border." *VDARE.* June 04, 2003. Accessed May 22, 2018. https://www.vdare.com/articles/swept-away-north-of-the-border.

absent when it came to her fellow Europeans in Greece who saw their lives destroyed because of debts owed to German banks.

Indeed, the MSM is openly celebrating the potential of the refugee crisis as a way to deconstruct nationhood, especially in Germany. *Der Spiegel* snickered that Germans will simply have to "get used to the idea that they live in a country of immigration" and abandon "the next illusion ... that there is such a thing as controlled immigration." This is necessary to create a more "cosmopolitan and generous" "New Germany" and "fundamentally change" the country.[7]

Evidently, the Obama strategy of deconstructing one's own country has crossed the Atlantic.

Of course, there is a problem with all this: European leaders, including Angela Merkel, were *already* admitting that multiculturalism had failed, even before this crisis.[8] Famously multicultural, generous, and ethnomasochist nations such as Sweden have been unable to "integrate" their Third World populations.

And even in the face of unabashedly overt repression, nationalist parties are surging across the continent.

From the gang wars in the *banlieues* of France to the grenade attacks in Malmö, Sweden, we already have all the evidence we need to see how this latest attempt at "integration" is going to play out. A few months from now, there will be the inevitable articles in the MSM quoting "underprivileged" Arab and African immigrants who are having a hard time competing in the First World country.

Rather than becoming the recipients of gratitude, countries such as Sweden, Germany, and France who accept these refugees will find

---

7   Der Spiegel Staff. "Dark Germany, Bright Germany: Which Side Will Prevail Under Strain of Refugees? — SPIEGEL ONLINE — International." *Der Spiegel*. August 31, 2015. Accessed May 18, 2018. http://www.spiegel.de/international/germany/spiegel-cover-story-the-new-germany-a-1050406.html.

8   "Nicolas Sarkozy Joins David Cameron and Angela Merkel View That Multiculturalism Has Failed." *Daily Mail*. February 11, 2011. Accessed May 18, 2018. http://www.dailymail.co.uk/news/article-1355961/Nicolas-Sarkozy-joins-David-Cameron-Angela-Merkel-view-multiculturalism-failed.html.

themselves the targets of riots, political agitation, and extremist political movements.

And that's the best-case scenario. As ISIS is already bragging about how they are using the refugee crisis to smuggle in operatives, it doesn't take much to imagine a far worse fate for the great nations of Europe.

Not surprisingly, some people are beginning to notice that the best way to deal with the "crisis" is to try to avoid it altogether by getting out of the EU while you still can. And so a new poll shows that a majority of the British people want to leave the European Union altogether and strongly prefer David Cameron's handling of the crisis to Angela Merkel's moralizing.[9]

Like the Empire in *Star Wars*, the more the EU tightens its grip, the more "captive nations" may slip through its fingers.

In the short term anyway. The likely response from most European governments to opposition to refugees will be to ban criticism of immigration, put up more institutional barriers against anti-immigration parties, and essentially entrench the existing political order until it can complete the process of electing a new people. And unless leaders such as Merkel can actually be replaced in the years to come, the powers that be may pull it off.

Ironically, authentic European unity will be forged in the years to come by the battle of European patriots who work together against the European Union itself. Patriots from England to Poland understand that they face the same struggle, confront the same enemies, and share the same goals.

If anti-immigration parties and activists can succeed in saving their countries from the immigrant invasion, it will be the end of the current European Union. But it will be the beginning of something far better — a Europe of the nations that will safeguard the future of its peoples, rather

9   Walters, Simon, and Glen Owen. "Britain Wants to Quit Europe: Shock New Poll Shows EU 'no' Camp Ahead for the First Time as Cameron Prepares to Face down Tory Rebels." *Daily Mail.* September 30, 2015. Accessed May 18, 2018. http://www.dailymail.co.uk/news/article-3223674/Britain-wants-quit-Europe-Shock-new-poll-shows-EU-no-camp-ahead-time-Cameron-prepares-face-Tory-rebels.html.

than drive blindly on with what the French writer Renaud Camus calls "The Great Replacement."

CHAPTER FIFTEEN

UnElecting a People

AMNESTY IS THE ULTIMATE FORM OF
"VOTER SUPPRESSION"

House Minority Leader Nancy Pelosi is refusing to admit that the Democrats need to change anything about their policies or their message in the wake of their historic defeat in the 2014 midterm elections. Instead, she thinks that the Democrats lost because "eligible voters did not vote in the election this year."[1]

While it's tempting to dismiss this as *Führerbunker-style* raving, Pelosi is actually foreshadowing the Democrats' next move — an all-out assault on election integrity, coupled with mass amnesty to overwhelm the historic American nation.

Underlying this blunt political calculus: the brutal reality that GOP's electoral strike against Obama's Minority Occupation Government was driven by a huge reliance on the white vote and enforcing laws against voter fraud, a reliance that will only increase in the elections to come. American elections are increasingly resembling a racial headcount.

Consider just some of the reports from this past cycle:

Kansas

Senator Pat Roberts and even Governor Sam Brownback survived a difficult political challenge spawned by Governor Brownback's insistence

---

1   Lillis, Mike. "Pelosi Delivers Postmortem to Her Troops." *The Hill.* November 07, 2014. Accessed May 18, 2018. http://thehill.com/homenews/house/223281-pelosi-delivers-postmortem.

on inflicting Beltway Right dogma on his struggling constituents.[2] Immigration patriot and Kansas Secretary of State Kris Kobach enjoyed an eighteen point victory, avoiding being dragged down by the state GOP's struggles.

One reason Brownback survived: the massive help he received from a national Republican Party which suddenly found itself defending Pat Roberts's Senate seat.[3]

But Brownback is also indebted to the stringent efforts of Kris Kobach to enforce the state's strict voter ID law — which led to thousands of would-be "voters," most of whom lean Democratic, not meeting the requirements.[4] The Main Stream Media calls this voter suppression — although Puerto Rico also requires a government-issued ID in order to vote, which is somehow accepted without controversy.

Virginia

Ed Gillespie confounded many expectations (including my own) and made a close Senate race in the Old Dominion, not conceding until November 7. Of course, one reason he was able to do this was his thinly veiled appeal to racial populism by defending the Washington Redskins name in the final weeks of the campaign.[5] Significantly, in the wake

2   Kirkpatrick, James. "What's the Matter With Kansas?— How Conservatism Inc. Is Blowing It In A Red State." *VDARE*. September 28, 2014. Accessed May 22, 2018. https://www.vdare.com/articles/whats-the-matter-with-kansas-how-conservatism-inc-is-blowing-it-in-a-red-state.

3   Brinker, Luke. "'Overwhelming Bombardment': How a Suddenly Competitive Senate Race Helped Sam Brownback Hang on in Kansas." *Salon*. November 07, 2014. Accessed May 18, 2018. https://www.salon.com/2014/11/07/%E2%80%9Coverwhelming_bombardment%E2%80%9D_how_a_suddenly_competitive_senate_race_helped_sam_brownback_hang_on_in_kansas/.

4   Gruver, Deb. "More than 21,000 Kansans' Voter Registrations in Suspense Because of Proof of Citizenship." The Wichita Eagle. October 31, 2014. Accessed May 18, 2018. http://www.kansas.com/news/politics-government/article3504228.html.

5   Kirkpatrick, James. "Ed Gillespie Tries a Hail Mary in Virginia — Backs NFL Redskins Name in New Ad." *VDARE*. October 27, 2014. Accessed May 22, 2018.

of Mark Warner's close victory, Democratic strategists are arguing that Warner should abandon his moderate (for a Democrat) outreach to white rural voters and focus on increasing turnout among white liberals and minorities.[6]

Georgia

Republican Senate candidate David Perdue won a victory without needing to go to a runoff because he acquired a sufficiently large share (74%) of the white vote. Chris Matthews recognized (but decried) the realities of racial headcounting in Southern politics when he shouted during a broadcast: "I feel like we're in South Africa! 27% of the white vote, and yet everybody says she [Democrat Michelle Nunn] needs 30. It's already written down somewhere exactly what your bar is for each community. I mean, it's pretty awful."[7]

Needless to say, this discomfort is nowhere to be found when MSM pundits discuss non-whites voting as a block.

As *VDARE* editor Peter Brimelow has noted:

Nationally in 2014, the GOP appears to have won about 60% of the white vote (*Exit polls: National House*, CNN.com, November 5, 2014). This is about what it won in the 2010 Tea Party midterms, and slightly better than the hapless Mitt Romney won in 2012.

But white turnout was higher than for Romney in 2012 — according to CNN, whites made up 75% of the voters in 2014, vs. some 72% in 2012.

---

https://www.vdare.com/posts/ed-gillespie-tries-a-hail-mary-in-virginia-backs-nfl-redskins-name-in-new-ad.

6 Portnoy, Jenna, and Rachel Weiner. "On His Way to a Slim Victory in a Changing Virginia, Warner May Have Wooed the Wrong Voters." *The Washington Post*. November 05, 2014. Accessed May 18, 2018. http://www.washingtonpost.com/local/virginia-politics/with-warner-ahead-vote-certification-begins-in-tight-virginia-senate-race/2014/11/05/4ffcff0c-6507-11e4-9fdc-d43b053ecb4d_story.html.

7 Griswold, Alex. "Matthews On Ga. Senate Race: 'I Feel Like We're In South Africa!' [VIDEO]." *The Daily Caller*. November 05, 2014. Accessed May 18, 2018. http://dailycaller.com/2014/11/04/matthews-on-ga-senate-race-i-feel-like-were-in-south-africa-video/.

To put this in perspective, remember that Reagan won 64% of the white vote in 1984 — and Nixon won 67% back in 1972.[8]

But even while the Republican Party relies upon a combination of strict voter identification laws, low turnout among minorities, and obtaining an ever-increasing share of the white vote, Beltway Right functionaries like *National Review*'s John Fund continue to promote the false hope that the GOP can somehow capture the votes of non-whites because they can "be appealed to on an individual basis."[9]

The GOP is thus unprepared for the powerful narrative taking shape within the MSM: the midterm elections are illegitimate because they were dominated by white voters and because it's too hard to vote.

Indeed, *The New York Times* ran a weird opinion column even before Election Day calling for midterms to be canceled because they "weaken the President."[10]

And since the GOP reclaimed the Senate majority on Tuesday, the anger has only increased:

• Amanda Marcotte at *Slate* sneered that the midterms were simply the "Revenge of the White Male Voter."[11]

• *Salon* patiently explained that "all the conventional wisdom you'll hear tonight is wrong: Republican gains are really proof of age-old ugliness."[12]

8   Brimelow, Peter. "2014 Midterms: Good News For GOP And Immigration Patriots — But No Decisive Breakthrough." *VDARE*. November 5, 2014. Accessed May 18, 2018. https://www.vdare.com/articles/2014-midterms-good-news-for-gop-and-immigration-patriots-but-no-decsive-breakthrough.

9   Fund, John. "More Non-White Voters for the GOP." *National Review*. November 07, 2014. Accessed May 18, 2018. https://www.nationalreview.com/2014/11/more-non-white-voters-gop-john-fund/.

10   Schanzer, David, and Jay Sullivan. "Cancel the Midterms." *The New York Times*. November 03, 2014. Accessed May 18, 2018. https://www.nytimes.com/2014/11/03/opinion/cancel-the-midterms.html.

11   Marcotte, Amanda. "Revenge of the White Male Voter." *Slate*. November 05, 2014. Accessed May 18, 2018. https://www.slate.com/blogs/xx_factor/2014/11/05/midterms_2014_64_percent_of_white_men_voted_republican.html.

12   Rosenberg, Paul. "It Is All Still about Race: Obama Hatred, the South and the Truth

• Elizabeth Drew writes in the *The New York Review of Books* that because certain sections of the Voting Rights Act no longer apply and voter ID laws are being enforced, "our elections are increasingly becoming illegitimate."[13]

The first step to restoring "legitimate" elections in the eyes of the Left: make sure that proof of citizenship or identification is not required in order to vote. And as usual, the courts are doing their dirty work. The Tenth Circuit Court of Appeals (Judges Jerome Holmes, George W. Bush nominee, Gregory Phillips, Obama nominee, and Carlos Lucero, Clinton nominee and author of the decision) ruled against Kris Kobach on November 7 and overturned a Kansas law that required proof of citizenship before registering to vote. This is only one of several court decisions against such laws.[14]

Worse, Barack Obama's forthcoming executive amnesty is being justified explicitly on the grounds that the people who voted in the midterms should be deliberately ignored.

Thus, William Saletan, fresh from pronouncing that the elections were actually a victory for the Left, now thinks that President Obama should counter by pushing through executive amnesty and governing in the interest of those who didn't vote. In his words, "Obama thinks there's an army of voters out there who stayed home Tuesday but can swamp Boehner's troops. And he's right."[15]

---

about GOP Wins." *Salon.* November 05, 2014. Accessed May 18, 2018. http://www.salon.com/2014/11/04/it_is_all_still_about_race_obama_hatred_the_south_and_the_truth_about_gop_wins/.

13 Drew, Elizabeth. "Why the Republicans Won." *The New York Review of Books.* November 11, 2014. Accessed May 18, 2018. https://www.nybooks.com/daily/2014/11/08/midterms-why-republicans-won/?insrc=wbll.

14 LaForgia, Elizabeth. "Federal Appeals Courts Overturns Citizenship Proof Rule for Kansas Voters." Jurist. November 8, 2014. Accessed May 18, 2018. http://www.jurist.org/paperchase/2014/11/federal-appeals-courts-overturns-citizenship-proof-rule-for-kansas-voters.php.

15 Saletan, William. "Obama Shouldn't Forget His Most Important Constituency: The Midterm's Nonvoters." *Slate.* November 06, 2014. Accessed May 18, 2018. https://www.slate.com/articles/news_and_politics/politics/2014/11/president_obama_should_govern_with_the_2016_electorate_in_mind_the_2014.html.

Lost in all the talk about "voter suppression" and the need to represent non-citizens is the fact that allowing fraudulent votes and importing a new population effectively disenfranchises *existing American citizens*.

And consciously acting to dispossess Americans through mass immigration after they have democratically expressed their opposition to it is an abuse of power far more serious than anything done by the government of George III.

To actively ignore the will of the voters and to consciously seek to "swamp" them is indistinguishable from the tactics of a foreign regime waging a war of conquest.

But then again — that's the point. The Obama Regime and its MSM cheerleaders have already decided that its chief obstacle is the actually existing American people.

Unfortunately, the only representation the American people currently have is in the compromised and weak Republican Congress. As even the Beltway Right is now admitting, impeachment is the only answer left if Obama goes through with his unilateral amnesty.

And if the GOP isn't willing to impeach, it will be complicit in the greatest act of voter suppression of all — effectively unmaking every vote the historic American nation cast in this past election, or in any election to come.

CHAPTER SIXTEEN

White Anti-Racists Attacked by Minorities

SURVIVORS WON'T LEARN, AND
FOR THE DEAD, IT'S TOO LATE

A German open borders activist was stabbed by his Muslim pets in one of the more "progressive" districts of Dresden. It's hard to feel too bad for him. After all, this activist is precisely the kind of person who would sneer and snark at German villagers losing their homes because the government thinks it's amusing to replace them.

Twenty-nine year old "Julius G." involved himself in political activism while reading his degree in industrial engineering Technical University of Dresden. Now he may have fallen victim to his own politics, as the refugee advocate was attacked while waiting for friends in Dresden's Neustadt, known as the city's "left wing", or "alternative" quarter.

Germany's *Bild-Zeitung* reports police were called to Pizza 5 on Alaunstraße on Saturday after a group of six to eight men jumped the student in the early hours and stabbed him twice in the back, leaving him in a serious condition. A police spokesman said: "Several police vans searched the surrounding area, unfortunately without success. According to witnesses, the attackers were said to be North Africans"…

The student didn't think the motivation was robbery, as nothing was taken after the stabbing. Explaining he campaigned for the rights of refugees, he explained: "It makes me very sad that I was attacked by precisely this group"…

Speaking to Saxony's *Sächsische Zeitung* newspaper, the unidentified student said he had also campaigned against the Patriotic Europeans Against the Islamisation of Europe movement (PEGIDA), which was founded and maintains its power base in conservative Dresden.[1]

This isn't the first case of its kind in what used to be the home of the European people. A Leftist woman was allegedly raped by migrants and was actually ordered to not report the case, lest the narrative be compromised:

> It is claimed she was trapped in a shower block near the camp but loud music meant her cries for help went unheard during the horror attack.
>
> The woman was told not to report the alleged crime by colleagues working for far-left group No Borders, according to reports.
>
> They are said to have told her speaking out would have damaged their cause – to support freedom of movement and oppose migration controls.[2]

Where are the feminists? Probably too busy complaining about some fraternity guy accidentally making eye contact, or Donald Trump "raping" them through the television.

Much like fake hate crimes on campus and "narrative collapse," the "liberal mugged by reality" is its own genre of crime. Matt Yglesias was "randomly" attacked by thugs in both Washington, D.C., and Amsterdam, though he suffered nothing more than some lost money and some bruises.[3] Sometimes, the consequences are far more severe.

For example, Kevin Sutherland was a self-described "millennial" who graduated from American University and became a political activist for the Left. His Twitter feed is what you would expect:

1   Lane, Oliver JJ. "'It Makes Me Very Sad' Says Open Borders Activist Brutally Stabbed by Migrant Gang." *Breitbart*. October 15, 2015. Accessed May 18, 2018. http://www.breitbart.com/london/2015/10/15/makes-sad-says-open-borders-activist-brutally-stabbed-migrant-gang/.

2   Parfitt, Tom. "Woman 'gang-raped in Refugee Camp Ordered to Stay SILENT by No-borders Activists'." *Express*. October 07, 2015. Accessed May 18, 2018. https://www.express.co.uk/news/world/610376/woman-gang-raped-refugee-camp-activists-Italy-border-France-Ventimiglia.

3   Sailer, Steve. "Was the Beating of Matthew Yglesias a Hate Crime?" iSteve. May 15, 2011. Accessed May 18, 2018. https://isteve.blogspot.com/2011/05/was-mugging-of-matthew-yglesias-hate.html.

- Celebrations of gay marriage[4]

- Sneering at Christians[5]

- Shilling for Bernie Sanders[6]

- Showily displaying how much he cares about #FreddieGray[7]

- Retweets of Ta-Nehisi Coates[8]

But then his Twitter feed stops abruptly in early July of 2015. This is because he was murdered by one of Obama's Sons, Jasper Spires, who stabbed him thirty or forty times on the D.C. metro in front of a horrified crowd. As several noted at the time, the crowd did nothing to help him.[9]

As it was just another "random" black-on-white murder, even the death of a politically connected left-wing activist barely registered as a blip in the D.C. scene. The only time he was mentioned was when his former boss, Democrat Jim Himes, attacked Governor Chris Christie for the "vile" act of using "Kevin's death to score political points." Christie

4   KevinSutherland. (2015, June 26). It's a great day for America! #lovewon ift.tt/1TTwR5x [Tweet]. https://twitter.com/KevinSutherland/status/614649725011263488

5   KevinSutherland. (2015, June 26). Cool story [Tweet]. https://twitter.com/ KevinSutherland/status/614465646047424512

6   KevinSutherland. (2014, September 16). CNN/National Journal Politics on Tap with Senator Burnie Sanders! (at @SixthEngine in Washington, DC) [Tweet]. https:// twitter.com/KevinSutherland/status/512010576974065665

7   KevinSutherland. (2015, April 28). "Did anybody recognize #FreddieGray when he was alive? Did you see him?" - @RepCummings ksut.co/1bPP7vp #BaltimoreRiots [Tweet]. https://twitter.com/KevinSutherland/status/593083088084819968

8   KevinSutherland. (2014, June, 12). If I were going to make a reparations plan, I would want to go to South Africa & see how it worked out — @ tanehisicoates #CaseforReparations [Tweet]. https://twitter.com/KevinSutherland/ status/477231341503668224

9   Hermann, Peter, Michael Smith, and Keith L. Alexander. "Horrified Passengers Witnessed Brutal July 4 Slaying aboard Metro Car." The Washington Post. July 07, 2015. Accessed May 18, 2018. https://www.washingtonpost.com/local/crime/victim-in-metro-slaying-stabbed-repeatedly-during-robbery-on-train/2015/07/07/8dd09132-249b-11e5-b72c-2b7d516e1e0e_story.html.

had used the young man's death as an example of the failure of liberals to prevent crime, and Himes took personal offense.[10] Of course, Himes had previously seen no problem in using the corpses of children from the Sandy Hook school shooting to argue for more gun control.[11]

Sutherland's death was seen as an act of merely private significance for his friends and family, without any further consequence. To derive a larger meaning would lead to uncomfortable conclusions about the racial realities of crime, and we simply can't have that. Similarly, to promote the attacks of Muslims even on those European traitors who are assisting their invasion might lead some people to question the wisdom of admitting millions of these people into Germany and other nations.

So don't expect these people to wake up, any more than Congressman Himes had his own views changed by his own intern being ripped apart in the middle of the nation's Capital. "Despite the apparently random violent attack by the migrants, the activist was adamant the stabbing shouldn't be used for political ends."[12]

Better for a few left-wing activists to die than for Leftists to have their beliefs challenged by uncomfortable facts.

10 Terkel, Amanda. "Congressman To Chris Christie: Stop Using My Intern's Murder For Political Gain." *The Huffington Post*. July 18, 2015. Accessed May 18, 2018. https://www.huffingtonpost.com/entry/jim-himes-chris-christie-kevin-sutherland_us_55a93901e4b0896514d1333c.

11 "Himes Statement on Gun Violence Prevention, Six Months After Sandy Hook Shooting." Congressman Jim Himes. June 14, 2013. Accessed May 18, 2018. https://himes.house.gov/media-center/press-releases/himes-statement-gun-violence-prevention-six-months-after-sandy-hook.

12 Lane, Oliver JJ. "'It Makes Me Very Sad' Says Open Borders Activist Brutally Stabbed by Migrant Gang." *Breitbart*. October 15, 2015. Accessed May 18, 2018. http://www.breitbart.com/london/2015/10/15/makes-sad-says-open-borders-activist-brutally-stabbed-migrant-gang/.

CHAPTER SEVENTEEN

Cuckservative Logic

MITT ROMNEY'S FRAME OF DEFEAT

Mitt Romney was not the worst of the bunch in the 2012 election. He was fairly solid in the lead up to the vote, strongly supported mandatory E-Verify, and said he would end the lawsuit against Arizona's SB 1070. Based on this, Ann Coulter said Romney was worth voting for, maybe even in 2016. Yet by our overall standards, Romney was still an immigration wimp, strong only because of how milquetoast the rest of the field was. And whatever fortitude he showed in the election collapsed after his defeat, as Romney has gone out of his way to shill for amnesty and concern troll about "tone."

In the latest example of the Decline and Fall of Mitt, 2012's loser had an interview with Barack Obama's strategist David Axelrod (!) during which he intoned the following:

"I think Donald Trump has said a number of things which are hurtful — and he has said that they were 'childish' in some respects — and I think [they] will be potentially problematic either in the primary or a general election," Romney said.

"And they relate to things he's said about women, and things he's said about members of the news media, things he's said about Hispanics," he added. "I think he'll have some challenges if he proceeds to the next stage..."

Speaking with Axelrod, Romney further predicted that Trump's heated remarks about illegal immigration could create obstacles for whomever their party nominates next year. Trump frequently accuses the Mexican government of sending "rapists" and other criminals across the US border.

"Donald Trump has a big megaphone, and I think that some of the things he's said, particularly about Hispanics, will be problematic — certainly for him if he were to go to the next stage — but for whoever our nominee is," Romney said.

However, Romney suggested that former Florida Gov. Jeb Bush (R), who has a Mexican-American wife and speaks Spanish, and Sen. Marco Rubio (R-Florida), a Cuban-American who is also fluent in Spanish, could deflect those concerns among Hispanic voters in the general election.

"Now, if our nominee happened to be someone like Marco Rubio or Jeb Bush, who have strong Hispanic roots themselves and connections themselves, that might not be as big an issue. But if it were someone else who didn't have those connections, why, it could probably remain as a shadow over their campaign," he said.[1]

There's something nauseating about displays of weakness. I can't help but feel a little sick to my stomach every time Jeb Bush minces up to the microphone to beg Hispanics to like him and plaster that sickly, pleading grin on his face. But this might be even worse. Let's break it down:

1. First, Mitt is making these comments trashing his own party's leading candidate not just to a Democrat, but to the Democrat who masterminded his defeat. This is the equivalent to the guy who was just dumped kissing up to his ex's new boyfriend.

2. Romney uses the word "problematic" unironically, which is simply unacceptable for a man of the Right.

3. Mitt makes the assertion that Marco Rubio or Jeb Bush would be more effective in winning over Hispanic voters. But there's no evidence for this. In fact, Trump is getting more support from Hispanics than Jeb Bush is.[2]

What Romney is showing here is that he accepts the Leftist frame on racial politics. Republicans are supposed to appeal to minority voters

---

1   Campbell, Colin. "Mitt Romney Just Ripped Donald Trump's 'hurtful' Comments and Predicted They'll Cast a 'shadow' over the Race." *Business Insider*. October 16, 2015. Accessed May 18, 2018. http://www.businessinsider.com/mitt-romney-david-axelrod-donald-trump-hurtful.

2   "Trump Still Leads National GOP Field, But Disaster in General." Public Policy Polling. July 22, 2015. https://www.publicpolicypolling.com/wp-content/uploads/2017/09/PPP_Release_National_72215.pdf.

as members of minority groups. But because minorities *qua* minorities (even Asians now) are presently defined by their status as victims of racist whites, the only way Republicans can approach them is apologetically. The GOP tries to compensate with vague "pro-growth" rhetoric about capitalism and opportunity, but most non-whites *want more government intervention in the economy*, regardless of the late Jack Kemp's fantasies or how many times the increasingly pathetic Rand Paul calls himself a "Detroit Republican."

Thus, tone policing like Romney is doing here doesn't actually do anything to win minority voters. It simply comes off as condescending. Republicans simultaneously appear weak and cynical, seemingly trying to pawn off minorities with some cheap rhetoric.

In contrast, Trump is appealing to non-white Americans as *Americans*. And while many racialized Hispanics, blacks, Asians, Jews, and self-hating whites are disgusted by this appeal to an inclusive but still implicitly white American identity, there are probably more non-whites who are willing to get behind a pro-American, anti-immigration candidate than there are non-whites who care about "enterprise zones" in urban centers.

Trump's strategy isn't just a better way to appeal to minority voters, it's the *only* way to appeal to minority voters from the Right. And more importantly, it doesn't mean you have to behave like a cuckservative, groveling and demeaning yourself before people who hold you in contempt.

PART TWO

SIGNS OF
LIFE

CHAPTER ONE

SEN. JEFF SESSIONS
Winning Fight to Make GOP a
"National Conservative" Party

The Main Stream Media is missing the real story on the Republican Party's suicidal push for an Amnesty/Immigration Surge. The Party may be on the brink of a sweeping realignment — and the critical transformative figure is Senator Jeff Sessions of Alabama.

This realignment is likely because, regardless of the outcome of the upcoming battles over legalizing the tens of millions of illegal infiltrators in Occupied America, the Republican leadership has already failed. Key Treason Lobby figures within the GOP are clearly feeling the heat. Even if the disaster of an Amnesty/Immigration Surge passes sometime in 2014, the GOP base is well aware of the treachery of its own leadership and is looking for alternatives.

Thus, according to Neil Munro of *The Daily Caller* (whose days as a journalist within the Beltway Right are surely numbered), House Majority Leader Eric Cantor frantically changed the subject when pressed by CBS reporter Major Garrett "if the GOP plan would allow the 12 million illegal immigrants to get citizenship." Instead, Cantor began babbling about "job growth and the lack of job growth," without making any connection between those subjects and the likely consequences of flooding the labor market with helots.[1]

Meanwhile, Paul Ryan has attempted a bit of misdirection by claiming

---

1   Munro, Neil. "GOP Leaders Hide Immigration Plans." *The Daily Caller*. February 03, 2014. Accessed May 18, 2018. http://dailycaller.com/2014/02/03/gop-leaders-hide-immigration-plans/.

that it is "clearly in doubt" whether Congress can pass an immigration bill this year.[2] However, what is significant is that this tactic is openly being called out *as* possible misdirection.

The Republican leadership's sudden cowardice has been triggered by the surprisingly stiff resistance of the GOP House Caucus to passing amnesty. According to Jonathon Strong of *Breitbart*, a closed-door session of Republican Congresscritters revealed that 80% were opposed to moving on a bill this year. Speaker John Boehner and Ryan were apparently both restrained in their rhetorical support for amnesty in this meeting, as ordinary Congressman trust neither Barack Obama to enforce security measures nor the leadership's promises that an Amnesty/Immigration Surge would be politically beneficial.[3]

Hilariously, Ryan is even saying that for an immigration bill to go anywhere, it has to be based on "security first, no amnesty" and only "then we might be able to get somewhere."[4] Mickey Kaus catches Ryan outright lying about this: "distorting and dissembling weren't getting the job done, I guess."[5]

The conclusion: the Republican leadership isn't composed of "leaders" at all. GOP Congressmen are not listening to the likes of Boehner, Ryan, and Cantor. Speaker Boehner resembles one of those late Roman Emperors who is a prisoner of his own soldiers.

So, who could command the loyalty of the troops? The answer:

2   York, Byron. "Are Immigration Reformers Talking down Chances so Opponents Will Drop Guard?" *Washington Examiner*. February 03, 2014. Accessed May 18, 2018. https://www.washingtonexaminer.com/are-immigration-reformers-talking-down-chances-so-opponents-will-drop-guard/article/2543330.

3   Strong, Jonathon. "Did Showdown Kill Boehner's Immigration Dreams?" *Breitbart*. January 31, 2014. Accessed May 18, 2018. http://www.breitbart.com/big-government/2014/01/31/did-showdown-kill-boehners-immigration-dreams/.

4   Chadbourn, Margaret. "U.S. Immigration Bill 'in Doubt' This Year, Republican Ryan Says." *Reuters*. February 02, 2014. Accessed May 18, 2018. https://www.reuters.com/article/us-usa-immigration-republicans/republican-ryan-says-u-s-immigration-bill-in-doubt-this-year-idUSBREA110GU20140202.

5   Kaus, Mickey. "Psst! Ryan's Lyin'..." *The Daily Caller*. February 04, 2014. Accessed May 18, 2018. http://dailycaller.com/2014/02/03/psst-ryans-lyin/.

Senator Jeff Sessions of Alabama, who is blazing a new and promising trail for the Republican Party politically, and ultimately more important, ideologically.

In a break with precedent, Senator Sessions organized a secret meeting on January 23 with staffers from over a dozen House offices to sabotage the GOP leadership's amnesty plans. The invitation sent from Senator Sessions's office bragged that "Over here in the Senate working for Senator Sessions, we learned a lot last year about the strategies employed by the powerful forces pushing bad immigration policies — and how to counter them."[6]

The result: a well-organized insurgency during the much-ballyhooed immigration strategy session of the House of GOP. Armed with anti-amnesty talking points by Senator Sessions and his staff, House Republicans had a detailed set of responses to every single predictable talking point that could have been offered by the pro-amnesty Republican leadership.

Senator Sessions and his staff also set a trap for the Republican leadership by pointing out that any compromise solution would ultimately have "loopholes and waivers that could be utilized by or granted to illegal aliens by the Obama administration."[7] Boehner, Ryan, and Cantor would essentially have to publicly declare that they trust President Obama more than they trust their own base.

In terms of political power over the House GOP, Senator Sessions is the *real* Republican leadership.

Sessions is arguing for a fundamental reframing of the way the conservative movement views the immigration issue. In contrast to libertarian and Conservatism Inc. court eunuchs who view the historic American nation as kulaks to be dispossessed, Sessions is saying that the core

---

6   Boyle, Matthew. "House Conservatives Plot Takedown of GOP Leaders' Amnesty Plans." *Breitbart*. January 24, 2014. Accessed May 18, 2018. http://www.breitbart.com/big-government/2014/01/23/immigration-backlash-builds-in-house/.

7   Boyle, Matthew. "Exclusive: Sessions Arms House Republicans Against Boehner Immigration Push." *Breitbart*. January 29, 2014. Accessed May 18, 2018. http://www.breitbart.com/big-government/2014/01/29/exclusive-sen-sessions-arms-house-republicans-against-misleading-pro-amnesty-talking-points/.

principle of real immigration reform should be "helping millions of job-less Americans get back to work." As Sessions put it, "President Obama and Senate Democrats have uniformly embraced an immigration plan that would devastate wages and working conditions for millions of strug-gling Americans to benefit a small cadre of lobbyists and CEOs."[8]

Nor is this some recent deviation for Sessions. As he said in Novem-ber:

> America is not an oligarchy... A Republic must answer to the people... Con-gressional leaders must forcefully reject the notion, evidently accepted by the president, that a small cadre of CEOs can tailor the nation's entire immigra-tion policy to suit their narrow interests.[9]

This argument is political dynamite to the corporate lobbyists and low-rent sophomoric collaborationists who comprise what passes for the American Right.

And the argument is spreading.

Senator Ted Cruz, who was noticeably reticent when the Senate passed the Gang of Eight's version of the Amnesty/Immigration Surge, is now sounding a populist, even class-warfare note. Thus, Cruz said recently: "Rather than responding to the big-money lobbying on K Street, we need to make sure working-class Americans show up by the millions to reject Obamacare and vote out the Democrats."[10]

This type of attack is being echoed by other congressional opponents of amnesty, to the distress of the Republican Party's nominal leaders who want to deliver for the Chamber of Commerce.

---

8   Walker, Brenda. "Senator Jeff Sessions Voices Immigration Principles." *VDARE*.
    January 18, 2014. Accessed May 23, 2018. https://www.vdare.com/posts/senator-jeff-sessions-voices-immigration-principles.

9   Munro, Neil. "Sen. Sessions Slams Obama, CEOs on Immigration." *The Daily Caller*.
    November 25, 2013. Accessed May 18, 2018. http://dailycaller.com/2013/11/25/sen-sessions-slams-obama-ceos-on-immigration/.

10 Munro, Neil. "Amnesty Fight Stirs GOP Fight over Voters' Wages." *The Daily Caller*.
    February 03, 2014. Accessed May 18, 2018. http://dailycaller.com/2014/02/01/amnesty-fight-stirs-gop-fight-over-voters-wages/.

Thus, Republicans have the rare opportunity to be on the right side of an economically populist issue. Immigration increases are opposed by the majority of lower-income and middle-income voters, and by political moderates and conservatives. Furthermore, a plurality of African-Americans also oppose the higher levels of immigration proposed in the House and Senate bills.[11]

If it continues to spread in influence, the political philosophy of Jeff Sessions would represent the first serious reintroduction of National Conservatism in American politics since the (deliberate) destruction of Pat Buchanan.

The main obstacle of course: the money provided by the open borders donor class.

But with the slow-motion collapse of Chris Christie, the GOP establishment's Great Wide Hope, the 2016 field is wide open. The battle over the Amnesty/Immigration may prove simply the first clash in a greater war to define the future of the Republican Party.

Senator Sessions has already dealt the Treason Lobby a serious setback. If he can rally the House GOP to defeat Obama and Boehner's amnesty push, he will take his place as the most important leader of the American Right since Ronald Reagan.

And with a fractured 2016 field, Sessions may have a great opportunity to save the future of his party — and his country.

---

11 Munro, Neil. "Poll: Wealthy, Liberals Unite to Support Increased Immigration." *The Daily Caller*. February 10, 2014. Accessed May 18, 2018. http://dailycaller. com/2014/01/20/wealthy-liberals-unite-to-support-increased-immigration/.

CHAPTER TWO

Why I Support
Scottish Independence

ANY DEVOLUTION IS BETTER THAN THE
GLOBALIST STATUS QUO

Yes, Scottish "nationalism" is less an expression of cultural pride than a Leftist power grab. Yes, and yes again, it's supported by hypocritical, unreconstructed socialists who support mass immigration, the European Union, and hatred of the English. Despite all of that (and even though it distresses *VDARE* editor Peter Brimelow) I believe that immigration patriots in America and abroad should support a "Yes" vote — because our biggest enemy is not "the Left," but the status quo.

First, the bad news. Although the great Pat Buchanan hailed the Scottish bid for independence as a testament to the enduring strength of ethnonationalism,[1] Alex Salmond's Scottish National Party, the driving force behind the independence referendum, could better be called traitors to Scotland than authentic patriots. Salmond explicitly and enthusiastically favors more immigration, even claiming that an independent Scotland will be a contrast to a United Kingdom which he claims (ludicrously) is too restrictive. Under the SNP, the expression "no true Scotsman" may change its meaning from a logical fallacy into a real question of identity.[2]

---

1   Buchanan, Pat. "What Would Braveheart Do?" Patrick J. Buchanan, Official Website. September 16, 2014. Accessed May 18, 2018. https://buchanan.org/blog/braveheart-6964.

2   Chorley, Matt. "Could Independent Scotland Become a Backdoor into England for Thousands of Immigrants? How Salmond Plans to Open Borders to 24,000 Every Year." *Daily Mail.* September 17, 2014. Accessed May 23, 2018. http://www.

The ostensible justification for Scottish independence is that Scotland lacks sufficient power in the government of the United Kingdom. However, from a historical point of view, Scotland actually wielded a disproportionately great amount of power during the time of the British Empire and still serves as the base for the Labour party and the home of recent Prime Ministers like Gordon Brown.

The bid for "independence" also seems farcical given that the SNP is suggesting to voters that they can both join the European Union *and* keep the pound as their currency. Evidently, the SNP wants to trade "foreign" rule from Westminster for far more foreign rule from Brussels — but it doesn't want to use the Euro. The European Union says that such a Rube Goldberg scheme of government is not going to happen anyway, as Scotland will not be permitted to instantly join the European Union and will have to use the Euro.[3] These are fundamental questions about the future of the country — and the SNP has no answers.

One thing unites this odd combination of "nationalism" and eagerness to join the bureaucratic colossus of the European Union: hatred for the English. Scottish nationalists have used physical intimidation and what could even be called "xenophobic" rhetoric including ethnic slurs in attempts to drive out the English.[4]

Not for the first time, it seems that Europeans can only get into the tribal spirit when it is directed against other Europeans.

And as few can argue that Scotland is really "oppressed" by England,

---

dailymail.co.uk/news/article-2759128/An-independent-Scotland-celebrate-soaring-immigration-How-SNP-s-plan-open-borders-24-000-year-offer-backdoor-England. html.

3   Johnson, Simon. "Spanish Warn Independent Scotland Would Get Euro Not Pound." *The Telegraph*. September 16, 2014. Accessed May 18, 2018. https://www.telegraph. co.uk/news/uknews/scottish-independence/11099167/Spanish-warn-independent-Scotland-would-get-euro-not-pound.html.

4   Adams, Guy. "Homes Vandalised, Accused of Stealing Jobs and an Atmosphere of Discriminatory 'Intimidation': The Savage Racism Turning Scotland into a No-go Zone for the English." *Daily Mail*. September 06, 2014. Accessed May 18, 2018. http:// www.dailymail.co.uk/news/article-2745565/Savage-racism-turning-Scotland-no-zone-English.html.

it seems that boredom is as much a driving force behind the referendum as anything else.

The ultimate motivation behind the Scottish independence drive is the effort by a clique of Leftist politicians to give themselves essentially permanent power. Extremist socialists are enthusiastically campaigning for independence.[5] One argument is that Left-leaning Scottish voters will never again have to worry about a Tory government and Scotland will be able to implement the Swedish-style far-Left government that many seem to want. As *American Renaissance* editor Jared Taylor, who is opposed to independence, writes:

> A vote for independence is being sold as a vote for more welfare — even though Scotland already gets more money back from Britain than it pays in taxes. Scots want more handouts, and think they'll get them from an independent Scotland.[6]

I offer no counter to any of this. Why then, do I hope the Saltire will soon fly throughout the land? Three reasons.

First, only independence can break Scotland's dependent culture.

Jared Taylor is right to charge that Scottish nationalism is driven by "money grubbing," not an authentic desire to be free. However, Scotland is not being offered a choice between a welfare state and a more efficient system. It is being offered a choice between a welfare state subsidized by England and a state they have to pay for themselves.

Indeed, as a last minute effort to support the pro-Union vote, lead-

---

5   Sharkov, Damien. "Independence Diary: Scottish Socialists Push for Yes Vote to Smash 'British Imperialist State.'" *Newsweek*. February 29, 2016. Accessed May 18, 2018. http://www.newsweek.com/scottish-socialists-push-yes-vote-smash-british-imperialist-state-271013.

6   Taylor, Jared. "Scotland Should Stay in the Union." *American Renaissance*. September 18, 2014. Accessed May 18, 2018. https://www.amren.com/news/2014/09/scotland-should-stay-in-the-union/.

ers of every major British political party have promised more money and powers for Scotland if it votes no.[7] A no vote would ensure that destructive policies continue — paid for by the English.

In contrast, as Nick Land writes,

> Beginning its new life as a hotbed of socialist lunacy, an independent Scotland would be forced — very rapidly — to grow up, which of course means moving sharply to the right. The more theatrical the transitional social crisis, the more thoroughly leftism-in-power would be humiliated. … A quantum of leftist insanity will have been extinguished, since its condition of existence was a relation of political dependency.[8]

If Scotland votes no, the checks keep coming — and Leftism endures.

Second, Scottish independence opens the door to the redemption of England.

At a stroke, the removal of Scotland from the Union ensures conservative (small "c") domination over England — as the loathsome George Galloway points out.[9]

Suddenly, it becomes far more realistic to speak of Nigel Farage achieving real power in Parliament — although UKIP may have to change its name. It also increases the likelihood of England leaving the European Union, and achieving real independence for itself. Scottish independence won't "free" the Scots — it will free the English.

---

7   "Scottish Independence: Cameron, Miliband and Clegg Sign 'No' Vote Pledge." BBC. September 16, 2014. Accessed May 18, 2018. https://www.bbc.co.uk/news/uk-scotland-scotland-politics-29213418.

8   Land, Nick. "Go Scotland." Xeno Systems (blog), September 09, 2014. Accessed May 23, 2018. http://www.xenosystems.net/go-scotland/.

9   Harris, John. "Scottish Referendum: George Galloway on Tour to Say 'Naw' to Independence." The Guardian. March 26, 2014. Accessed May 18, 2018. https://www.theguardian.com/politics/2014/mar/26/scottish-referendum-george-galloway-naw-tour-independence-no-vote.

Most importantly, it opens up the possibility of revolutionary change in Europe — which is desperately needed, sooner rather than later.

As a Sign of Contradiction, the same powerful forces that support mass immigration are violently opposed to Scottish secession. George Galloway and other elements of the British Left are largely opposed because Scottish independence will rekindle nationalism, even if it is momentarily framed as a politically correct variant.

George Soros, who made his fortune by disrupting the British economy, is now suddenly concerned about secession because he wants "increased unity."[10] And Tyler "Cheap Chalupas" Cowen is upset that the people are being asked to vote on independence in such a "blatant" form, rather than being guided carefully by their betters about what they should support.[11]

It may be the case that it is marginally wiser for Scotland to remain in the Union for largely pragmatic reasons. However, the British people as a whole have nothing to gain from stability: even the mass rape of English girls in Rotherham has led to no systematic change.

And time is running out in demographic terms if the British Isles are to be something other than a northern outpost of the Dar-al-Islam.

My calculation: Scottish secession would empower other movements across the Continent, including more forthrightly ethnonationalist ones like that in Flanders. And as mass immigration is largely an elite-driven phenomenon pushed from the top down, almost *any* devolution works to the advantage of immigration patriots in strategic terms — especially

---

10 Boyle, Catherine. "Soros Wades in to Scotland Debate." *Yahoo! Finance.* September 11, 2014. Accessed May 18, 2018. https://finance.yahoo.com/news/soros-wades-scotland-debate-065717367.html.

11 Cowen, Tyler. "Creative Ambiguity, Scottish Independence, and Sudden Death." *Marginal Revolution.* September 17, 2014. Accessed May 18, 2018. https://marginalrevolution.com/marginalrevolution/2014/09/creative-ambiguity-scottish-independence-and-sudden-death.html.

when the European Union is showing no eagerness to absorb these new states.

Scottish-born Gavin McInnes may well be right when he charges that Scottish nationalism is driven by "hate" of England — and is, as he puts it, "crap."[12] But so is the system that they have now — and the system that rules the rest of Britain and all of Europe.

The British Union is no longer about Empire, but about subsidizing decadence. The Death of the West is happening and we are out of time to slow the decay through cautious conservatism.

If devolution and secession is the wave of the future, immigration patriots should ride the tide and embrace the new possibilities it offers.

---

12 McInnes, Gavin. "Scottish Independence Is Crap." *Taki's Magazine*. September 12, 2014. Accessed May 18, 2018. http://takimag.com/article/scottish_independence_is_crap_gavin_mcinnes/print#axzz5Foj57U1t.

CHAPTER THREE

TRUMP ANNOUNCES RUN FOR PRESIDENT

SLAMMED BY THINKPROGRESS FOR MENTIONING IMMIGRATION

After years of teasing the press, Donald Trump is officially running for President, exactly as *VDARE*'s Matthew Richer bravely predicted.[1] One can't help but think The Donald thought his announcement would be greeted by rapturous applause. Instead, there's been barely concealed fury from the Main Stream Media.

Some people say he's not a serious candidate. But the argument over "seriousness" is one I can't take seriously. Hillary Clinton is widely favored to be the next President and I have yet to find anyone who can name one actual accomplishment of her time as First Lady, Senator, or Secretary of State.

Some say he's just a shallow salesman. But I'd rather a salesman than someone like Paul Ryan, who cynically and shamelessly lies to his own supporters.

Yet the MSM seems angriest because Trump mentioned immigration. I take great joy in quoting from *ThinkProgress* below:

> "When do we beat Mexico at the border?" Trump asked the crowd at his announcement at his namesake Trump Tower in New York City. "They are not

---

1   Richer, Matthew. "For Better Or Worse, Donald Trump May Be The Only Immigration Patriot Running For President." *VDARE*. April 12, 2015. Accessed May 18, 2018. https://www.vdare.com/articles/for-better-or-worse-donald-trump-may-be-the-only-immigration-patriot-running-for-president.

our friend, believe me. ... The U.S. has become a dumping ground for every-body else's problems. ... When Mexico sends its people, they are not sending their best. They are not sending you. They are sending people that have lots of problems, and they are bringing those problems to us. They are bringing drugs and they are bringing crime, and they're rapists.

"Some, I assume are good people. But I speak to border guards and they tell us what we are getting," Trump continued. "They are not sending us the right people. It's coming all over South and Latin America and it's coming probably from the Middle East. But we don't know because we have no pro-tection and we have no competence. We don't know what is happening and it has got to stop and it has to stop fast."

Trump also indicated that he would build a "great, great wall on the southern border" and that he would undo the president's executive action known as the Deferred Action for Childhood Arrivals (DACA) program.[2]

Would it be better if more "mainstream" Republican candidates were making these arguments? Well, yes. But such is donor control over the Republican Party that only someone with his own source of funding can say these kinds of things. And it will be fun to watch him criticize the other Republican candidates.

Besides, who is the Beltway Right to complain? Trump has been giv-en speaking slots at CPAC (even as conservative intellectuals are chased away), has partnered with conservative movement organizations like Americans for Limited Government, and regularly appears on Fox News. Any conservative whining that Trump is not "serious" has to explain why he was apparently "serious" enough to be used as a source of media atten-tion and funding in the past.

And who actually is a "serious" Republican candidate with well-thought-out positions? Jeb Bush?

2   Lee, Esther Yu Hsi. "Watch Donald Trump Go Full Nativist In Presidential Campaign Launch." *ThinkProgress.* June 16, 2015. Accessed May 18, 2018. https://thinkprogress. org/watch-donald-trump-go-full-nativist-in-presidential-campaign-launch-d5459a57e994/.

CHAPTER FOUR

America's Jacobin Moment

WILL IT INSPIRE A COUNTER-REVOLUTION?

The Supreme Court mandated gay marriage for all fifty states, in what is being celebrated as a bold stand for equality. Of course, all the Supreme Court really did is ratify the opinion of the Ruling Class: big business, the Main Stream Media, and the academic and bureaucratic establishments.

Regardless of its merits as policy, the Court's decision on marriage was undeniably a judicial *coup d'état* by America's homegrown Jacobins. It capped what may have been the worst week in history for movement conservatives. Just to review what else happened in the last few days:

- The Republican Congress joined with President Obama to pass the catastrophic Trans-Pacific Partnership, a policy firmly opposed by the conservative base. Largely because of its infringements on immigration policy and American sovereignty, conservative activist Phyllis Schlafly called it "the worst bill Congress has ever passed."[1]

- The Confederate flag was removed from monuments, statehouses, and even national parks. The only politicians who appeared to defend the flag were Democrats. As the modern Republican Party is based in the South and depends heavily on increasing white turnout, the TPP and the Confederate flag are a one-two punch to any Republican hopes of turning out its white base in the 2016 elections.

- The Supreme Court, led by Bush appointee John Roberts, saved the Affordable Care Act ("Obamacare") for nakedly political reasons.

---

1 "Schlafly Slams 'worst Bill Congress Has Ever Passed.'" *WND*. June 23, 2015. Accessed May 18, 2018. http://www.wnd.com/2015/06/schlafly-slams-worst-bill-congress-has-ever-passed/.

Voters who delivered a crushing victory for the GOP in the midterm elections must be wondering what the point was.

Yet this week did not just reveal the impotence of the Beltway Right. It also saw the beginning of a truly frightening witch-hunt that reveals how members of the historic American nation will not just be politically dispossessed but personally punished for any views perceived as out of step with the emerging Third World America.

And we got a sneak peek of the tactics to come.

Truth is no defense — you can be punished for mentioning "Hatefacts"

The scapegoating of the Council of Conservative Citizens (CCC) for the murderous actions of Dylann Roof continued, even though the CCC's "motivation" consisted of nothing more than pointing out the racial realities of crime. *VDARE* uses the term "hatefact" to describe objectively truthful statements that are nonetheless perceived as offensively politically incorrect. This week saw the term lose its ironic connotation. Truthfully reporting crime is now enough for one to be accused of having "allegedly inspired" a killer — and the MSM won't even bother to get the name of your group right.[2]

Needless to say, if the same rules applied to the MSM's far less accurate and objective coverage of police shootings and the violence that has resulted, you could count the number of innocent journalists on one hand.

Dissident groups will have their tax-exempt status revoked

Part of the MSM's campaign against the CCC consists of "point and

---

2   Dodrill, Tara. "Kyle Rogers: Conservative Christian Council Leader Denies Dylann Roof Connection." *The Inquisitr*. June 24, 2015. Accessed May 18, 2018. https://www.inquisitr.com/2198845/kyle-rogers-conservative-christian-council-leader-denies-dylann-roof-connection/.

sputter" articles about the CCC's tax exempt status. Some of these are even coming from ostensibly conservative websites such as *Newsmax*.[3]

Of course, it won't just be race-realist organizations that will have their tax-exempt status revoked. It will also be any churches that refuse to host a gay wedding. In fact, President Obama's Solicitor General admitted this would be an "issue" if the Court legalized gay marriage.[4] Black churches, many of which openly engage in electioneering, will continue be exempt from the rules everyone else has to follow — a reality taken for granted by lawyers operating in the non-profit area.[5]

Economic Strangulation will be encouraged by the MSM

The MSM, far from encouraging a robust debate on important issues, largely exists to choke out dissent. This includes strangling the finances of dissident groups and trying to prevent them from getting advertisers.

In a recent example, Jared Taylor's New Century Foundation lost advertising revenue from *Newsmax* and Taboola when *USA Today* wrote an article denouncing groups that ran advertisements on sites "who helped inspire one of America's most notorious killers."[6] Interestingly, one of the

3   Clyne, Melissa. "Supremacist Group Tied to SC Shootings Has Tax-Exempt Status." *Newsmax*. June 26, 2015. Accessed May 18, 2018. https://www.newsmax. com/Newsfront/conservative-citizens-supremacist-tax-exempt-irs/2015/06/26/ id/652325/.

4   Bailey, Sarah Pulliam. "Could Religious Institutions Lose Tax-exempt Status over Supreme Court's Gay Marriage Case?" *The Washington Post*. April 28, 2015. Accessed May 18, 2018. https://www.washingtonpost.com/news/acts-of-faith/wp/2015/04/28/ could-religious-institutions-lose-tax-exempt-status-over-supreme-courts-gay- marriage-case/.

5   Howley, Patrick. "Eric Holder, IRS Officials Coached Tax-exempt Black Ministers on How to Engage in Political Activity." *The Daily Caller*. September 16, 2013. Accessed May 18, 2018. http://dailycaller.com/2013/09/13/eric-holder-irs-officials-coached- tax-exempt-black-ministers-on-how-to-engage-in-political-activity/.

6   Cabrera, Cristina, and David Mastio. "Cash Flood Puts Politicos, Advertisers in Bed with Racists: Column." *USA Today*. June 25, 2015. Accessed May 18, 2018.

"research assistants" for the hit piece was one Jenna Adamson, a fellow for the "conservative" Collegiate Network.

The Purges Will Continue (Until Morale Improves)

The jihad against the Confederate Flag defied satire as sites including Amazon, eBay, and Google banned sales of the battle flag. Communist and even Nazi memorabilia are still available, however, though presumably the latter will eventually be banned. It remains to be seen if "offensive" books will be purged, but as the fatal step has already been taken against a symbol perceived as "mainstream" only a week ago, that kind of censorship can't be far behind.

Even people who want to remain apolitical find themselves being caught up in the online terror campaign. For example, *every* Civil War game once available on the App Store for use on the iPhone has now been purged, meaning that developers have just had their work randomly destroyed.[7] If merely having a Confederate flag in a game about the Civil War is beyond the pale, what isn't?

And, needless to say, the life-destroying purges against individuals for single posts on social networking or membership in certain groups are accelerating. For example, a police officer was just fired for a "selfie" featuring Confederate flag underwear. Interestingly, the officer was not fired for releasing a picture of himself in his underwear (which was obviously unprofessional) but because he was associated with a symbol of "hate and oppression." If he had been wearing a shirt or a Confederate re-enactor uniform, presumably there would have been the same result.[8]

---

https://www.usatoday.com/story/opinion/2015/06/25/white-supremacist-websites-business-oversight-column/29184499/.

7 Lazarides, Tasos. "Apple Removes All American Civil War Games From the App Store Because of the Confederate Flag." *TouchArcade.* August 31, 2017. Accessed May 18, 2018. http://toucharcade.com/2015/06/25/apple-removes-confederate-flag/.

8 Miller, Michael E. "North Charleston Cop Fired for Posing in Confederate Flag Underwear on Facebook." *The Washington Post.* June 26, 2015. Accessed May 18, 2018. https://www.washingtonpost.com/news/morning-mix/wp/2015/06/26/north-charleston-cop-fired-for-posing-in-confederate-flag-underwear-on-facebook/.

Two police officers in Alabama had also been fired for their partici-
pation in the pro-Southern League of the South, before Roof's ram-
page.[9]

Leftists traditionally claim negotiation is possible even with terrorists.
Former Republican and current Democratic candidate for President Lincoln Chafee even said he would negotiate with ISIS.[10] Yet now it seems
that acknowledging the sacrifice of those who died defending the Southern Confederacy is *verboten*. Even grave desecration is being advocated
by elected officials.[11]

How should Americans and especially Southerners respond to this
unprecedented cultural offensive? Partially, they are trapped by their allegiance to the Republican Party.

Because Democrats have written off rural whites and because rural
whites have no political home, many believe there is no political price
to be paid for the anti-Confederate *Kulturkampf*. Both economically and
culturally, many whites are simply being cut out of the system.

But, paradoxically, this provides an opportunity for people willing to
create new alternatives. One example of unintended consequences in action: the surge in sales for Confederate flags after the bans by major online
retailers. Smaller flag stories, including, presumably, the "Patriotic Flags"
store advertised on the CCC's website, are reaping the benefits.

And we can imagine a political equivalent. From the candidacy of

9   Blidner, Rachelle. "Two Alabama Cops Ousted for Membership in Confederate Hate
    Group." *New York Daily News*. June 20, 2015. Accessed May 18, 2018. http://www.
    nydailynews.com/news/national/2-alabama-cops-ousted-confederate-hate-group-
    ties-article-1.2264937.

10 Weigel, David, and Ben Brody. "Lincoln Chafee Talks Peace with Islamic State,
    Forgiveness for Edward Snowden, and the Metric System for All." *Bloomberg*.
    June 03, 2015. Accessed May 18, 2018. https://www.bloomberg.com/news/articles/
    2015-06-03/lincoln-chafee-talks-peace-with-isis-forgiveness-for-edward-snowden-
    and-the-metric-system-for-all.

11 Starnes, Todd. "Memphis Mayor Wants to Dig Up Dead Confederate War General."
    Townhall. June 26, 2015. Accessed May 18, 2018. https://townhall.com/columnists/
    toddstarnes/2015/06/26/memphis-mayor-wants-to-dig-up-dead-confederate-war-
    general-n2017895.

Donald Trump in the GOP to Jim Webb in the Democrats, the 2016 election could see the rebirth of Sam Francis's Middle American Radicals, as mostly white voters in both parties look for an alternative that is increasingly closed off to them.[12] As political repression and cultural indoctrination becomes more repressive and stifling, the spirit of revolt may emerge in surprising ways as people search for alternatives to another Bush vs. Clinton election.

Completely unexpectedly, *Roe v. Wade* triggered a Right To Life movement that now terrifies GOP operatives. Two generations ago, George Wallace transformed the American political system and pointed the path to GOP nation-wide victories that its operatives have only just recently forgotten.

Here's hoping. After all, we already have the perfect symbol for a good old-fashioned rebellion.

---

12 Francis, Sam T. "From Household to Nation." *Chronicles*, March 1996, 12-16. Accessed May 22, 1996. http://www.unz.com/print/Chronicles-1996mar-00012/.

CHAPTER FIVE

We Are All Donald Trump Now

LEFT MOVES TO BAN TRUTH ABOUT IMMIGRATION

The Overton Window is a political theory describing how ideas go from the margins to mainstream, from "unthinkable" to "policy." But in today's anti-America, a Reverse Overton Window is visibly at work: existing law, policy, majority opinion, legal terms like "illegal alien" and established traditions like flying the Confederate Battle Flag are suddenly decreed to be beyond the pale for all good-thinkers.

Case in point: the unprecedented political and economic terror campaign being waged against Republican presidential candidate Donald Trump for stating the facts about immigrant crime. And this characteristically totalitarian Cultural Marxist drive reveals an American political and economic system increasingly defined by ever more blatant hatred of the historic American nation in general and of white males in particular.

During The Donald's presidential announcement, he made the now-famous comment that the United States is not receiving the "best" people from Mexico, but instead people who are bringing "problems," including "rapists," "crime," and "drugs" — although he stipulated "some, I assume, are good people." Right on cue, Kate Steinle of San Francisco was murdered by José Inez Garcia Zarate (aka Juan Francisco López-Sánchez), an illegal immigrant who was deported five times but chose to return to the City by the Bay because of its liberal Sanctuary City policies.[1]

Yet instead of forcing the Democrats on the defensive over their

---

1   Barnard, Cornell. "EXCLUSIVE: Pier 14 Suspect Admits to Shooting." ABC7 San Francisco. July 05, 2015. Accessed May 19, 2018. http://abc7news.com/news/exclusive-accused-san-francisco-killer-admits-to-crime/830325/.

treasonous refusal to enforce existing immigration law and to import Third World criminals, Trump's statement has become a "hatefact" — scandalous by virtue of its political incorrectness.

Though Trump acknowledges he has suffered heavy financial damage from canceled contracts, and is also falling all over himself to deny that he's a racist, he has refused to back down on his comments.[2] His key talking point, "I can't apologize for the truth," is a more forceful repudiation of political correctness than anything a Republican politician has said in years.[3]

Needless to say, Republican presidential candidates like Rick Perry and Jeb Bush have declared they were "offended" by Trump's remarks.[4] But other Republican candidates, including Ben Carson, Rick Santorum, and Ted Cruz, have defended or at least expressed sympathy with Trump's remarks. Most recently, the appalling Republican National Committee Chairman Reince Priebus took the quintessentially Stupid Party step of calling Trump to ask him to stop saying such popular things, but Trump with characteristic irrepressibility has claimed Priebus merely told him he had hit a "nerve."[5]

By refusing to cave on his remarks, Trump has shifted the dynamics of the race and instantly catapulted himself to the status of a front-runner. He may even have inspired some legislative action: Representative Duncan D. Hunter (the son of former Congressman and presidential

2   Trump, Donald J. "Trump: I Have Lost a Lot, But I'm Right About Mexico." *Newsmax.* July 06, 2015. Accessed May 18, 2018. https://www.newsmax.com/Newsfront/trump-mexico-first-person-statement/2015/07/06/id/653706/.

3   Key, Pam. "Trump on Mexico Comments: 'I Can't Apologize for the Truth.'" *Breitbart.* July 05, 2015. Accessed May 18, 2018. http://www.breitbart.com/video/2015/07/05/trump-on-mexico-comments-i-cant-apologize-for-the-truth/.

4   Chalfant, Morgan. "Jeb Bush, Rick Perry 'offended' by Donald Trump's Remarks on Mexican Immigrants." Red Alert Politics. July 05, 2015. Accessed May 18, 2018. http://redalertpolitics.com/2015/07/05/jeb-bush-rick-perry-offended-donald-trumps-remarks-mexican-immigrants/.

5   Diamond, Jeremy. "Trump: RNC Call Was 'congratulatory.'" CNN. July 09, 2015. Accessed May 18, 2018. https://www.cnn.com/2015/07/08/politics/donald-trump-reince-priebus-immigrants-rnc/index.html.

candidate Duncan L. Hunter) is introducing legislation that will restrict funding to "sanctuary cities."[6]

Yet powerful forces are moving to shut Trump down, and, by extension, drive anyone who shares a patriotic position on immigration out of public life. Hillary Clinton has called for the Republican Party to repudiate him because his position should not be allowed in the presidential campaign. And she might just get her wish: Republican donor John Jordan is trying to spearhead a campaign to keep Trump out of the debates.[7]

As the GOP is now nothing else but a donor-driven party, Trump may face an uphill battle to be allowed to participate, regardless of the popular support he receives.

Right now, television channels including (but not limited to) NBC, ESPN, and Univision, companies including Macy's and the craft brewer 5 Rabbit Cerveceria, various participants and performers in the Miss USA pageant, and local governments including the City of New York have all tried to cut ties with Donald Trump and sever business relationships with him. The PGA Tour has also moved its Grand Slam of Golf event from Trump National golf course.[8]

Many of these groups are also eager to make shrill statements through their spokespeople about Trump's supposed "hatred" of Latinos.[9]

And individuals with a social media presence are also getting involved. Mostly-white open-borders advocate and former celebrity Eva Longoria,

6   May, Caroline. "GOP Rep. Slated To Introduce Legislation Targeting Sanctuary Cities." *Breitbart*. July 07, 2015. Accessed May 18, 2018. http://www.breitbart.com/big-government/2015/07/07/gop-rep-slated-to-introduce-legislation-targeting-sanctuary-cities/.

7   "Top GOP Donor Wants Donald Trump Banned from First Debate." *Breitbart*. July 07, 2015. Accessed May 18, 2018. http://www.breitbart.com/big-government/2015/07/07/top-gop-donor-wants-donald-trump-banned-from-first-debate/.

8   "PGA of America Pulls Tournament from Trump National L.A." *Breitbart*. July 07, 2015. Accessed May 18, 2018. http://www.breitbart.com/sports/2015/07/07/pga-of-america-pulls-tournament-from-trump-national/.

9   Hongo, Hudson. "A Comprehensive List of Everyone Trying to Sever Ties With Donald Trump." *Gawker*. July 1, 2015. Accessed May 18, 2018. http://gawker.com/a-comprehensive-list-of-everyone-trying-to-sever-ties-w-1715314213.

who finds it profitable to Live Action Role Play as an oppressed mestizo as her career fades, even managed to fulfill Godwin's Law by comparing Donald Trump to Hitler.[10]

Of course, this campaign is hardly a natural occurrence. The Cultural Marxist pressure group Media Matters, which, like the Southern Poverty Law Center, defines political success as simply censoring or intimidating opposition groups out of existence, is leading a "Dump Trump" campaign on social media.[11] The campaign is designed to destroy Trump by forcing companies to sever licensing agreements with him and to sabotage his brand by smearing him as a "racist."

Exactly as predicted, the Main Stream Media is also going after Trump's construction business for employing illegals, even though their presence proves his point that immigration laws are not being enforced.[12]

For his part, Trump has triumphantly declared that he has the "silent majority" behind him. But that may be part of his problem. An institutional failure of democracy is that a highly mobilized and organized minority receiving concentrated benefits can easily defeat a loosely organized majority that pays diffuse costs.

Trump faces a coalition of groups, including the ethnic lobbies, cheap labor lobbies, and specific Republican donors, who are willing to do whatever it takes to ensure America never enforces its immigration laws. In contrast, Republican primary voters are atomistic, distracted by more than a dozen other competing candidates, and brow-beaten by a hopeless

10 Jones, Kipp. "Eva Longoria Compares Donald Trump to Hitler." *Breitbart*. July 01, 2015. Accessed May 18, 2018. http://www.breitbart.com/big-hollywood/2015/07/01/eva-longoria-compares-donald-trump-to-hitler/.

11 Lee, Kurtis. "Another Company Dumps Trump as Controversy Threatens to Bite into His Brand." *Los Angeles Times*. July 02, 2015. Accessed May 18, 2018. http://www.latimes.com/nation/politics/la-na-donald-trump-fallout-20150702-story.html.

12 Olivo, Antonio. "At Trump Hotel Site, Immigrant Workers Wary." *The Washington Post*. July 06, 2015. Accessed May 18, 2018. https://www.washingtonpost.com/local/they-say-they-arrived-in-the-us-illegally-now-theyre-working-on-trumps-dc-hotel/2015/07/06/9a785116-20ec-11e5-84d5-eb37ee8eaa61_story.html.

Beltway Right that believes immigration is less important than issues like the Export-Import Bank.

What's worse, Trump faces an interlocking series of academic, media, and political institutions that consistently promote an open-borders narrative and create online mobs to punish dissenters. Curtis Yarvin, AKA "Mencius Moldbug," has coined the term "The Cathedral" to describe the institutions that function as a 21st century equivalent to an established church. The Cathedral has the ability to create an artificial consensus on issues, even when the vast majority of people disagree with the opinions of the media and political class. The result is a culture of fear where anyone, at any time, might face economic destruction at the hands of unstable people whipped into a frenzy by the media.

Thus, even though the majority of Americans, and certainly the majority of Republicans, agree with Trump that immigration laws should be enforced, his opinion is treated as out of bounds. (Yarvin too was essentially forced out of a software conference because of his unrelated political writings.)[13]

Trump is important because he represents the first figure with the financial, cultural, and economic resources to openly defy elite consensus. If he can mobilize Republicans behind him and make a credible run for the Presidency, he can create a whole new media environment for patriots to openly speak their mind without fear of losing their jobs.

What's more, if enough Americans rally to him because of his contrarian populism, it could encourage businesses to return to or even seek out the Trump brand, marking one of the first times a top-down effort to discredit someone for racial sensitivity has backfired.

Donald Trump, to his own surprise, is finding that America is no longer a free country. Yet he seems determined not to play by the rules of the MSM and not to accept the artificial consensus of the political class.

---

13 Bokhari, Allum. "Strange Loop Tech Conference Bans Software Engineer Over Political Views." *Breitbart.* June 05, 2015. Accessed May 18, 2018. http://www.breitbart.com/london/2015/06/05/strange-loop-tech-conference-bans-software-engineer-over-political-views/.

For that reason, the campaign of Donald Trump is no longer about public policies, the Republican nomination, or even the Presidency.

It's about who governs this country — the Main Stream Media (and whosoever controls it) or the American people.

CHAPTER SIX

VIKTOR ORBÁN:

HUNGARY FOR HUNGARIANS,
EUROPE FOR EUROPEANS

Victor Orbán, who has a somewhat mixed record when it comes to supporting Western patriots,[1] triggered the enemies of Europe again by delivering a powerful speech in which he declared that Hungary belongs to Hungarians and Europe to Europeans:

"The real threat is not coming from the war zones but from the depths of Africa", the Prime Minister highlighted. "With the disintegration of the countries of North-Africa, the defence line which once protected Europe, and which absorbed the masses of people coming from the interior of Africa, has evaporated", he explained.

"What we have at stake today is Europe, the European way of life, the survival or disappearance of European values and nations, or their transformation beyond recognition", the Prime Minister pointed out. "We would like Europe to be preserved for the Europeans", he stated. "But there is something we would not just like but we want because it only depends on us: we want to preserve a Hungarian Hungary", he stressed.[2]

Is this supposed to be a bad thing? If it was referring to any other continent

---

1 Feher, Margit. "Hungary Bans Conference by U.S. Group It Calls 'Racist.'" *The Wall Street Journal.* September 29, 2014. Accessed May 23, 2018. https://www.wsj.com/articles/hungary-bans-conference-by-u-s-group-it-calls-racist-1412021984.

2 Mariann, Őry, and Jancsó Orsolya. "Orbán: Europe Is at Stake." *Magyar Hírlap.* July 25, 2015. Accessed May 18, 2018. http://magyarhirlap.hu/cikk/31400/Orban_Europe_is_at_Stake.

and civilization, it would be a truism. As some American conservatives are being forcibly reminded by their base, the nation isn't a cheap combination of some dirt, floating abstract "values," and a piece of paper that the government doesn't follow anyway. The nation is the people. When the people are dispossessed and deconstructed, the nation ceases to exist.

Europe faces an existential threat with the immigration invasion from Africa. The decisions Western leaders take in the coming years will determine whether Africa stops at the Mediterranean or the Baltic Sea. Orbán recognizes this. Other leaders either do not, or, more likely, actively favor the transformation taking place because it will strengthen the power of the political class.

They are assisted in this effort by the media. For example, at *The Guardian*, one Cas Mudde, who specializes in pathologizing the "radical right" (i.e., normal people), is screaming for the European Union and the United States to go after Orbán. He writes:

> While Orbán lacks the eloquence, and classical training, of Enoch Powell, make no mistake: this speech was more significant that [sic] Powell's infamous Rivers of Blood speech of 1968. While Powell was a member of the Tory shadow cabinet, a position he lost because of the speech, Orbán is the almighty ruler of Hungary — more or less jokingly referred to as Orbánistan by his opponents. He doesn't just warn about "the survival or disappearance of European values and nations", he organises xenophobic referendum campaigns and builds walls on his borders — roughly 25 years after the Iron Curtain was lifted in, of all places, Hungary.[3]

Several points.

1. Notice how warning about the "survival or disappearance of European values and nations" is apparently a bad thing. Why? Isn't preventing such an occurrence the first responsibility of any Western leader?

2. "Xenophobic referendum campaigns" where people get to vote on issues like

---

3 Mudde, Cas. "The Hungary PM Made a 'rivers of Blood' Speech ... and No One Cares." *The Guardian*. July 30, 2015. Accessed May 18, 2018. https://www.theguardian.com/commentisfree/2015/jul/30/viktor-orban-fidesz-hungary-prime-minister-europe-neo-nazi.

immigration are also bad apparently. I suppose Mudde wants the American system, where there is a referendum and if people vote the "wrong" way, the courts simply toss it out and say that it doesn't count. Because that's how democracy works.

3. Building a wall to prevent an unwanted invasion is different from building a wall to keep people in the country. Do we really have to spell this out? Incidentally, the Iron Curtain was about suppressing the independence of Eastern European countries and making sure the truly important decisions were made outside the country. Sounds a bit like the European Union.

4. Orbán is referred to as the "almighty ruler of Hungary," and his Hungary as "Orbánistan." But elsewhere in the piece, Mudde speculates that Orbán is simply using an "opportunistic strategy in order to fend off the Jobbik challenge."[4] Which is it? Is he an "almighty" God-Emperor of the Magyars or a threatened democratic politician responding to the concerns of his constituents in order to stay in power?

5. Enoch was right.

One more excerpt:

> As leaders from around the world descended on Paris to speak in defence of free speech, however hypocritical they were, the Hungarian PM used the #JeSuisCharlie demonstration to launch an anti-immigration campaign that is becoming more problematic by the day.[5]

So, unlike other politicians who posed for the cameras and then pursued the same suicidal policies, Orbán took action against an obvious security threat. Incidentally, anyone who uses the term "problematic" unironically is a terrible person.

What's interesting about the contemporary Western debate about mass immigration is that pro-invasion advocates no longer bother denying the effects of their policy. The eradication of traditional Western nations and the dispossession of Western peoples is held to be a self-evident good. Indeed, *they* are allowed to talk about the motivations and inevitable effects of their policies, it's just unacceptable when "nativists" point them out.

---

4   Ibid.
5   Ibid.

CHAPTER SEVEN

Donald Trump: Last Chance for Conservatism

OR FIRST SIGN OF WHITE IDENTITY POLITICS? MAYBE BOTH

Trump unstumped: The Donald now has the largest lead of any Republican this election cycle, according to a recent poll which shows that the real estate developer is beating his nearest competitor (Ben Carson) by sixteen points. He has displaced Scott Walker to take the lead in Iowa and, perhaps even more telling, has reversed his unfavorability ratings there in an unprecedented way.[1] The Beltway Right is unleashing a desperate attack against him, warning that he "is antithetical to the modern conservative movement."[2] (True!)

But the truth is that Trump represents a last chance for "conservatism" to remain relevant in American politics. And the borderline hysterical reaction against him reveals the embarrassing fact that political victory, or even influence, is less important to many Conservatism Inc. types than being seen as respectable in the eyes of elite liberal opinion.

Indeed, the problem with Trump seems to be that he may actually serve the interests of the Republican base — something deemed unacceptable inside the Beltway.

1   Cillizza, Chris. "This Iowa Poll Shows Just How Amazing Donald Trump's Rise Has Been." *The Washington Post.* August 30, 2015. Accessed May 18, 2018. https://www.washingtonpost.com/news/the-fix/wp/2015/08/30/this-iowa-poll-shows-just-how-amazing-donald-trumps-rise-has-been/.

2   Rubin, Jennifer. "The Anti-Trump Angst Grows." *The Washington Post.* August 30, 2015. Accessed May 18, 2018. https://www.washingtonpost.com/blogs/right-turn/wp/2015/08/30/the-anti-trump-angst-grows/.

Thus, Redstate co-founder (and notorious plagiarist)[3] Ben Domenech writes that Trump is a threat to the "classically liberal" American Right, one which "synthesizes populist tendencies and directs such frustrations towards the cause of limited government." Trump, he intones, represents a turn towards "white identity politics" instead of "freedom," and a possible regression to the populist European Right, which must be avoided. After all, "in rare places like Hungary, we see what happens when the populist-right actually wins, and it isn't pretty."[4]

Perhaps Domenech is angry that Hungary's Viktor Orbán actually built a fence, instead of lying to voters like our Republican leaders do. But Domenech's larger concern is that the American Right may reorient itself towards expressing the "narrow" interests of whites "in opposition to the interests of other ethnic groups… in a marked departure from the expansive view of the freedoms of a common humanity."[5]

Until the nation-breaking 1965 Immigration Act, of course, "whites" would have been called "Americans."

And there's an obvious air of unreality to all of this. To Domenech's first point, what glorious victories for "limited government" has the American conservative movement actually achieved? The intrusion of the federal government into daily life and the constant growth of state power has not been restricted or even significantly slowed despite a half century of effort and repeated Republican victories.

This growth in government power and the collapse of local authority has been justified on the grounds of promoting multiculturalism and fighting supposed white racism. Domenech seems to suggest that instead of combating hostile Leftist identity politics with identity politics from the Right, conservatives should limit themselves to mutterings about

3   Bailey, Jonathan. "The Ben Domenech Scandal." *Plagiarism Today*. March 26, 2006. Accessed May 19, 2018. https://www.plagiarismtoday.com/2006/03/24/the-ben-domenech-scandal/.

4   Domenech, Ben. "Are Republicans For Freedom or White Identity Politics?" *The Federalist*. August 31, 2015. Accessed May 18, 2018. http://thefederalist.com/2015/08/21/are-republicans-for-freedom-or-white-identity-politics/.

5   Ibid.

"classical liberalism." But such a tactic appears increasingly disconnected from reality. Much as when the Beltway Right talks about Christianity, classical liberal principles are only invoked when it is time to explain to the pawns why they aren't allowed to actually expect forceful or successful political action from their political representatives.

As you've probably already guessed, *National Review*'s Kevin Williamson is making this case even more explicitly. Incredibly, he couples it with sneers at the rise of the Sweden Democrats, now the most popular party in Sweden and the only democratic opposition to a forthrightly authoritarian government seemingly obsessed by the desire to replace its own people. Williamson writes:

> As with the case of Donald Trump in the United States, the Sweden Democrats illustrate that when responsible parties will not confront the issue of uncontrolled immigration, then irresponsible parties will...
>
> [T]here is a large overlap between those who put immigration restriction at the center of their agenda and those who oppose free trade, and they share the assumption that economic interactions with foreigners absent government guidance toward the "national interest" is necessarily destructive. It is not that there is no such thing as the national interest: We have an intense and necessary interest in what's going on in Pyongyang at the moment, and what happens in Syria, whether our borders are secure, whether our banking regulations put us at a global disadvantage. But there isn't a legitimate national interest in having boffins in Washington stand between a fellow in Pittsburgh who wants to buy a pair of sneakers and a guy in Mindanao who wants to sell them to him.[6]

But if the nation-state is regarded as a legitimate institution, issues such as good jobs, quality of life, trade deficits, and self-sufficiency are more important than simply achieving a low cost of labor. Such issues are at least as "legitimate" as what's happening overseas.

Moreover, what we are witnessing in both the United States and in

6   Williamson, Kevin D. "National Fronts." *National Review*. August 24, 2015. Accessed May 18, 2018. https://www.nationalreview.com/2015/08/donald-trump-bernie-sanders-national-socialism-immigration/.

Europe is nothing less than a civilizational crisis, enabled and defended by the so-called "responsible" parties. In this context, for a self-described conservative to mention an "intense" national interest in Pyongyang or Syria isn't just misguided; it's obscene.

And yet so much of the Beltway Right commentary on Trump is simply an extended whine that The Donald is somehow making the GOP look bad.

Thus, *National Review* editor Rich Lowry sniffs: "Trump is such a forceful communicator that he comes off as some sort of throwback alpha male, whereas Bush is such an earnest wonk he looks and sounds like a sensitive dad from a contemporary sitcom."[7]

Is being an alpha male supposed to be a bad thing? Well, perhaps to Lowry.

Meanwhile, George Will worries that Trump will lead to a focus on the white vote instead of the minority vote, which is supposedly a necessity because the share of the electorate that is white is shrinking. Of course, as he admits, even Romney was unable to win many minority voters: "Minorities generally detected Republican ambivalence, even animus, about them. This was before Trump began receiving rapturous receptions *because* he obliterates inhibitions about venting hostility."[8]

But if this is the case, then what is the point of pursuing the minority vote? Wouldn't it make more sense to mobilize the white vote?

No one seems to want to answer this question. Instead, the underlying motivation for the hostility against Trump is, quite clearly, a gut hostility towards his (white) supporters. Thus, Robert Tracinski can snark at *The Federalist* about "single-issue anti-immigration fanatics, Archie Bunker

7   Lowry, Rich. "The GOP Field That Failed." *Politico.* August 26, 2015. Accessed May 18, 2018. https://www.politico.com/magazine/story/2015/08/the-field-that-failed-121785.

8   Will, George F. "The Havoc That Donald Trump Wreaks — On His Own Party." *The Washington Post.* August 26, 2015. Accessed May 18, 2018. https://www.washingtonpost.com/opinions/the-havoc-that-donald-trump-wreaks--on-his-own-party/2015/08/26/7418c2c8-4b4c-11e5-84df-923b3ef1a64b_story.html.

types, [and] outright racists" among Trump's supporters in a piece urging conservatives to get behind another candidate.[9]

Unfortunately for Conservatism Inc., this snarking won't help when even a candidate like Jeb Bush has to get those white voters to turn out for the general election. Every Republican campaign will have to rely on "dog whistling" to some extent, and even GOP candidates who try to avoid race altogether will find that their positions do quickly take on racial overtones.

Trump matters because he is connecting the largely symbolic rhetoric of the GOP with actual appeals to the concrete interests of grassroots white conservatives on immigration, trade, and jobs. Politics is about who, not what. Trump's strategy of mobilizing voters behind an explicitly nationalist agenda may prove harder to contain than Conservatism Inc. expects.

The hard truth is that the legacy of William F. Buckley is failure. Because of the massive demographic shift that American cuckservatives enabled when they purged men such as Sam Francis, Pat Buchanan, and Peter Brimelow, the future of American politics is, as Francis predicted, ethnopolitics.[10]

The Left is already practicing this, and as the Obama Administration shows, is becoming quite successful. Republicans either need to adapt or find themselves replaced and irrelevant in the emerging post-America. If they had wanted to talk only about "classical liberalism," they should have stopped Third World immigration a few decades ago.

Trump offers a compromise position with his patriotic vision of renewed American greatness. But Conservatism Inc. may honestly prefer to remain politically correct and lose rather than be "offensive" and win. In effect, they may prefer running out the clock on Anglo-America in order

9   Tracinski, Robert. "Who Are Donald Trump's Supporters?" *The Federalist.* August 27, 2015. Accessed May 18, 2018. https://thefederalist.com/2015/08/26/who-are-donald-trumps-supporters/.

10   Nelson, Brent. "The Method Of Samuel T. Francis: From Burnham To Ethnopolitics." *The Occidental Quarterly* 5, no. 2 (Summer 2005): 37-48. Accessed May 23, 2018. https://www.toqonline.com/archives/v5n2/TOQv5n2Nelson.pdf.

to squeeze out consultants' fees and board directorships for a few more election cycles.

In that case, ultimately, the dreaded specter of "white nationalism" will move from the margins to the mainstream as the only alternative to a permanent Leftist (and anti-white) regime.

And, as *New York Times* slightly-better-than-token-conservative columnist Ross Douthat recently implied,[11] the Beltway Right will only have itself to blame.

11 Douthat, Ross. "Donald Trump, Traitor to His Class." *The New York Times.* August 29, 2015. Accessed May 18, 2018. https://www.nytimes.com/2015/08/30/opinion/sunday/ross-douthat-donald-trump-traitor-to-his-class.html.

CHAPTER EIGHT

TRUMP VICTORIOUS

AS GOP TRANSFORMED INTO A NATIONAL CONSERVATIVE PARTY

In the end, it wasn't even close. Donald Trump won a crushing victory in Indiana with over 50% of the vote, leading Ted Cruz to suspend his campaign for President. To the shock and horror of the Conservatism Inc. establishment (whom you could actually watch melting down in real time on Twitter), Donald Trump is the presumptive GOP nominee.

How much does Trump owe his Indiana victory to immigration? Exit polls ranked immigration as a top issue, but not *the* top issue, coming in well behind the Economy/Jobs, Government Spending, and Terrorism.[1] But this is misleading. *All* of the top three issues are directly related to immigration. Moreover, Trump's views on immigration are part of a larger nationalist narrative which is attractive to voters. As one voter put it, Trump is "for us."[2]

And Trump's own supporters certainly thought immigration was important. Exit polls showed slightly less than half of all Republican primary voters said most illegal immigrants should be deported to the country

---

1   Mascaro, Lisa. "Exit Polls: Immigration Not a Top Issue for Indiana Republicans." *Los Angeles Times*. May 03, 2016. Accessed May 18, 2018. http://www.latimes.com/politics/la-na-live-updates-indian-exit-polls-immigration-fades-as-top-issue-for-ind-1462311663-htmlstory.html.

2   "Immigration, Social Security on the Minds of Indiana Voters on Primary Day." Fox News. May 3, 2016. Accessed May 18, 2018. http://www.foxnews.com/politics/2016/05/03/immigration-social-security-on-minds-indiana-voters-on-primary-day.html.

they came from. Of those voters, 64% voted for Trump, with 34% going for Cruz and only 1% for Kasich.[3]

The scale of Trump's victory was such that it essentially ended the Republican primary race. And many commentators acknowledged, Tuesday night was a historic moment, marking the transition from a "conservative" Republican Party to a "nationalist, populist" one.

Jonathan Chait moaned, "[O]n the ground, Republican politics boils down to ethno-nationalistic passions ungoverned by reason." Chait blamed conservatives for not doing enough to tone-police their movement:

> The paranoid mendacity of Joe McCarthy, the racial pandering of Barry Goldwater, Richard Nixon, and George Bush, the jingoism and anti-intellectualism of Ronald Reagan, George W. Bush, and Sarah Palin — all these forces have embodied the essence of American conservative politics as it is actually practiced (rather than as conservative intellectuals like to imagine it). Trump has finally turned that which was always there against itself.[4]

Ignore the virtue-signaling and hysteria. Chait actually does have a sort of point here. Conservatism Inc. always has to appeal to nationalism and populism to win elections. However, the point is that *they didn't actually mean it* — it was simply a way to get the rubes to vote Republican. Once safely in office, the likes of Eric Cantor and Paul Ryan get back to cutting taxes for the rich, outsourcing jobs, opening the borders, and getting mired in pointless foreign wars.

Trump has destroyed this calculus, perhaps forever.

Josh Barro at *Business Insider*, who predicts a crushing Trump defeat, is nonetheless correct when he writes:

> Trump is the candidate who finally figured out how to exploit the fact that much of the Republican voter base does not share the policy preferences of

---

3   "Indiana Republican Entrance/Exit Poll." CBS News. June 9, 2016. Accessed May 18, 2018. https://www.cbsnews.com/elections/2016/primaries/republican/indiana/exit/.

4   Chait, Jonathon. "Trump Has Won and the Republican Party Is Broken." *New York Magazine*. May 3, 2016. Accessed May 18, 2016. http://nymag.com/daily/intelligencer/2016/05/trump-has-won-and-the-republican-party-is-broken.html.

the Republican donor class, and that it is therefore possible to win the nomination without being saddled with their unpopular policy preferences.

He will not be the last candidate to understand this.[5]

Trump did reject some of the elements of orthodox conservatism, notably support for so-called free trade and cutbacks for Social Security and Medicare. However, Barro and many of the #NeverTrump Conservative Inc. functionaries miss the mark when they say that Trump is a truly dramatic departure from conservatism.

After all, Trump's most stubborn opponent was Cruz, who aped Trump on both immigration and trade. Trump has been blasted by neoconservatives for calling for an America First foreign policy. But the *Washington Post*'s Jennifer Rubin, who for some unknown reason still postures as a "conservative," blasted Ted Cruz back in December on the same grounds — after Cruz used the America First phrase during a Republican debate, Rubin kvetched the Texas Senator had "sank further into the far-right brew of isolationism and xenophobia."[6]

More than any of Trump's other opponents, it was Cruz who clung the closest to Trump throughout the primaries. All it enabled him to do was beat out Jeb Bush, Marco Rubio, *et al.* Any attempt at a post-Trump purge of those forces that made Trump possible would have to start with Cruz himself.

Conor Friedersdorf, who can fairly be described as a cuckservative, sniffs:

> Look again at some of the figures who've done the most to signal that Trump is acceptable, or even that he is preferable: Sarah Palin, Sean Hannity, Rush Limbaugh, Joe Arpaio, higher-ups at Breitbart.com, Bill O'Reilly, Ann Coulter. It isn't as if no one warned the right about the dangers these people posed to

5   Barro, Josh. "The Crisis in the Republican Party Is Even Worse than It Looks." *Business Insider.* May 03, 2016. Accessed May 18, 2018. http://www.businessinsider.com/donald-trump-nomination-gop-crisis-2016-5.

6   Rubin, Jennifer. "Ted Cruz's Vision Turns Ugly." *The Washington Post.* December 16, 2015. Accessed May 18, 2018. https://www.washingtonpost.com/blogs/right-turn/wp/2015/12/16/ted-cruzs-vision-turns-ugly/.

their coalition. Few heeded the warnings. Until they recognize their error and grapple with it, they are unlikely to rebuild a coalition that is worthy of electing a president.[7]

Obviously, it's easy for Friedersdorf to make a career counter-signaling against the members of his own party. But it's much harder to win an election. Assuming the likes of Friedersdorf could even purge the Hannities and Limbaughs of the world, who would still exist to mobilize the grass-roots? How could this reformed Republican Party win elections?

What's more, Ted Cruz would not exist without figures like Palin or Limbaugh. Obviously, Friedersdorf doesn't like Cruz much more than he likes Trump. But the #CruzCrew types swearing they will never vote for Trump don't have much to go on other than their dislike of Trump personally. The main reason Cruz lasted as long as he did is because he tried to compete with Trump's positions on National Question issues.

In the next few days, there will be plenty of commentary about the death of "moderate" Republicans. But it's precisely grass-roots "moderate" Republicans who have been the most fanatic Trump supporters. What's really happening is not the victory of some sectional candidate or some "anti-establishment" figure. It's a realignment within the Republican Party.

Trump is taking the nationalist impulses that the Republican Party has used for years and putting them at the forefront of his new political movement. He's downplaying some of the hardcore social issues which conservatives have already lost on anyway. He's abandoning rhetoric about slashing programs that actually benefit the Republican Party's core constituents. And he's tapping into a narrative of national redemption which is deeply felt all over the country.

There's nothing about Trump's message which is opposed to "conservatism" at its most primal level. Trump wants to preserve the cultural existence of the American nation-state. Conservatism Inc. defends "conservatism" as a word, but has utterly lost touch with the people they are

---

7   Friedersdorf, Conor. "How the Party Decided on Trump." *The Atlantic*. May 03, 2016.
    Accessed May 18, 2018. https://www.theatlantic.com/politics/archive/2016/05/how-
    gop-influencers-cued-voters-to-choose-donald-trump/480294/.

supposed to defend. For all their invocations of "principle," they appear entirely self-interested and corrupt.

Now, the Republican base has caught on. They have chosen to displace the Beltway Right entirely. And they don't want the same old goofy slogans — but a nationalist movement that will actually fight for them.

It's about time. After all, the "conservative movement" can't say they weren't warned.

CHAPTER NINE

TRUMP'S STRATEGY:
Confront Main Stream
Media. It's Working

The fight now is not about who will be the next President of the United States. It is about whether the American nation will continue to exist. And this battle pits confrontational conservatives like Donald Trump against anti-American "protesters" working to deny our country a future — in alliance, increasingly blatantly, with the Main Stream Media in its role as "keeper of the Cultural Marxist narrative."

On Tuesday, May 31st, Trump threw the gauntlet at the feet of the Main Stream Media with an extraordinary press conference blasting the assembled reporters for what he said was their biased coverage.[1] While ostensibly about his fundraising for veterans, the real aim of Trump's press conference was to target the MSM as such.

"Is this what it's going to be like covering you if you're president?" asked one reporter plaintively. Trump fired back: "Yeah, it is. I'm going to continue to attack the press."[2]

In the aftermath, reporters who spent last week writing navel-gazing articles about how nasty it is to get mean Tweets from anonymous Twitter

---

1   Stokols, Eli, and Nolan D. McCaskill. "Trump Taunts Media to Its Face." *Politico*. May 31, 2016. Accessed May 18, 2018. https://www.politico.com/story/2016/05/trump-veterans-donations-223730.

2   Waldman, Paul. "Donald Trump Declares War on the Press." *The Washington Post*. May 31, 2016. Accessed May 18, 2018. https://www.washingtonpost.com/blogs/plum-line/wp/2016/05/31/donald-trump-declares-war-on-the-press/.

accounts with anime avatars began kvetching about how they are under mortal threat from the "anti-democratic" Trump.[3]

This, of course, is nonsense. Hillary Clinton hasn't even bothered to hold a press conference in months.[4] The real sin: Trump calling out reporters as political actors in their own right rather than pretending that they are unbiased observers.

And this calling-out is what grassroots conservatives want to hear. As Marco Rubio might say, let's "dispel" with this fiction that most journalists are any different from far-Left open-borders activists. They share the same premises, push the same narrative, and conceal evidence which contradicts the story they are trying to promote. After years of pro-immigrant sob stories and selective reporting, patriotic Americans are right to distrust the MSM.

The hard reality for reporters is that more people trust Trump than the "lying press." According to Gallup, Americans have even less confidence in newspapers and television news than they do in banks — notwithstanding the financial crisis.[5] According to a survey from the Pew Research Center, 65% of Americans say the national news media impacts the country negatively.[6] As Rush Limbaugh enthused:

> That was the kind of press conference Republican voters have been dying to see for who knows how many years…

3   Wemple, Erik. "Trump's Crazy, Insane, Nonsensical, Bonkers and Anti-democratic Press Conference." *The Washington Post*. May 31, 2016. Accessed May 18, 2018. https://www.washingtonpost.com/blogs/erik-wemple/wp/2016/05/31/trumps-crazy-insane-nonsensical-bonkers-and-anti-democratic-press-conference/.

4   Wolfgang, Ben. "Hillary Clinton Yet to Hold Single Press Conference in 2016." *The Washington Times*. May 31, 2016. Accessed May 18, 2018. https://www.washingtontimes.com/news/2016/may/31/hillary-clinton-yet-to-hold-single-press-conferenc/.

5   Jones, Jeffrey M. "Confidence in U.S. Institutions Still Below Historical Norms." Gallup. June 15, 2015. Accessed May 18, 2018. http://news.gallup.com/poll/183593/confidence-institutions-below-historical-norms.aspx.

6   "Beyond Distrust: How Americans View Their Government." Pew Research Center. November 23, 2015. Accessed May 18, 2018. http://www.people-press.org/2015/11/23/beyond-distrust-how-americans-view-their-government/.

[H]ow many years have people been begging for a Republican to just once take on the media the way Trump did? All the way from the premise, to the details, to the motivation, he took 'em all on…

But the media, the media totally wants Hillary Clinton to win, but they're so conflicted. The cable networks, since this thing ended, have been devoted to the press conference and how Trump was mean to them and how Trump insulted them and how Trump criticized them.[7]

One of the most important elements driving this fury against the MSM: the absurd double standards surrounding the protests directed against Trump. While the MSM casually calls Trump a "fascist," reporters ignore or even cover for startling acts of violence directed against his supporters and police. It's no surprise many Trump supporters are beginning to suspect reporters and protesters to be practically in partnership.

Trump's strategy of confrontation was on display again recently in Albuquerque, New Mexico. Screaming protesters waved Mexican flags, started fires, and even attacked police horses. One particularly apropos image: a group of Hispanic protesters holding obscene signs cursing Trump, with one even calling to "Free El Chapo." Next to that was a young girl holding a sign claiming, "I am not a rapist or drug dealer!"[8] Well, obviously not. But a drug dealer is still more respectable in the eyes of the MSM and academia than someone who simply calls for enforcing immigration laws.

Indeed, even as the fires and flags burned and the blood flowed, the MSM worked quickly to pin the blame on Trump. Partially, this was done through the passive language so beloved by reporters — it wasn't violent protesters who created chaos at the Trump rally; it was the Trump rally itself which somehow "turned" violent. Here are just three examples:

---

7   Limbaugh, Rush. "The Press Conference Republican Voters Have Wanted to See for Years." *The Rush Limbaugh Show*. May 31, 2016. Accessed May 18, 2018. https://www.rushlimbaugh.com/daily/2016/05/31/the_press_conference_republican_voters_have_wanted_to_see_for_years/.

8   Hunter, Derek. "Mexican Flag-Waving Mob Attacks Police, Horses Outside Trump Rally [VIDEO]." *The Daily Caller*. May 25, 2016. Accessed May 18, 2018. http://dailycaller.com/2016/05/25/activists-and-illegal-aliens-attack-police-horses-outside-trump-rally-video/.

- "Donald Trump's Campaign Rally In New Mexico Turns Violent," by Sara Jerde, Talking Points Memo, May 24, 2016. https://talkingpointsmemo.com/livewire/trump-rally-new-mexico-violent.

- "New Mexico Trump Rally Turns Violent," by Sarah Fisher, TruthRevolt, May 25, 2016. https://www.truthrevolt.org/news/new-mexico-trump-rally-turns-violent.

- "Albuquerque Trump Rally Turns Violent," by Daniel Chacon, *The New Mexican*, May 26, 2016. http://www.santafenewmexican.com/news/local_news/albuquerque-trump-rally-turns-violent/article_5e5dd5a2-c5ac-5811-8e44-29cb21e56a29.html.

It was the same story a few days later when Trump held a rally in San Diego. Trump's presence and rhetoric about immigration (i.e., build the wall and enforce the law) was held to be responsible for the chaos, rather than the people who actually perpetrated it.[9]

On television and in the press, reporters lectured Trump and his supporters about "civility" and worked hard to present a deliberately misleading version of events. One reporter for Telemundo, the fifth column Spanish-language network inside the United States, was even caught staging the news by covering up obscenities to present an attractive image of young children holding a Mexican flag.[10]

What makes Donald Trump different is that he refuses to let this narrative be perpetuated. He tweeted, "The protesters in New Mexico were thugs who were flying the Mexican flag. The rally inside was big and beautiful, but outside, criminals!" The tweet has received over 13,000 retweets and 35,000 likes, large numbers even for Trump's Twitter account.[11] Trump's campaign

---

9   "Violence as Trump Brings Immigration Rhetoric to Border." CBS News. May 28, 2016. Accessed May 18, 2018. https://www.cbsnews.com/news/donald-trump-protesters-violent-california-rally-gop-election-2016/.

10 T., Brett. "Watch: Telemundo Cameraman Helps Trump Protesters Holding Mexican Flag Upside-down." *Twitchy.* May 28, 2016. Accessed May 18, 2018. https://twitchy.com/brettt-3136/2016/05/28/watch-telemundo-cameraman-helps-trump-protesters-holding-mexican-flag-upside-down/.

11 realDonaldTrump. (2016, May 25). The protesters in New Mexico were thugs who were

also slammed the MSM for consistently blaming Trump. As Trump campaign manager Corey Lewandowski put it: "Mr. Trump and the campaign do not condone violence. The campaign rallies are attended by tens of thousands of people, and it's no surprise the dishonest media is intent on focusing on a few professional agitators."[12] Trump's ability to call his enemies what they are is emboldening his supporters. As one man who attended the New Mexico rally said: "This was not a protest, this was a riot. These are hate groups."[13]

Donald Trump's strategy of confrontation is highlighting the reality that Fourth Generation War has already begun in the United States. From New Mexico to Chicago, the anti-American Left and the revanchist street soldiers of foreign countries are making their intentions all too clear. The MSM is doing their best to pretend anti-Trump protesters are the mainstream and Trump is the extremist. But simply showing the protesters on the screen reveals the fanatical hatred for America, and for whites, driving the anti-Trump Left.

And that's why the more Trump takes his patriotic message into the heart of the enemy's domain, the more Americans rally to his cause.

In his famous "Liberty or Death" speech, Patrick Henry mocked those who believed the American Revolution hadn't already started. "Gentlemen may cry 'Peace, peace,' but there is no peace! The war is actually begun!"[14]

---

flying the Mexican flag. The rally inside was big and beautiful, but outside, criminals! [Tweet]. https://twitter.com/realDonaldTrump/status/735465352436408320.

12 McLaughlin, Seth. "Protests Backfire as Anti-American Images Push Undecided Voters to Trump." *The Washington Times.* May 30, 2016. Accessed May 18, 2018. https://www.washingtontimes.com/news/2016/may/30/donald-trump-rally-protests-backfire-as-anti-ameri/.

13 "Protests Turn Violent Outside Trump Rally in New Mexico." *Newsmax.* May 25, 2016. Accessed May 18, 2018. https://www.newsmax.com/Politics/US-GOP-2016-Trump-Rally/2016/05/25/id/730558/.

14 Henry, Patrick. "Give Me Liberty Or Give Me Death." Speech, Virginia, Richmond, March 23, 1775. Accessed May 18, 2018. http://www.constitution.org/col/war_inevitable.htm.

And so it has. The only question is how long the Main Stream Media can continue to conceal the obvious truth.

Donald Trump is doing his best to ensure their time of living on lies will soon be at an end.

CHAPTER TEN
Cuckservatives Call Retreat After Dallas Shooting. Will Trump?

On July 7, 2016, at a Black Lives Matter protest in Dallas, Texas, five policemen were shot and killed. Another nine officers were wounded — along with two civilians. This was done single-handedly by Micah Xavier Johnson, an African-"American" who considered it an act of vengeance against America law enforcement, whom he believed to be killing unarmed blacks with impunity.

The bodies were barely cold when leading cuckservatives were already rushing to triangulate between the hate group Black Lives Matter and the American policemen struggling to contain a low-level insurgency. To those familiar with The Stupid Party and Conservatism Inc., no such display of cowardice could be surprising. But will Donald Trump follow, either by caving himself — or by picking a cuck-compromised figure like Newt Gingrich as his Vice President?

Trump's initial reaction after the shootings in Dallas was sound. Hours before Hillary Clinton responded, Trump offered "prayers and condolences" to "all of the families" "devastated by the horrors we are all watching take place in our country."[1] In a longer response posted to his Facebook page, Trump called for the restoration of "law and order" and decried the worsening of racial tensions. He also called for "strong leadership, love, and compassion."[2] Especially given that many European-Americans

1 realDonaldTrump. (2016, July 8). Prayers and condolences to all of the families who are so thoroughly devastated by the horrors we are all watching take place in our country [Tweet] https://twitter.com/realDonaldTrump/status/751370918027489280.

2 Trump, Donald. (2016, July 8). [Facebook] https://www.facebook.com/DonaldTrump/posts/10157277205810725.

voted for Barack Obama because they thought he would heal the racial divide, this is a sober and highly appropriate response.

In contrast, Hillary Clinton tossed off a tweet a few hours later saying she mourned for police officers who had a "sacred duty to protect peaceful protesters."[3]

Even in the immediate aftermath of the shooting, this was a kind of passive-aggressive critique of the police — essentially saying the loss of life was tragic *because* cops were needed to "protect" the Black Lives Matter activists protesting them. Protect from whom? That same day, as the narrative already had begun to shift, Hillary pinned the blame on whites for the violence, saying, "White Americans need to do a better job of listening when African Americans talk about the seen and unseen barriers you face every day."[4]

Of course, back in reality, as political harassment causes policing to be formally or informally withdrawn, African-Americans are being increasingly victimized by violent crimes *at the hands of other African-Americans*:

> Under intense pressure, the Chicago police cut their pedestrian stops by 90 percent and murders are up 60 percent. When the Baltimore police virtually stopped making drug arrests after the Freddie Gray riots, murders shot up by 63 percent. They are up 54 percent in Washington, DC, and 65 percent in Milwaukee. If no blacks at all are arrested there will be no appearance of bias. Is that what Mr. Obama wants?[5]

Not surprisingly, resistance to law enforcement officers is also increasing, as criminals feel emboldened to disobey orders. Ominously, officers report that mobs have begun to gather whenever they try to detain

3   HillaryClinton. (2016, July, 8). I mourn for the officers shot while doing their sacred duty to protect peaceful protesters, for their families & all who serve with them. -H [Tweet] https://twitter.com/HillaryClinton/status/751401960381767680.

4   HillaryClinton. (2016, July, 8). White Americans need to do a better job of listening when African Americans talk about the seen and unseen barriers you face every day. [Tweet] https://twitter.com/HillaryClinton/status/751542474972291072.

5   Taylor, Jared. "The Dallas Killings Were Inevitable." American Renaissance. July 08, 2016. Accessed May 18, 2018. https://www.amren.com/features/2016/07/the-dallas-killings-were-inevitable/.

someone who is breaking the law. The Main Stream Media is cheer-leading this frenzy, which will almost certainly lead to further violence before the summer is over.

Unfortunately, it is simply not clear that the black community as a whole has the will or character to resist this death spiral, regardless of the fact that blacks themselves are its first victims.

Some commentators on the Right have identified the obvious and condemned the Left and the MSM's campaign of incitement. Rush Limbaugh featured Heather Mac Donald prominently on a recent show and gave her a great deal of time to explain the obvious lies underlying the Black Lives Matter campaign.[6]

But other conservatives have already begun giving aid and comfort to this burgeoning terrorist campaign against police and European-Americans. Useless goober Matt Lewis, always eager to curry favor with his Leftist friends, picked this moment to virtue signal as a Woke White Man coming to terms with his own privilege:

> In the era of Facebook Live and smart phones, it's hard to come to any conclusion other than the fact that police brutality toward African-Americans is a pervasive problem that has been going on for generations. Seriously, absent video proof, how many innocent African-Americans have been beaten or killed over the last hundred years by the police — with little or no media coverage or scrutiny?
>
> I was brought up to reflexively believe the police. To give them the benefit of the doubt. This was before everyone had a camera — and before my own personal experience would demonstrate to me that not all cops are heroes (though some certainly are).[7]

As a reward (no doubt eagerly anticipated), Lewis then got to appear on

6   Limbaugh, Rush. "Heather Mac Donald Talks About Her Essential Book: The War on Cops." *The Rush Limbaugh Show.* July 08, 2016. Accessed May 18, 2018. https://www.rushlimbaugh.com/daily/2016/07/08/heather_mac_donald_talks_about_her_essential_book_the_war_on_cops/.

7   Lewis, Matt K. "A Confession..." *The Daily Caller.* July 08, 2016. Accessed May 18, 2018. http://dailycaller.com/2016/07/08/a-confession/.

National Public Radio to discuss how "smartphones" and regular record-ing of incidents have changed views of police.[8]

But of course, Lewis has it precisely backwards. In the last few years, smartphones and video camera footage have actually provided a truthful perspective on events which otherwise would have been misrepresented or completely disappeared by the MSM. Millions of Americans around the country have witnessed black mobs causing chaos at fast food restau-rants, concerts, and other public spaces, often interspersed with feral cries of "World Star!" (World Star Hip Hop is a website that ostensibly features rap videos but more often features black Americans videotaping their own violent acts.)

For example, the "Epic Beard Man" case of several years ago would undoubtedly have been presented as a "racist" assault by a white man on an innocent African-American were it not for the existence of a video proving that the black man started the fight.[9]

Similarly, the "Knockout Game" is another viral phenomenon that the MSM tries to deny but which millions of Americans know is real because they've seen it.

"Smartphone" culture has provided the MSM with material for var-ious coordinated campaigns designed to incite black hostility against whites. But as we've seen in so many cases, once further citizen report-ing reveals the facts behind each case, "narrative collapse" sets in and the morality play of "innocent blacks victimized by racist whites" falls apart. Sometimes, as in the George Zimmerman case, it even turns out a white guy wasn't involved at all.

But if the MSM can control the information that is released, it can keep the original narrative of white guilt going. Thus, in the eyes of the

8   Martin, Rachel. "Matt Lewis: Smartphone Era Challenges Americans' Established Perceptions On Race And Policing." NPR. July 10, 2016. Accessed May 18, 2018. https://www.npr.org/2016/07/10/485432464/matt-lewis-smartphone-era-challenges-americans-established-perceptions-on-race-a.

9   Hart, Alexander. "Epic Beard Man, The MSM, And Citizen Reportage." *VDARE.* February 23, 2010. Accessed May 17, 2018. https://www.vdare.com/articles/epic-beard-man-the-msm-and-citizen-reportage.

MSM, releasing information which undermines the myth of black victimization is far more immoral than inciting murder against police officers.

Thus, when Matt Drudge made the obvious connection between Black
Lives Matter and the murders in Dallas, *Slate* showed far more anger towards Drudge then it did towards the murders themselves. Isaac Chotiner, one of the typical Cultural Marxist writers who functions in a state
of shrieking hysteria, screeched, "The Drudge Report, a highly-trafficked
sewer of right-wing racism and hate, led its hate with the despicable headline 'Black Lives Kill.'"[10]

But what is truly remarkable is how David French, the man Bill Kristol
floated as the "true conservative" alternative to Trump, bought the exact
same premise. "I just deleted my Drudge app," he preened. His action was
seized on by "conservatives" who are far more concerned about the threat
of Donald Trump than violence against police officers.[11]

French, practically a cuckservative icon, is surprising no one with his
actions. Of more concern is Newt Gingrich, still (apparently) one of the
leading candidates to be Donald Trump's Vice President. Gingrich com-
mented just after the shooting:

> It took me a long time, and a number of people talking to me through the
> years to get a sense of this. If you are a normal white American, the truth is
> you don't understand being black in America and you instinctively under-es-
> timate the level of discrimination and the level of additional risk.[12]

This is obscene. "Normal white Americans," to use Gingrich's phrase, also

10 Chotiner, Isaac. "Racist Responses to Tragedies Like Dallas Do More than Stoke
    Hatred. They Rob Us of Our Ability to Grieve." *Slate*. July 08, 2016. Accessed May
    18, 2018. https://www.slate.com/blogs/the_slatest/2016/07/08/racist_response_to_
    dallas_shootings_and_the_human_desire_to_grieve_the_dead.html.

11 Darcy, Oliver. "After Dallas, Conservatives Rebel against the Drudge Report."
    Business Insider. July 10, 2016. Accessed May 18, 2018. http://www.businessinsider.
    com/conservatives-drudge-report-dallas-2016-7.

12 Sheinin, Aaron Gould. "Newt Gingrich: White Americans 'don't Understand Being
    Black in America.'" *The Atlanta Journal-Constitution*. July 8, 2016. Accessed May 18,
    2018. https://politics.myajc.com/blog/politics/newt-gingrich-white-americans-don-
    understand-being-black-america/WhjQxDN8uslD895nbA8XTL/.

deal with "additional risk" simply by being around blacks. The desire to escape disproportionately high levels of black crime — levels which are now increasing again — is the dominant factor determining settlement patterns within the United States.

And even as Gingrich and his fellow cuckservatives posture to win Leftist favor, white Americans are being gunned down by Black Lives Matter supporters, with little sympathy or even recognition from the same reporters and activists shrieking for more concessions from the besieged historic American nation.

Americans should have the right to live free from fear in functioning communities that aren't plagued by thugs and murderers egged on by a sociopathic media and political class. What is needed is a leader who will resist this campaign of intimidation. Americans who are tired of Black Lives Matter's thuggery and outraged at the collapse of our cities are looking to Trump to be that leader.

Let's hope he stays worthy.

CHAPTER ELEVEN

IS EUROPE BURNING?

EVENTS PROPELLING TRUMP INTO WHITE HOUSE

"Events, dear boy, events," British Prime Minister Harold Macmillan supposedly said when discussing what political leaders most feared. No politician, however skilled, can predict the future. But they can manage expectations and perceptions. And that's precisely what Donald Trump did with his masterful speech at the 2016 Republican National Convention, creating a confirmation bias through which all future terrorist attacks will be interpreted. Since he spoke, Europe has been providing those events.

- Even as this is written, reports indicate an 84-year-old priest was beheaded in his church in Normandy, France, by two attackers claiming allegiance to the Islamic State.[1]

- The day before that, a Syrian refugee in Germany killed one woman and injured two other people by attacking them with a machete.[2]

- Also Monday, a "failed asylum seeker" attempted to suicide bomb a German music festival, with the BBC reporting it as "Syrian migrant dies in German

1   Hodge, Katie, and Jack Royston. "'They Slit His Throat Then Preached in Arabic': Nun's Horror as Sick ISIS Fiends Butcher Priest at Altar." *The Sun.* July 27, 2016. Accessed May 18, 2018. https://www.thesun.co.uk/news/1503398/the-isis-teen-who-filmed-himself-forcing-catholic-priest-84-to-kneel-before-cutting-his-throat-after-performing-sermon-in-arabic/.

2   Mortimer, Caroline. "German Machete Attack: Syrian Refugee Kills Woman and Injures Two Others in Reutlingen." *The Independent.* July 24, 2016. Accessed May 18, 2018. https://www.independent.co.uk/news/world/europe/german-machete-attack-stuttgart-reutlingen-crime-knife-attack-a7153561.html.

blast."[3] New reports indicate he pledged allegiance to the Islamic State.[4]

- Just a few days before that, we had a "German-Iranian" who killed nine people in Munich.[5]

- And only a few days before that we had the slaughter of at least eighty-four people in Nice, France as a truck barreled into a crowd celebrating Bastille Day. [6]

There was also breaking news of a shooting in the city of Malmo, Sweden, an area heavily colonized by Muslims. However, as yet there is no evidence whether this is a terrorist attack.

European authorities appear impotent in the face of these attacks. The French government said plaintively that the attacker in Nice radicalized "very rapidly" because of his exposure to online extremist Islamic propaganda.[7]

Today's murder of Father Jacques Hamel was even more stunning — one of the killers was *actually being monitored via an electronic*

3   Griswold, Alex. "BBC Headline on Suicide Bomber: 'Syrian Migrant Dies in German Blast.'" *Mediaite.* July 25, 2016. Accessed May 23, 2018. https://www.mediaite.com/online/bbc-headline-on-suicide-bomber-syrian-migrant-dies-in-german-blast/.

4   Waters, Angela. "Bomber Who Blew Himself up in Germany Pledged Allegiance to Islamic State." *USA Today.* July 26, 2016. Accessed May 18, 2018. https://www.usatoday.com/story/news/world/2016/07/25/bomber-who-blew-himself-up-germany-pledged-allegiance-islamic-state/87523386/.

5   Mekhennet, Souad, Stephanie Kirchner, and William Branigin. "Shooter Who Killed 9 in Munich Was 18-year-old with Dual Iranian German Nationality." *The Washington Post.* July 22, 2016. Accessed May 19, 2018. https://www.washingtonpost.com/world/german-police-seal-off-mall-area-in-munich-after-shots-fired/2016/07/22/6567e6d8-502c-11e6-a422-83ab49ed5e6a_story.html.

6   Rubin, Alissa J., Adam Nossiter, and Christopher Mele. "Scores Die in Nice, France, as Truck Plows Into Bastille Day Crowd." *The New York Times.* July 14, 2016. Accessed May 18, 2018. https://www.nytimes.com/2016/07/15/world/europe/nice-france-truck-bastille-day.html.

7   Birnbaum, Michael, and James McAuley. "Attacker in Nice Is Said to Have Radicalized 'very Rapidly.'" *The Washington Post.* July 16, 2016. Accessed May 19, 2018. https://www.washingtonpost.com/world/islamic-state-claims-responsibility-for-france-attack-in-nice/2016/07/16/4327456e-4ab9-11e6-8dac-0c6e4accc5b1_story.html.

tag because he had twice tried to join Islamic State forces in Syria.[8] What's worse, Adel Kermiche, one of the attackers, was considered a "normal teenager" with no particular interest in Islam who would "[drink] alcohol" until recently.[9]

The appalling conclusion: even with an Orwellian security regime and a heavy military presence on the streets of French cities, the French government can't (or won't) do anything against jihadists. What's more, given the ability of these kinds of terrorists to "self-radicalize" via the internet or extremists within the already huge Muslim diaspora communities, even the most intrusive surveillance program will fail to detect budding attackers.

Already, before the latest round of attacks, city councilors, gun shop owners, and figures in the intelligence community were all speaking about France as a nation on the verge of civil conflict.[10] The general lack of faith in civil authorities is not being helped by new allegations French Interior Ministry officials were attempting to doctor reports and cover up their incompetence.[11]

There are also rumblings in Germany. The governor of Bavaria said

8   Calderwood, Imogen. "'A War of Religions': Fury in France over How Known Jihadists on Terror Watchlist Were Allowed to Murder Priest as Sarkozy Calls for 'a Merciless Response.'" *Daily Mail.* July 26, 2016. Accessed May 19, 2018. http://www.dailymail.co.uk/news/article-3709237/A-war-religions-Fury-France-known-jihadists-terror-watchlist-allowed-murder-priest-Sarkozy-calls-merciless-response.html.

9   Nossiter, Adam, Alissa J. Rubin, and Benoît Morenne. "ISIS Says Its 'Soldiers' Attacked Church in France, Killing Priest." *The New York Times.* January 20, 2018. Accessed May 19, 2018. https://www.nytimes.com/2016/07/27/world/europe/normandy-france-church-attack.html.

10   Miller, Jonathan. "What Next? Could France Be Facing a Civil War?" CNBC. July 18, 2016. Accessed May 19, 2018. https://www.cnbc.com/2016/07/18/what-next-could-france-be-facing-a-civil-war.html.

11   McAuley, James. "Scandal Grows over Lack of Security on Night of Nice Terror Attack." *The Washington Post.* July 25, 2016. Accessed May 19, 2018. https://www.washingtonpost.com/world/europe/scandal-grows-over-lack-of-security-on-night-of-nice-terror-attack/2016/07/25/383e8916-5264-11e6-b652-315ae5d4d4dd_story.html.

Germany must "do whatever is necessary to protect our citizens" and spoke of his citizens as being fearful and on edge.[12]

Is this the new normal? Amazingly, French Prime Minister Manuel Valls says it may simply be that the French people "have to live with terrorism."[13]

It no longer seems absurd to say we are seeing the opening shots of a European civil war. Things that can't go on forever, don't — and it's impossible to imagine Western Europe will continue to tolerate almost daily terrorist attacks indefinitely.

At the very least, one might think the explosion of terrorism in the heartland of Western Civilization would at least be worthy of comment by our alleged political leaders in the Democratic Party.and it's impossible to imagine Western Europe will continue to tolerate almost daily terrorist attacks indefinitely.

At the very least, one might think the explosion of terrorism in the heartland of Western Civilization would at least be worthy of comment by our alleged political leaders in the Democratic Party.

However, the subject of terrorism and the existence of the Islamic State was not even mentioned on the opening night of the Democratic National Convention.

Donald Trump, speaking in Charlotte before a crowd of veterans, capitalized on this failure today:

> We need to change our foreign policy to focus on defeating and destroying ISIS, a word you didn't hear last night at the Democrat convention. You didn't hear it. They don't want to talk about it because in a very true way, they really established ISIS because of weakness… It's also essential that we suspend the refugee flows from Syria and other dangerous countries so we don't bring into the United States the same terrorism that our American soldiers are fighting overseas.[14]

---

12 "Germany Must Address Fears after Attacks, Says Bavaria Premier." BBC. July 26, 2016. Accessed May 19, 2018. http://www.bbc.com/news/world-europe-36897694.

13 Friedman, Uri. "Learning to Live With Terrorism." *The Atlantic*. August 15, 2016. Accessed May 19, 2018. https://www.theatlantic.com/international/archive/2016/08/terrorism-resilience-isis/493433/.

14 Diamond, Jeremy. "Trump Knocks Dems for Not Mentioning ISIS." CNN. July 26, 2016.

As Trump points out, we don't have a terrorism problem so much as an immigration problem. Yet at this moment Hillary Clinton is suggesting importing more Muslim refugees.

As we are learning in Europe, a large Muslim population practically guarantees more terrorist attacks because it provides a group of people susceptible to being radicalized by uncontrollable means, including books, social networking, or websites. In practice, once you have a large Muslim population, the danger of Islamic extremism and jihadism becomes a *permanent* fixture of your society.

But Clinton wants to make this danger a part of everyday American life as it is now in Europe.

There's been a notable reluctance by the Main Stream Media to cover these recent European attacks. Indeed, the slaughter and decapitation of a Catholic priest by Muslim terrorists in France was barely considered newsworthy at all by outlets like unless that population is physically removed.

But Clinton wants to make this danger a part of everyday American life as it is now in Europe.

There's been a notable reluctance by the Main Stream Media to cover these recent European attacks. Indeed, the slaughter and decapitation of a Catholic priest by Muslim terrorists in France was barely considered newsworthy at all by outlets like *the Huffington Post, Slate,* or *Salon,* all of which are giving far more attention to conspiracy theories about Vladimir Putin working to make Donald Trump President of the United States.

But the Lying Press can't cover up everything—especially as there is every indication more attacks are on the way.

And each new attack supports Trump's theme that the Obama Administration and Secretary of State Hillary Clinton unleashed global chaos and enabled the rise of the Islamic State. Furthermore, it forces Clinton to justify why she wants to invite more Muslim refugees into the country when even government surveillance is no guarantee against spontaneous

Accessed May 19, 2018. https://www.cnn.com/2016/07/26/politics/donald-trump-democratic-convention-isis/.

outbreaks of jihad. Not surprisingly, over half of Americans believe Donald Trump would handle terrorism better than her.[15]

Trump, and events, have maneuvered Clinton into campaigning as the candidate of continuity, the champion of the status quo. Each new attack shows millions of Americans that Trump's view of the world is fundamentally correct—while Clinton's alleged view (does she have opinions?) is not just mistaken but positively dangerous.

It's too early to say Trump is going to win simply because events are moving in his direction. But if the past two weeks are any indication, there'll have been another attack by the time this article goes to pixel.

15 Blanton, Dana. "Fox News Poll: Voters Trust Trump on Economy, Clinton on Foreign Policy, Nuclear Weapons." Fox News. May 20, 2016. Accessed May 19, 2018. http://www.foxnews.com/politics/2016/05/20/fox-news-poll-voters-trust-trump-on-economy-clinton-on-foreign-policy-nuclear-weapons.html.

CHAPTER TWELVE

TRUMP SUPPORTER MARTYRED

RIP THOMAS SHAW JR., SEVENTY-FIVE — STABBED BY TWENTY-ONE-YEAR-OLD BLACK MAN

Just another typical story out of 21st century post-America, where lives only matter if they can further the narrative. There was a man named Thomas Shaw Jr., an active citizen, businessman, father, grandfather, and great-grandfather. He had a family-owned plumbing, heating and air conditioning company which provided twenty jobs to his community. After he retired, he went into real estate.

Shaw was also well-known for being a vocal supporter of Donald Trump. Along with friends, he created the "Stumping for Trump" bus tour. One friend recalls: "We started this movement, the Stumping for Trump bus tours and Tommy drove his motorcoach all over, from the Wiregrass to Auburn. We'd pull up with music playing and t-shirts and Tommy loved it."[1]

Trump was also a kind of role model for Shaw, who by all accounts was a driven but generous man. One suspects Trump was the reason Shaw got into real estate after he retired:

> "He wanted to get the best people on office who would do the best job for the people of this state," [Shaw's best friend Ron] Creel added. "Donald Trump doesn't know this, but he was Tommy's mentor. And then when he decided to run for president, Tommy just lit up like a Christmas tree."

---

1   "Well-known Businessman Killed at Work Remembered by Many in River Region." WSFA 12 News. August 05, 2016. Accessed May 24, 2018. http://www.wsfa.com/story/32698700/well-known-businessman-killed-at-work-remembered-by-many-in-river-region.

Shaw was a founding member of the River Region Republican Club and one of the original members of the River Region Trump Supporters.

"He generously gave of his time and resources to volunteer for Republican candidates and causes, most recently as an integral member of the Trump Campaign in Alabama. Tommy was always ready to donate and drive his personal bus throughout Alabama and the southeastern states. It is rare to find such a committed and giving person. He will be greatly missed," said Pat Wilson, chairwoman of the Montgomery County Republican Executive Committee.[2]

At any other time in history, we'd call him a model citizen. But in Montgomery, Alabama (home of the Southern Poverty Law Center), collecting rent and traveling the streets in safety is one of those things you can simply no longer do. And in modern America, the Main Stream Media, academia, and the political elite endlessly incite hatred against people like Shaw. This trickles down to the system's client class, the seething dependents of Third World America's urban hellholes. And so, after a day collecting rent from his tenants, Shaw found himself approached by one of Obama's Gentle Giants, Corwin Walker, who stabbed him to death.

Shaw's name will not be a hashtag. There will be no huge protests or heavily funded activism efforts to demand justice for his murder. Indeed, don't speak up too loudly about the realities of crime in Montgomery or anywhere else in the country or else the $PLC will do its best to destroy your life. Noticing patterns is seen as far more immoral in our collapsing country than being a murderer. Just save your money and try to move away and isolate yourself from it all. (Until the feds dump a Section 8 housing development in your town, and you have to do it all over again.)

The funeral and burial have already taken place; let's remember them this November.

---

2   Ibid.

CHAPTER THIRTEEN

The Night Trump Won

I had lost faith.

My position all along had been that Donald Trump would lose the primary, but, if he somehow was nominated, would win the general election. Having spent too much time around professional "conservatives," I knew how deeply the respectable right despised our would-be God-Emperor. I assumed Conservatism Inc. would be able to prevent Trump from winning the nomination even if meant pulling a dirty trick at the convention. At the same time, I had enough distance from them to know that Hillary Clinton was a uniquely bad candidate. I overestimated Conservatism Inc. when it came to the primary. But at least I knew Conservatism Inc. was overestimating Hillary Clinton.

Still, the Access Hollywood tapes had shaken me.[1] Even though I rolled my eyes at the obvious attempt to drive Trump out of the race, I could well imagine other people falling for it. As we came into Election Night, I braced myself for defeat. I'd wait until Florida came in, I told myself, at which point I'd turn off the computer, throw the cell phone into another room, then take enough sleeping pills that I wouldn't need to face Hillary's America until tomorrow afternoon.

And yet, while I had lost faith, I hadn't lost hope. Three things kept the flame alive. First was the report of a friend from Michigan who told me about Trump posters covering white working-class districts – a sure sign, he said, that Trump would win the state despite all the pundits' scoffing.

---

1 "Trump Recorded Having Extremely Lewd Conversation about Women in 2005." October 07, 2016. Accessed March 28, 2019. https://www.washingtonpost.com/politics/trump-recorded-having-extremely-lewd-conversation-about-women-in-2005/2016/10/07/3b9ce776-8cb4-11e6-bf8a-3d26847eeed4_story.html.

Secondly, there was the cryptic letter FBI Director James Comey sent out days before the election announcing the re-opening of the investigation into Hillary Clinton. The quote from Hans Gruber in *Die Hard* came to mind: "You ask for miracles, I give you the F.B.I."

The final element was something more intangible but no less real. What Hunter S. Thompson penned about San Francisco in "the middle sixties" being a "very special time and place to be a part of" applied to our strange online world in the 2016 campaign. Every single thing that needed to happen had happened. Every break, no matter how unlikely, had gone Trump's way. Kek[2] was with us, and it really felt like we had tapped into some divine force that blew apart all obstacles in the path of the chosen one. It felt like the world was being resacralized, that our thoughts could change reality, that an entire movement was rising out of nothing. Surely this — whatever it was — couldn't fail us at the last moment. Surely, we couldn't get this far and lose it all.

And so as election night began, I tracked the results, eagerly, fanatically. I told myself I expected disaster. Yet somehow, in my deepest core, I just knew. When Frank Luntz confidently predicted early in the day that Hillary Clinton would be president, I somehow knew this wouldn't be true.

When I started hearing anecdotal evidence about unprecedented white turnout in areas around the country, it was simply confirmation of what I had been arguing for years. Hadn't I written countless times for VDARE.com about the potential for the Republican Party to build a governing coalition behind populist, nationalist policies designed to appeal to the white working class? Hadn't giants like Peter Brimelow, Steve Sailer, and Sam Francis been predicting just such a winning strategy for more than a decade?

Frantically reloading Twitter and /pol/,[3] refreshing at least three different sites to get the latest tallies, my cell phone suddenly began exploding with messages from dozens of people, some whom I hadn't spoken

---

2   See https://pepethefrogfaith.wordpress.com/.

3   /pol/ is the 'politically incorrect' subforum on the free speech anonymous message board called 4chan.

to in months. One issued a command: it was my duty to History to drop everything and get to the Trump Hotel in Washington D.C. Right now. Worry how to get inside when I get there.

Casually endangering my own life and the lives of around me, I kept lurking on /pol/, posting on *VDARE*'s Twitter account, and refreshing the vote counts while speeding around heavy northern-Virginia traffic. Of all nights, I was somehow able to secure a parking spot near the hotel. Already, there was a crowd both inside and outside the hotel.

Thanks to high-placed friends, I was able to gain entry and joined a circle of about a dozen friends drinking and staring intently at Fox News. There was a curious combination of arrogance and terror. Arrogance — because we had been proven right. (Or, rather, *they* had been proven right, because my natural pessimism was well known.) Terror — because it could still go so wrong.

Our consensus was that if he won Wisconsin, he would win the whole thing. Various chants started and faded throughout the crowd. "Make-America-Great-Again!" "U-S-A! U-S-A!" But the one that really did it was "Call it! Call it!" We shouted hatefully at the journalists hundreds of miles away. Objectively, I knew the networks weren't deliberately slow walking their state calls. Everyone remembers the nightmare the premature Florida call caused in 2000. Caution was prudent. Even if the networks were slow walking the calls, it wouldn't make any difference in the long run.

But remember — this was 2016. We were poring through thousands of emails to try to link Hillary Clinton to "Spirit Cooking" and esoteric cults.[4] We seriously wondered if the DNC had whacked Seth Rich.[5] The Clinton Foundation was at the center of an international smuggling

---

4   Levitz, Eric. "Report: Clinton Linked to Satanic Rituals Involving Kidnapped Children and Marina Abramovic." *New York Magazine.* November 04, 2016. Accessed March 28, 2019. http://nymag.com/intelligencer/2016/11/spirit-cooking-explained-satanic-ritual-or-fun-dinner.html.

5   Mole, Charlie. "Seth Rich: How a Young Man's Murder Attracted Conspiracy Theories." BBC. April 21, 2018. Accessed March 28, 2019. https://www.bbc.com/news/blogs-trending-43727858.

ring.[6] No conspiracy was too insane; no evidence too tenuous. In that environment, with that amount of tension, and with a liberal amount of whiskey, no conspiracy seemed too unlikely.

So when Wisconsin was called, it was like a spell breaking. As someone who was "Alt Right" before it was a thing, it was that moment I first realized that victory was even possible. Not just on that Election Night, but at any time.

To be on the "far right" when young is to doom yourself to being a Cassandra. You know, and you accept, that your prophecies will go unheeded. It's for that reason so many fall into extremist ideologies or wildly excessive critiques; you aren't going to win anyway, so why even consider political realities? I think for many of us, that was one of the reasons we supported him from the beginning: to paraphrase Tertullian, precisely *because* his victory was so unlikely, it was necessary to support Donald J. Trump. And then, somehow, we slowly began to realize that we could actually win this thing.

Thus, there was a sense of unreality at the moment of victory. It was the culmination of that magical, *literally* magical feeling that had been building over the past year, that certain laws no longer applied, that a new era had begun. *Novus ordo seclorum.* The resistance from within the conservative movement had been so fierce, and the hysteria from the leftists so unlimited, that it was likewise easy to imagine that "we" had just taken power, in the same sense as if we had marched on Rome or seized the Winter Palace. Maybe I'd be running an office in the Department of Homeland Security under Kris Kobach. Maybe he'd shut down the Antifa networks nationwide. Maybe Peter Brimelow would give the keystone address at CPAC next year! Anything seemed possible.

The celebration at the Trump Hotel was joyous but clichéd. I hugged strangers. I made new friends. I drank champagne and issued wild

---

6   Kaplan, Alex. "Return of Pizzagate: Pro-Trump Media Use FBI IG Report to Revive Conspiracy Theory." *Salon.* June 25, 2018. Accessed March 28, 2019. https://www.salon.com/2018/06/25/pro-trump-media-use-fbi-ig-report-to-bring-back-pizzagate_partner/.

declarations about eternal victory. And then a friend said we should go to the White House.

I vaguely remembered an incident from the 2000 election battle, when Republicans protested the Vice President's residence and chanted, "Get Out Of Cheney's House!" I expected something similar; a legion of Red Hats chanting "Get Out Of Trump's House!" American flags. Trump-brand champagne. The great MAGA army at the very moment of victory.

The reality was far different. The area in front of the White House was filled with Antifa, waving the flags-within-flags banner that heralds violence and chaos throughout the West. I witnessed a black Trump supporter set upon by a mob of Antifa who beat him until he was dragged to safety by a white Trump supporter — who was then detained by police. At the very moment of triumph, I had the same feeling I had had for most of my life — being part of a small minority, unable to openly express my views without fear of physical attack or economic ruin, and utterly unrepresented. Even the official moment of success in the early hours of the morning, when the President-Elect addressed the nation on the "complicated business" of his victory, seemed anti-climatic. I wasn't at a victory party, but walking the streets of the nation's capital, alone, somber, sober, and thoughtful. The high was over and the magic broken before Trump even declared victory.

The months following November were like awakening from a sleep induced by anesthesia. It was groping, and hesitant, and you were drifting in and out. But slowly, inevitably, despite your best efforts to enjoy your comfortable sleep, reality kept creeping in on you. The Cabinet appointments were a disappointment — no Kris Kobach, Lou Barletta, Jim Webb or some of the other names that had been floated. With the exception of Jeff Sessions, it was the same kind of Republicans that we would have gotten from Jeb Bush — and Goldman Sachs was well represented.

After a series of doxxings, the attack on Richard Spencer at the Inauguration, Hailgate, and then Charlottesville, the Alt Right lost its connection to the larger Trump movement. It was gradually isolated and stripped of much of its influence. Websites were taken offline; practically every site lost tens of thousands of dollars in revenue when we were deplatformed from fundraising services. Many of the figures who defined the Alt Right simply dropped off the face of the Earth before the onslaught of media counter-attacks, never to return.

Meanwhile, President Trump himself, while unquestionably the best president of my lifetime, was not the revolutionary change we had been hoping for. His main legislative accomplishment has been a tax cut any Republican would have pushed for, and as of this writing, there has still been no wall. There is no sense of urgency to his policies; he governs with the same sense of complacency as George Bush, seemingly forgetting his own rhetoric from the campaign about how mass immigration imposes a time limit on how long Republicans can continue to win elections without changing the demographic equation.

And yet, there is still a sense that we are at the beginning of something. As someone who had been involved in practical politics for more than a decade, I knew not to fall into the temptation of believing that political victory meant that the struggle was over. This election had seemed different somehow, but it wasn't. It was just another election. It was also an election that for the first time, *we* had won, and that still meant something.

The Republican Party is now Trump's Party. Despite how the MAGA movement has been co-opted, despite how the president himself has so often failed us, and despite the devastating blows given to the Alt Right, the American Right is with us on the fundamentals. The progress since 2014 has been unimaginable. The ecstasy and magic of that night in 2016 will never come again, just like your first love will never come again. Yet the time has come to put aside childish things and to build the movement that America deserves.

The current moment in the life of the American nationalist right is akin to that day when you realize you aren't a young man anymore. That sense of the unlimited and unbounded future is gone forever, yet there is also the pride of knowing you have really built something. As an adult, you have that singularity of purpose so often absent in youth. I see Election Night 2016 as the last night of my youth. It was the night my idealism, my revolutionary spirit, and my utopian hopes to see a president simply deliver us victory from the White House departed forever. Yet the immature young man who had those childish dreams was replaced in a matter of months by someone more realistic, effective, and dedicated. The same can be said of almost all those who survived the terrible bloodletting of 2017 and 2018. My course is set—as is yours, if you are reading these words.

As on the morning of Election Day 2016, I have no certainty in final victory. But I still have hope. And even more than I did on the night of Donald Trump's ascension, I have faith that the best days of our movement, our country, and our people still lie before us.

PART THREE

THE CURRENT
YEAR(S)

CHAPTER ONE

Nixonism Is Not Enough

TRUMP MUST ATTACK. ANCHOR
BABIES: NO, AFRIKANER REFUGEES: YES

A battle is won. But the war is just beginning. Let's hope President-elect Donald Trump knows what he's in for.

Reportedly, Donald Trump is already disappointing some of his followers by appointing villainous gnome Reince Priebus as his White House Chief of Staff. Republican National Committee Chairblob Priebus is the consummate Republican insider, an immigration wimp and hardly the kind of revolutionary figure many of Trump's grassroots supporters were hoping for. Priebus also cucked out during the faux Khizr Khan debacle, attacking Trump for supposedly going after an "off-limits" family.[1]

But this doesn't mean everyone should give in to despair — yet. The charitable reading: Priebus did, after all, help quell repeated efforts at rebellion from within the Republican Party, especially at the GOP Convention. It's also fair to assume that Priebus, whose political base is Wisconsin, had quite a bit to do with helping ensure Trump's shocking victory in that state and with bringing out Governor Scott Walker to support Trump openly near the end of the campaign.

If we know anything about Donald Trump, we know that he values loyalty. And whatever his initial sins and failures of nerve, Priebus has been loyal ever since Trump won the GOP nomination.

The White House Chief of Staff controls access to the President. Many

---

1 McCaskill, Nolan D. "RNC Chief Rebukes Trump: Khans 'Should Be Off Limits.'" *Politico*. August 01, 2016. Accessed May 19, 2018. https://www.politico.com/story/2016/08/priebus-trump-khizr-khan-226533.

national conservatives were hoping Steve Bannon, the current leader of *Breitbart*, would be appointed to the position. However, Bannon will instead be "Chief Strategist and Senior Counselor to the President."

Bannon of course has an independent political base and a media empire which he can use to put pressure on those who don't go along with his policy agenda. Already, Speaker Paul Ryan has been put on notice. Trump may be drafting the GOP establishment he once warred against to shepherd through policies deriving from, if not the Alt Right, at least the Alt Lite.

But Trump's path to success is narrow. The real danger: Donald Trump may turn out to be another President Nixon. Like President-elect Trump, Nixon won by targeting the Main Stream Media and mobilizing the silent majority. Like Trump, Nixon had no patience with political correctness; indeed, he expressed in private views about race, Leftist extremism, and even Jewish influence which would no doubt startle the new President-elect. And, like Trump, Nixon was the favorite enemy of campus protesters who regarded him as the symbol of an entire social order that progressives wanted to overthrow.

To this day, even on the Alt Right, Nixon serves as a symbol of defiance. But Nixon's actual legacy is Title IX, the EPA, and anti-white racial preferences (i.e., Affirmative Action).

The Main Stream Media and the activist Left (where distinguishable) have already made it clear that they will be working to destroy President-elect Trump and his government from day one. Trump will be facing furious, sustained opposition from both the top (the elite media) and the bottom (street protesters). Any efforts by GOP insiders like Priebus to "compromise" with such forces will only lead to disaster.

After all, in future elections Trump will no longer be able to claim the fuzzy mantle of "change." We can also expect he will be criticized for retaining some insiders (like Priebus) when he promised to "drain the swamp," even though such compromises are inevitable.

Trump's shocking victory overshadowed the relatively swift loss of Colorado and Nevada Tuesday night, and Trump's margins in Wisconsin,

Michigan, and Pennsylvania were too narrow to be relied on in 2020. As we already see, the Left is going to be going nuts for four years. "Bush Derangement Syndrome" is going to seem like nothing.

What can Trump do? The new President must quickly move to shift both the Overton Window and the underlying dynamics of political power. He has to be constantly on the offensive, not giving his enemies (and they are enemies) a moment's rest.

This will involve attacking on several fronts. But most importantly, it means taking strong action on immigration and showing no weakness. Thus far, the signs are promising and Trump has earned at least a modicum of trust.

Some MSM reports are already trying to gaslight Trump supporters into saying he's betraying them. Chief among them is a report that Trump is backing down from a wall to a "fence" in certain areas. This isn't really true. What matters is that the border barrier is effective. Obviously, it may take different forms in different places. With appointees like Kris Kobach, Lou Barletta and Jeff Sessions on the transition team, Trump supporters should be confident we're going to see the wall.

Trump has also said he will begin immediate deportations of "criminal" aliens. While he has also said some illegal aliens will be permitted to stay behind, that is a battle for another day. Deportations right off the bat are a good start.

But this isn't enough. Trump needs to not just keep his campaign promises, but also put his enemies off balance. So, here's a quick checklist for Steve Bannon and President-elect Trump to consider:

1) Strategic Deportation

The MSM's narrative about "mass deportation" was always a red herring. A "deportation force" would be great, but really, it already exists. What's more important is furthering self-deportation through the kinds of policies we've exhaustively documented here at *VDARE*, including mandatory E-Verify, workplace raids, and enforcing laws against hiring illegals.

But at least some deportations are necessary. President Trump needs to tell immigration authorities to deport those arrogant illegals who are appearing on television, speaking at political conventions and even appearing before Congress on *day one*.

At the top of the list: Jose Antonio Vargas, an occupier who has spent his entire life trying to deconstruct our nation and identity. No muss, no fuss, no press conference. Out, out, out!

The rest will get the message.

2) Birthright Citizenship

Closing the Anchor Baby loophole is the single most important policy change that need to be implemented if America is to be saved. All enforcement mechanisms, even deporting all illegals, are simply delaying the inevitable unless the lie of birthright citizenship is abolished. Both Trump and Vice-President-elect Mike Pence have advocated the abolition of birthright citizenship in the past. However, there was disturbingly little mention of this near the end of the campaign.

According to an analysis by *The Daily Caller*, there will be another seven million eligible voters because of birthright citizenship by 2032. This will be enough to wipe out the Trump Coalition unless it is headed off right away.[2] Trump must act quickly and also ensure any justices appointed to the Supreme Court will correctly interpret the 14th Amendment in regard to this issue.

3) Flip the Script on Refugees

After initially wobbling, Trump has been solid in opposing the importation of Muslim refugees to the United States. However, even this is ultimately a defensive action — the providing against "preventable evils" that

---

2   Caruso, Justin. "6.8 MILLION: How Birthright Citizenship Is Changing US Elections." *The Daily Caller*. November 05, 2016. Accessed May 19, 2018. http://dailycaller.com/2016/11/05/6-8-million-how-birthright-citizenship-is-changing-u-s-elections/.

Enoch Powell said was "the supreme function of statesmanship" in his great 1968 immigration speech.[3]

But it's time to take the offensive. At CPAC in 2013, Donald Trump spoke about accepting high-skilled immigration from European nations.[4] He should now announce the United States is willing to accept only refugees of European descent from a once-Western nation, South Africa. After all, who can say that Afrikaners are not being oppressed by their government, are not at risk for violence, or being discriminated against on a massive scale?

This would send a powerful symbolic message. And, at the very least, we might end up with the abolition of the "refugee" racket — which is just an expedited, subsidized special immigration program for politically favored groups that makes no sense morally or politically.

Each of these policies contains risk. But power is fleeting and this opportunity will never come again.

It is no exaggeration to say what is at stake is whether the United States of America will continue as a First World country. A defensive strategy will lead to another Nixon Administration. Compromise with declared enemies is a non-starter. Trump has no choice but to go on the attack.

Peace was never an option.

3   Powell, Enoch. "Rivers of Blood." Speech, Annual General Meeting of the West Midlands Area Conservative Political Centre, England, Birmingham, April 20, 1968. Accessed May 18, 2018. https://www.vdare.com/articles/like-the-roman-i-seem-to-see-the-river-tiber-foaming-with-much-blood.

4   Levy, Pema. "Trump: Let In More (White) Immigrants." *Talking Points Memo*. March 15, 2013. Accessed May 19, 2018. https://talkingpointsmemo.com/dc/trump-let-in-more-white-immigrants.

CHAPTER TWO

The Empire Strikes Back

THE MAIN STREAM MEDIA'S THREE-POINT PLAN
TO RECAPTURE THE NARRATIVE

For most of human history, power was rooted in possession of land. After the Industrial Revolution, power lay in controlling in the means of production. But today, the main source of power is control of information.

Having the power to control information (what Steve Sailer calls "The Megaphone") gives you the ability to determine what issues will be discussed, what viewpoints are considered legitimate, and who is allowed to participate in polite society. It ultimately allows you to push an entire code of morality on others. And morality is, ultimately, a weapon more terrible than can be found in any arsenal.

The 2016 election was ultimately a battle between the commanding heights of media (newspapers, networks, and web portals) and what we could call the guerrillas of media (/pol/, forums, hackers, trolls, and independent media outlets like *VDARE*). The latter lacked power on their own, but they united behind Donald Trump, a man whose brand was so well established that the establishment couldn't ignore him. It was Fourth Generation Warfare — this time over information.

And just as guerrillas have been frustrating established armies all around the world on real-world battlefields, so did the online commandos frustrate and eventually overcome the seemingly invincible Fourth Estate.

But this victory wasn't inevitable. From day one, the MSM tried to destroy Donald Trump, including his business empire, because of his stated views on immigration.

Since that failed, they have started turning on his supporters by means of three tactics.

First, a blatant attempt to pathologize dissent — especially the Alt Right.

Soon after the election, the Leftist *ThinkProgress* blog announced that the "alt-right" should only be called "white nationalist" or "white suprema-cist."[1] The Associated Press dutifully echoed this pronouncement days later, warning journalists not to use the term and instead to stick to pejo-ratives.[2]

This is an Orwellian attempt to literally eliminate crimethink through linguistic control. Of course, no such guidelines will apply to non-white identitarian groups such as the National Council of La Raza, which will continue to be called an "advocacy group" or "progressive grass-roots im-migration-reform organization."

Secondly, a meme has been invented about so-called "Fake News," which will be used to shut down dissident media outlets.

Needless to say, most of the rationale for this is not just fake, but obvi-ously, comically, wrong. Thus, *The Washington Post* reported that *VDARE* (along with many other sites) was a "Russian propaganda effort," an accu-sation based on no evidence at all.[3] We ask: where is our vodka?

1   "EDITORS' NOTE: *ThinkProgress* Will No Longer Describe Racists as 'alt-right.'" *ThinkProgress*. November 22, 2016. Accessed May 19, 2018. https://thinkprogress. org/thinkprogress-alt-right-policy-b04fd141d8d4/.

2   Griffiths, Brent. "AP Issues Guidelines for Using the Term 'alt-right.'" *Politico*. November 28, 2016. Accessed May 19, 2018. https://www.politico.com/story/2016/11/ use-alt-right-or-white-nationalism-associated-press-231889.

3   Timberg, Craig. "Russian Propaganda Effort Helped Spread 'Fake News' During Election, Experts Say." *The Washington Post*. November 24, 2016. Accessed May 19, 2018.   https://www.washingtonpost.com/business/economy/russian-propaganda-

Rolling Stone, which pushed one of the most disgusting hoaxes in modern journalism with their story of a supposed rape at the University of Virginia,[4] is having meetings with President Obama to discuss "fake news."[5] Meanwhile, algorithms are already being introduced to distinguish between "verified" and "non-verified" news sources. It can be assumed that only Leftist sites will receive verification on social media.

There *is* "fake news," and it is annoying, to be sure. There were plenty of cringey stories about non-existent celebrity endorsements of Trump in the last cycle, for instance. But most "verified" or "mainstream" sources today don't actually report but simply "point and sputter," or actually conceal real news. For example, even after the journalists got what they wanted out of the latest National Policy Institute conference, the MSM *still* couldn't restrain themselves from simply making things up out of whole cloth by claiming that Richard Spencer questioned the very humanity of Jews.[6]

Actual attacks on Trump supporters are not covered, while unsourced, unverified claims of a wave of "hate crimes," which mostly consist of handwritten notes most likely composed by the supposed "victims," or other incidents so trivial that normal people wouldn't even notice them, dominate the headlines.

This is a far more insidious form of "fake news" than anything "the

---

effort-helped-spread-fake-news-during-election-experts-say/2016/11/24/793903b6-8a40-4ca9-b712-716af66098fe_story.html.

4   "UVA Frat Sues Rolling Stone For $25 Million Over Rape Hoax." *The Federalist*. November 10, 2015. Accessed May 19, 2018. http://thefederalist.com/2015/11/10/uva-frat-sues-rolling-stone-for-25-million-over-fake-rape-story/.

5   Sailer, Steve. "Rolling Stone's Fake News Impresario Jann Wenner Interviews President-Eject Obama About the Scourge of Fake News." *VDARE*. November 30, 2016. Accessed May 19, 2018. https://www.vdare.com/posts/rolling-stones-fake-news-impresario-jann-wenner-interviews-president-eject-obama-about-the-scourge-of-fake-news.

6   Dooghy, Roger. "NPI's Spencer vs. Politico's Hirsh, Etc.—Why Trump Calls The Media 'Dishonest And Corrupt.'" *VDARE*. November 24, 2016. Accessed May 19, 2018. https://www.vdare.com/articles/npis-spencer-vs-politcos-hirsh-etc-why-trump-calls-the-media-dishonest-and-corrupt.

Russians" are promoting. And what about the lie of "hands up, don't shoot"?

Another example: Mainstream outlets are evidently comfortable leveling wild charges that Steve Bannon is somehow a "white nationalist." On the evidence, Bannon is actually a civic nationalist who has specifically denounced racism and, if anything, is showing troubling signs of moving towards the "DemsRRealRacist"-style talking points which led Conservatism Inc. to disaster. There are absolutely no statements by Bannon actually calling for, say, a white ethnostate.

In contrast, Rep. Keith Ellison, candidate to head the DNC, actually *has* called for a black ethnostate.[7] However, this has not prevented him from being "normalized" and celebrated by the "mainstream" media.

The logical conclusion of all of this:

Thirdly, the Trump victory is clearly leading to *increased* attempts at outright repression.

Or, as *VDARE* editor Peter Brimelow told the NPI conference, "What we are going to see in the next few years is an intensified Reign of Terror."[8]

For example, *BuzzFeed*'s latest masterpiece of journalism: the shocking revelation that reality stars Chip and Joanna Gaines attend a church that disagrees with homosexual marriage.[9] You know — like every Christian church for about 2,000 years. The obvious agenda is to get the show canceled, or to get the Gaines to disavow their own pastor.

---

7   Caruso, Justin. "Keith Ellison Once Proposed Making A Separate Country For Blacks." *The Daily Caller*. November 28, 2016. Accessed May 19, 2018. http://dailycaller.com/2016/11/26/keith-ellison-once-proposed-making-a-separate-country-for-blacks/.

8   Brimelow, Peter. "Brimelow At NPI: Trump's America — The Next Shoe Will Drop In 2020." *VDARE*. November 23, 2016. Accessed May 19, 2018. https://www.vdare.com/articles/brimelow-at-npi-trumps-america-the-next-shoe-will-drop-in-2020.

9   Aurthur, Kate. "Chip And Joanna Gaines's Church Is Firmly Against Same-Sex Marriage." *BuzzFeed*. November 29, 2016. Accessed May 19, 2018. https://www.buzzfeed.com/kateaurthur/chip-and-joanna-gaines-church-same-sex-marriage.

This is the major goal of most "journalism" today — to get someone
fired or to get someone to disavow someone. The Southern Poverty Law
Center makes a lucrative income from policing speech. And journalists
today are no different than the $PLC. They do not report, they do not pro-
vide information, and, rather than ensuring freedom, they are the willing
tools of repression.

And this repression only goes one way.

If you wouldn't invite some Communist demonstrator into your meeting, why would you invite a MSM journalist? They have the same beliefs,
the same motivations, and they increasingly rely on the same tactics.
Aside from the occasional throwing of feces, the preferred tactic of "Antifa" consists in pearl-clutching blog posts; how is the MSM any different?

The repression is accelerating. Reddit is now moving to censor pro-
Trump content on its site.[10] Having been purged from Twitter, many free
speech supporters are moving to GAB, so *The New York Times* is trying to
get that shut down too.[11] And Kellogg (among others) pulled its ads from
Breitbart after Trump's election, because the site was not "aligned with its
values as a company."[12]

Since the election, journalists have been paying tribute to their own
courage, promising to hold Trump accountable. But there is no greater
enemy to free speech than reporters. Shutting down the networks and
shuttering the newspapers would be a boon to independence of thought,
not an obstacle.

For his own sake, to defend his own administration, Trump has to

10 "'Toxic' Trump Trolls: Reddit Vows to Take 'Aggressive' Action." RT. December 1,
    2016. Accessed May 19, 2018. https://www.rt.com/usa/368892-reddit-ceo-trump-
    users/.

11 Hess, Amanda. "The Far Right Has a New Digital Safe Space." *The New York Times.*
    November 30, 2016. Accessed May 19, 2018. https://www.nytimes.com/2016/11/30/
    arts/the-far-right-has-a-new-digital-safe-space.html.

12 Yu, Roger. "Kellogg to Join Others in Removing Advertising on *Breitbart.*" *USA
    Today.* November 30, 2016. Accessed May 19, 2018. https://www.usatoday.com/
    story/money/business/2016/11/29/kellogg-join-others-removing-advertising-
    breitbart/94619068/.

delegitimize the MSM, just as he did during the campaign. He should continue to use his Twitter account and speak straight to the people. He should not hold press conferences with national MSM, and should speak only to local reporters before holding rallies. If Twitter bans him, as Leftists are urging, he should nationalize it as a utility and make it a free speech zone.

And Trump's supporters need to act the same way. Stop giving reporters access. Stop pretending you can play the MSM for your own benefit. Stop acting like these people are anything other than hostile political activists whose only interest in life is to make yours worse.

Stop giving them what they want.

Your career, family, and entire life may depend on it. The life of the nation certainly does.

CHAPTER THREE

Automation + Immigration =
White Identitarianism

HAVE OUR RULERS REALLY THOUGHT THIS THROUGH?

The purpose of the Lying Press is to tell Americans why they are not allowed to resist their dispossession. Thus, just before Christmas, *The New York Times* contemptuously informed its readers that immigration and globalization are not the real threat to jobs — automation is. Therefore, according to labor economists quoted by *NYT*, we need "retraining programs, stronger unions, more public-sector jobs, a higher minimum wage, a bigger earned-income tax credit, and, for the next generation of workers, more college degrees."[1]

Otherwise, people might do something unacceptable — like start "blaming immigrants."

Yet in the long term, the United States is heading towards financial disaster as entitlement programs and health care costs will push the debt to ruinous levels. More handouts and entitlements are hardly likely to solve the problem unless they are paid for with massive tax increases, which would stifle already languid economic growth. And the current state (and cost) of higher education hardly makes "more college degrees" a panacea.

Furthermore, declining unions and falling wages are not separate from the phenomenon of mass immigration. From the perspective of the

---

1   Miller, Claire Cain. "The Long-Term Jobs Killer Is Not China. It's Automation." *The New York Times*. December 21, 2016. Accessed May 19, 2018. https://www.nytimes.com/2016/12/21/upshot/the-long-term-jobs-killer-is-not-china-its-automation.html.

Chamber of Commerce, the whole point of immigration is that it's a politically correct form of union-busting, driving down the wages of both skilled and unskilled workers.

And the Left goes along with this because it dispossesses the hated European-Americans.

The same motivations are at play in Europe. In Germany, the vast majority of the traitor Merkel's refugees are both unemployed and unemployable.[2] The costs are ruinous and there is no end to the migration in sight.

The so-called "anti-fascists" demanding more refugees are just the union-busting Pinkerton Detectives of today. The impact of their actions is to ensure the corporations they pretend to hate get the cheap workers they want.[3]

Still, Miller's *New York Times* article brings up an important point — especially when it notes that while automation in the past created new jobs, "experts are beginning to worry that this time could be different."[4] We are coming to a point where, even absent mass immigration, vast swathes of the population will essentially be unemployable and entire industries will be stripped of workers.

Nearly half the jobs in Idaho will be automated in the next twenty years.[5] The difficult but well-paying jobs in the oil industry are gone

2   McGee, Patrick. "Survey Reveals Germany's Top Companies Employ Just 54 Refugees." *Financial Times.* July 15, 2016. Accessed May 19, 2018. https://www.ft.com/content/d5d0bb96-49a8-11e6-8d68-72e9211e86ab.

3   "German Conservatives Seek Minimum Wage Exceptions for Refugees." *Reuters.* September 29, 2015. Accessed May 19, 2018. https://www.reuters.com/article/us-europe-migrants-germany-wages/german-conservatives-seek-minimum-wage-exceptions-for-refugees-idUSKCN0RT0LU20150929.

4   Miller, Claire Cain. "The Long-Term Jobs Killer Is Not China. It's Automation." *The New York Times.* December 21, 2016. Accessed May 19, 2018. https://www.nytimes.com/2016/12/21/upshot/the-long-term-jobs-killer-is-not-china-its-automation.html.

5   Kennison, Heather. "Will Your Job Be Automated? Nearly Half in Idaho Will Be in the next 20 Years." *Idaho Statesman.* December 28, 2016. Accessed May 19, 2018. http://www.idahostatesman.com/news/business/article123450979.html.

forever. Truck drivers will soon be under threat. Even industries like construction may no longer need workers.

This is not just something which will affect the West. Some countries, such as Japan, already seem to be adjusting to the new order. But others will face greater challenges.

In China, vast robot factories are being constructed for manufacturing, which have the potential to replace "millions" of workers.[6] Almost 70% of jobs in India are threatened by automation, with an astonishing 77% in China slated to go. As the president of the World Bank observed, the traditional path of development "from increasing productivity of agriculture to light manufacturing and then to full-scale industrialization may not be possible for all developing countries."[7]

In many countries, one of the most likely responses is a basic minimum income. Cyprus has something like it already.[8] Finland is experimenting with it.[9] Communities in Scotland are investigating trial programs for it.[10] The Indian government is also taking steps to move towards such a program.[11]

---

6   Knight, Will. "Inside China's Effort to Replace Millions of Manufacturing Workers with Robots." *MIT Technology Review*. November 18, 2016. Accessed May 19, 2018. https://www.technologyreview.com/s/601215/china-is-building-a-robot-army-of-model-workers/.

7   "Automation Threatens 69% Jobs in India: World Bank." *The Hindu*. November 01, 2016. Accessed May 19, 2018. http://www.thehindu.com/business/Industry/Automation-threatens-69-jobs-in-India-World-Bank/article15427005.ece.

8   Hazou, Elias. "GMI Net Widened to Offer More Assistance." *Cyprus Mail*. July 10, 2015. Accessed May 19, 2018. https://cyprus-mail.com/2015/07/10/gmi-net-widened-to-offer-more-assistance/.

9   Tanner, Jari. "Finland to Pay Unemployed Basic Income of $587 per Month." *AP News*. January 02, 2017. Accessed May 19, 2018. https://apnews.com/441e12c324b04d549c13366c891fe8d0/Finland-to-pay-unemployed-basic-income-of-$587-per-month.

10   Glaze, Ben. "Scotland Could Trial Giving Every Citizen a Minimum Income." *Mirror*. January 02, 2017. Accessed May 19, 2018. https://www.mirror.co.uk/news/uk-news/scotland-could-trial-giving-every-9553198#.

11   Colson, Thomas. "The Indian Government Is about to Endorse Giving All Its Citizens

The Swiss recently voted down a proposal to implement a guaranteed basic income,[12] so there is nothing inevitable about this — in the short term. But in the long term, it seems like it will become a political necessity.

A major part of the Trump coalition were factory workers, coal miners and other working-class voters worried about their jobs being eliminated or outsourced. When almost *everyone* becomes a part of that threatened class, populism will increase even more.

And as the barista at Starbucks with a degree in English Literature and $80,000 in student loan debt can tell you, just sending more people to college isn't going to do anything to help.

However, the implications go beyond populism. Ultimately, democracy itself will be called into question. A remarkably small number of people will be contributing in terms of technological progress or economic growth. In the post-work world, the vast majority of people will simply be consumers, passively absorbing increasingly degraded cultural products catering to their worst instincts. But because of universal suffrage, these masses will still have the political power to direct more public goods their way, even as the entire system becomes financially unsustainable. A major crisis is all but inevitable.

And adding to the instability: mass immigration. Even if we concede, for the sake of argument, that automation, not immigration, is the real threat to jobs, adding millions more Third Worlders onto Western infrastructure and social safety networks which are already buckling is practically a guarantee of permanent social conflict. It also increases the amount of competition for those few remaining jobs.

And because all men are not created equal, class distinctions will also largely be based on racial and cultural differences, and will be

<hr>

Free Money." *Business Insider.* January 03, 2017. Accessed May 19, 2018. https://www.businessinsider.com.au/india-indian-government-set-to-endorse-universal-basic-income-free-money-economic-survey-2017-1.

12 "Switzerland's Voters Reject Basic Income Plan." BBC. June 05, 2016. Accessed May 19, 2018. http://www.bbc.com/news/world-europe-36454060.

interpreted as such. After all, those liberal arts college graduates the Left loves so much don't really know how to do anything else.

Which brings us to the final factor: identity. Francis Fukuyama posited in *The End of History and the Last Man* that liberal democracy may be the end of Hegelian History because it best satisfies the human desire for "recognition." But the "Who? Whom?" conflicts of identity are likely to increase if people can no longer attain dignity through their profession.

"Alienation," as Marx defined it, will be even worse, because individuals won't even be contributing to the production of commodities. And added to this economic alienation: cultural alienation, as Western nations will be filled with an ever-increasing number of economically useless Third Worlders eager to claim public goods through the ballot box and sharing nothing in common with Europeans.

The only outlet First World people will have left: identitarian movements. They will reclaim their dignity and reassert their identity as human beings by going "back to blood" and seeking meaning through religious, cultural, and ethnic activism. What's more, many of them will have nothing better to do and will have no fear of having their "basic right" of a minimum income stripped away.

We are already seeing this in Europe. For example, the almost-comically radical Islamist preacher Anjem Choudary worked full time as an organizer and agitator because he received welfare payments from the very government he was trying to overthrow.[13] He's only one of many.

History is about to restart. The end of work, mass immigration, mass unemployment, and the primal need for human recognition are likely to explode in a worldwide Age of Identity. It will confront every Western nation with unprecedented challenges. Preventing the ethnic and cultural conflicts which will rip our civilization apart is the defining issue of the next century.

---

13 Dodd, Vikram. "Anjem Choudary: A Hate Preacher Who Spread Terror in UK and Europe." *The Guardian*. August 16, 2016. Accessed May 19, 2018. https://www.theguardian.com/uk-news/2016/aug/16/anjem-choudary-hate-preacher-spread-terror-uk-europe.

But our leaders seem determined to just make matters worse. After all, if automation is inevitable, then why are they making the inevitable problems so much more volatile by continuing mass immigration?

If we are governed by people this stupid and/or malicious, perhaps "a little rebellion now and then" is a good thing after all.

CHAPTER FOUR

Why It Makes Sense For Donald Trump To Reconcile Andrew Jackson And Henry Clay

Recently, President Trump visited Andrew Jackson's grave on the 250th anniversary of his birth and laid a wreath upon it. Then, at a rally in Louisville in Kentucky, Trump also praised Henry Clay.

This led to predictable snarking from reporters because Clay and Jackson had one of the fiercest political rivalries in American history. The ferociously anti-Trump *Time* magazine also took the opportunity to hit President Trump:

> "Henry Clay believed in what he called the 'American system,' and proposed tariffs to protect American industry and finance American infrastructure," Trump said. "Like Henry Clay, we want to put our own people to work. ... Clay was a fierce advocate for American manufacturing. He wanted it badly, he said, very strongly, free trade. ... He knew all the way back, early 1800s, Clay said that trade must be fair, equal, and reciprocal. Boom."
>
> Experts say that Trump's assessment of Clay's belief that the country would prosper when industry at home grew is correct, yet Clay's ideas weren't based on helping American workers. In that sense, he diverged from the populist idol who has been a frequent touchstone for Trump: Andrew Jackson, whose portrait hangs in the Oval Office.
>
> "They were absolutely feral enemies," says Fergus Bordewich, author of *America's Great Debate: Henry Clay, Stephen A. Douglas, and the Compromise that Preserved the Union.* "They absolutely hated each other, they shared almost no views in common."[1]

---

1   Waxman, Olivia B. "Donald Trump Praises Henry Clay in Louisville: What to Know."

But this misses the point. It's like saying that Alexander Hamilton or Thomas Jefferson would side with John McCain or Maxine Waters today. In today's America, or more accurately, today's post-America, the real battle is between nationalism and globalism and between those who want to preserve the historic American nation and those who want to replace it with the Third World. And in this climate, a Jackson and Clay synthesis makes a lot of sense.

After all, what is Andrew Jackson best known for today? Jackson was an aggressive American nationalist who fought the Indians, prized the Union, and generally exemplified the fighting spirit of the Scotch-Irish who settled the American frontier.

Clay was also an American nationalist, albeit one who prized high tariffs and infrastructure improvements. But from a contemporary point of view, both would be characterized on the side of "nationalists," those who put loyalty to the American nation-state ahead of attachments to foreign nations or a global system of international capitalism.

In Clay and Jackson's time, the battle was between those who were opposed to an Eastern establishment who wanted investment in infrastructure and a national bank, and those who thought that that was supporting a system of privilege. But today, the issue is that our economic, political and culture elite has no loyalty nor even identification with this country. Both Clay and Jackson would be horrified by this.

What's more, on racial views, the real focal point of American politics and culture today, Clay and Jackson were on the same side. Kevin Williamson at *National Review* once predicted that Democrats would never rename the Jackson-Jefferson Day dinners because the cries of "racism" were just being driven by partisanship. He was wrong. The battle over figures like Jackson and Jefferson comes from a deeper political and cultural conflict, and these dinners were eventually renamed. Jackson's status as a Democrat is less important to modern progressives than his status as a "racist."[2]

Time. March 21, 2017. Accessed May 19, 2018. http://time.com/4707867/donald-trump-henry-clay-andrew-jackson/.

2 Kirkpatrick, James. "It's About Race, Not Party — Democrats Ban Jefferson-Jackson

Similarly, Henry Clay was one of the founding members of the American Colonization Society, which sought to send free blacks back to Africa and help them establish colonies there.[3] At the time, one could argue this was an altruistic attitude to take — and it was viewed as a compromise position on the issue of slavery. But it hardly fits with modern views about multiculturalism. Clay would be savaged as a "racist" today. Indeed, Rand Paul used his very first speech in the Senate to criticize Henry Clay for not doing enough to fight slavery.[4]

Today, it makes a lot of sense to talk about Clay and Jackson as leaders in different factions of a larger American nationalism which they identified with the core European-American population. Indeed, the times demand we reconcile their legacies.

Trumpism, in a sentence, is Andrew-Jackson-style populism in the service of a Henry-Clay-style program. And that's what America needs today.

Dinner." *VDARE*. July 23, 2015. Accessed May 19, 2018. https://www.vdare.com/posts/its-about-race-not-party-democrats-ban-jefferson-jackson-dinner.

3   Lubinskas, James P. "A Troublesome Presence." *American Renaissance* V. 9 No. 8 (August 1998): 1; 3-5. Accessed May 18, 2018. https://www.amren.com/news/2011/10/a_troublesome_p/.

4   Stiles, Andrew. "Rand Paul's Maiden Speech: The Question of Compromise." *National Review*. February 02, 2011. Accessed May 19, 2018. https://www.nationalreview.com/corner/rand-pauls-maiden-speech-question-compromise-andrew-stiles/.

CHAPTER FIVE

The Moral Of New Orleans

AMERICANS CAN'T LIVE WITH THESE PEOPLE

In 2017, the murder rate in New Orleans is up 70% compared to 2016. The police say it is driven partially by the heroin epidemic, which is fueled by Mexican drug traffickers. Police are also having a harder time solving murders, with less than a third being cleared — a phenomenon New Orleans Police Department (NOPD) Superintendent Michael Harrison blamed on victims not cooperating with police.[1] This is not an uncommon phenomenon in America's post-Western cities, where police are perceived as the enemy even by the non-white populations that are merrily slaughtered by their own co-ethnics.

So, naturally, the city fathers of New Orleans think the real threat to the "community" is some statues.

Mayor Mitch Landrieu sent workers to tear down the Battle of Liberty Place monument, the first of four statues which will be torn down. "We will no longer allow the Confederacy to literally be put on a pedestal," he chirped. Construction workers were sent in under cover of night, wearing masks, guarded by police snipers.[2]

The parallel to the iconoclasm of ISIS is inescapable.

Obviously, the anti-white agitators will not stop with their terrorist

---

1   Curth, Kimberly. "NOPD: Murder Rate up 70%." FOX 8. April 27, 2017. Accessed May 19, 2018. http://www.fox8live.com/story/35272439/nopd-murder-rate-up-70.

2   Selk, Avi. "New Orleans Removes a Tribute to 'the Lost Cause of the Confederacy' — with Snipers Standing by." *The Washington Post*. April 24, 2017. Accessed May 19, 2018. https://www.washingtonpost.com/news/post-nation/wp/2017/04/24/new-orleans-removes-a-tribute-to-the-lost-cause-of-the-confederacy-with-snipers-standing-by/.

tactics after they purge the Big Easy of Southern heroes. A statue of Joan of Arc has already been attacked.[3]

The leader of the "Take 'Em Down" group, black academic Malcolm Suber, is a comfortable member of the Parasite Class, working at the Historically Black College Southern University. *The New York Times* notes that he is already targeting statues of George Washington and blandly observes he is an "avowed Marxist-Leninist."[4]

The nonchalance with which the Main Stream Media reports the political extremism of Leftists is in dramatic contrast with the witch-hunting zealotry driving its coverage of the Alt Right and the Trump phenomenon. Since Donald Trump's election, the MSM has grown increasingly hysterical and apocalyptic in its desire to control speech and dox Alt Right and Trump supporters. Like the Southern Poverty Law Center, the MSM seems to believe it has the right to determine not just who or what is "mainstream," but also what is allowed to be said and who is allowed to have a job.

In increasingly feminized and emotional language, wrist-flapping campaigns have been targeted at various members of the Trump Administration including Jeff Sessions, Steve Bannon and, now, former *Breitbart* reporter Julia Hahn, a White House aide. At *The Intercept*, Peter Maass explicitly compares her to Muslim extremists because Hahn wants to enforce American immigration laws and not replace the population—essentially the same positions held by every other American who has ever lived until about a decade ago. He sniffs: "Julia Hahn's opposites are not the young and impressionable Muslims who adopt hate-filled ideas about infidels. They are her mirror image."[5]

---

3   Boyd, Kevin. "Is Joan Of Arc The Next Target For Take 'Em Down NOLA?" *The Hayride*. May 04, 2017. Accessed May 19, 2018. https://thehayride.com/2017/05/joan-arc-next-target-take-em-nola/.

4   Fausset, Richard. "Tempers Flare Over Removal of Confederate Statues in New Orleans." *The New York Times*. May 07, 2017. Accessed May 19, 2018. https://www.nytimes.com/2017/05/07/us/new-orleans-monuments.html.

5   Maas, Peter. "White Fear in the White House: Young Bannon Disciple Julia Hahn Is a Case Study in Extremism." *The Intercept*. May 07, 2017. Accessed May 19, 2018. https://

Similar campaigns are also being waged against various Alt Right activists, most of whom have neither political nor financial power. In contrast, the extreme ties of major political figures such as Congressman Keith Ellison are never discussed pejoratively.[6]

Obviously, the fact that the Left never has to disavow its own radicals is a major tactical advantage. And while conservatives love to complain about the double standard, they have yet to internalize a far darker truth: journalists know *exactly* what Antifa and other anti-white and left-extremists believe. *But they agree with them*, and are using their journalism (which is a tactic, not a profession) to further these ends.

It is no longer possible to take the frenzied agitprop campaigns of the likes of Maass at face value. Objectively, there is no difference between him and the Antifa screaming obscenities in the street.

The desire of many conservatives and nationalists across the Right to simply operate in the same unapologetic way as the Left, in defiance of the self-appointed policing role of Conservatism Inc., was one of the powerful drives behind the Trump campaign. Of course, since Trump's election and his baffling decision to staff his administration with many of the same Conservatism Inc. types who opposed him, that alliance has splintered.

But one place where it had largely held up was in the increasing street battles between Left and Right. During the repeated protests in Berkeley, both explicitly ethno-nationalist and civic nationalist groups joined forces against Antifa protesters.[7] Mainstream conservatives are also now explicitly denouncing Antifa — a practically unthinkable development only a few years ago.

---

theintercept.com/2017/05/07/white-fear-in-the-white-house-young-bannon-disciple-julia-hahn-is-a-case-study-in-extremism/.

6   Kirkpatrick, James. "Zero Black Congressmen Disavow Keith Ellison's Plan For A Black Ethnostate." *VDARE*. December 1, 2016. Accessed May 19, 2018. https://www.vdare.com/posts/zero-black-congressmen-disavow-keith-ellisons-plan-for-a-black-ethnostate.

7   Kirkpatrick, James. "The Battle(s) Of Berkeley — Someone Is Going To Get Killed. Where Is Trump?" *VDARE*. April 16, 2017. Accessed May 19, 2018. https://www.vdare.com/articles/the-battle-of-berkeley-and-what-comes-next.

Yet even there the alliance may now be over. After Berkeley, tensions between the constitutionalist Oath Keepers organization and the Alt Right have been rising — not that this will prevent the Oath Keepers from also being called "racist."

And when opponents of removing New Orleans's Confederate monuments rallied over the weekend to defend them, the only violence which resulted was between civic nationalists and identitarians. A mysterious figure waving an American flag and a suit of armor, promptly dubbed the "Cuck Knight," reportedly attacked pro-Confederate protesters, and was punched out. The MSM celebrated this as an example of the "far right" tearing itself apart through a "purity spiral."[8]

However, this seemingly petty skirmish actually does represent a far deeper divide within the American Right which elected Donald Trump. For some Trump supporters, The Donald was simply the best person to beat Hillary and implement Republican policies. For others, notably for the Alt Right and for many immigration patriots, Trump was simply an avatar of a larger movement which recognized that all politics in America has become identity politics and that this politics is a zero-sum game. These supporters aren't interested in cutting the taxes of the rich or slashing entitlement programs. They want a more fundamental, existential change.

The American Left, dominated as it is by Cultural Marxism and united almost solely by anti-white animus, already sees politics this way. Note that the MSM's rage at the Republican Party's health-care bill was less about the actual content of the legislation than by how many white men in Congress voted for it.[9]

The Beltway Right and its remaining hapless followers don't seem to understand that the American identity is already fatally deconstructed.

---

8   Menegus, Bryan. "So Begins the Alt-Right Purity Spiral." Gizmodo. May 08, 2017. Accessed May 19, 2018. https://gizmodo.com/so-begins-the-alt-right-purity-spiral-1795017211.

9   Filipovic, Jill. "The White Guys Are Back in Charge." CNN. May 06, 2017. Accessed May 19, 2018. https://www.cnn.com/2017/05/05/opinions/health-care-photo-white-men-filipovic/index.html.

Even discussing what is best for America on issues such as taxes, health care or the economy seems pointless when there is no longer any agreement on what the nation itself is.

And that's why the events in New Orleans are ultimately more important even than what is happening in Congress today. The "Marxist-Leninists," motivated by their hatred of European-Americans and determined to destroy their symbols, simply can't be spoken of as belonging to the same people as the historic American nation. Therefore, it's not just pointless but obscene to speak about how conservatives can appeal to such types.

Unfortunately, that's also why the battle over the Confederate statues strikes me as a rearguard action. New Orleans has, in a deeper sense, already been lost. Perhaps it is time to take down these statues of European heroes ourselves and move them somewhere else. And time to rename Washington, D.C. and take down the father of our country's monuments too. Not as a surrender to the egalitarians, but because the cities themselves are no longer worthy of American heroes. As Gregory Hood put it:

> What greater dishonor can we give him [George Washington] than associating him with the gaggle of plutocrats, criminals, and traitors who presume to rule us? What greater proof can we show of the ultimate failure of the American Revolution than how we have turned his name into the epithet on the lips of millions of white Americans?[10]

These dead statues have more inherent worth than the living rulers of these Third World embarrassments.

And in the face of the endless hate emanating from these people and their servants in the streets and in the press rooms, actual Americans may have to recognize that, if we want to survive, we can no longer live together with them, or allow them to have authority over us in any way.

---

10 Hood, Gregory. "Rename Washington." *American Renaissance*. June 19, 2014. Accessed May 24, 2018. https://www.amren.com/news/2014/06/rename-washington/.

CHAPTER SIX

Treason To What?

I'M WITH THE RUSSIANS, THEY HATE
US LESS THAN THE MEDIA DOES

"Traitor!" screamed Keith Olbermann after Donald Trump fired FBI Director James Comey, though Olbermann himself was calling for Comey's resignation months ago.[1] Protesters scream the President is a "traitor" at public rallies. Michael Moore has been calling Trump a "Russian traitor" practically since he was inaugurated.[2]

Of course, this begs an obvious question. Traitor to *what*? In an "America" which no longer has a definable culture, language, ethnos, history, identity or rule of law, what is there left to betray?

The open celebration of what any other generation would have called "treason" reveals how fully self-discrediting the Russian "interference" narrative is. John Harington famously quipped: "Treason doth never prosper: what's the reason? Why, if it prosper, none dare call it treason." The "Russian interference" narrative is false, because the fact that it can be loudly denounced without being shut down for being the equivalent of "racist" or "xenophobic" shows that Russia isn't very powerful within our government and society.

In contrast, our government and media seem not only to tolerate

---

1   Athey, Amber. "Olbermann Says Trump Is Either An 'Idiot' Or A 'Traitor.'" *The Daily Caller.* May 09, 2017. Accessed May 19, 2018. http://dailycaller.com/2017/05/09/olbermann-yates-an-american-hero-trump-a-traitor-video/.

2   Vladimirov, Nikita. "Michael Moore to Trump: 'Vacate You Russian Traitor.'" *The Hill.* February 14, 2017. Accessed May 19, 2018. http://thehill.com/blogs/in-the-know/319504-michael-moore-to-trump-vacate-you-russian-traitor.

openly subversive or even hostile actions by foreign governments against the United States, but celebrate them.

Consider:

- The Mexican government makes open claims to sovereignty over both American citizens and territory and promotes the migration of its nationals in order to chip away at American independence.[3]

- A seemingly endless flow of Chinese, motivated by racial and national loyalty, are leaking American defense technology to their homeland; the MSM buries the stories out of fear of being called racist.[4]

- Saudi Arabia funds terrorist groups and networks within the United States and Europe, yet the same American military which the federal government won't use to secure our own border is used to guard the Kingdom.5 (And of course, Huma Abedin, Hillary Clinton's close aide, has strong ties to the Saudi government.)[6]

- Israel defines itself as a Jewish state, has a border wall, and has a powerful lobby in this country which has a huge amount of influence in both political parties. Israel's hold on American foreign policy, and the willingness of many American Jews to vote or oppose certain politicians based on the depth of their support for the Jewish State, is completely understood and taken for granted by the American public.

3 Wall, Allan. "Said In Spanish: Meddling Mexico Promotes Drive To Help Mexican Immigrants Become U.S. Citizens — And Voters; Etc." *VDARE*. December 23, 2015. Accessed May 19, 2018. https://www.vdare.com/articles/said-in-spanish-meddling-mexico-promotes-drive-to-help-mexican-immigrants-become-u-s-citizens-and-voters-etc.

4 McGregor, Michael. "FBI Video Warning About Spying for China Stars White College Student." *American Renaissance*. April 25, 2014. Accessed May 19, 2018. https://www.amren.com/news/2014/04/fbi-video-warning-about-spying-for-china-stars-white-college-student/.

5 Greer, Scott. "How Is Putin's Russia Worse Than Saudi Arabia?" *The Daily Caller*. December 26, 2015. Accessed May 19, 2018. http://dailycaller.com/2015/12/22/how-is-putins-russia-worse-than-saudi-arabia/.

6 Sailer, Steve. "Huma Abedin and the Saudi Lobby." *VDARE*. July 25, 2012. Accessed May 19, 2018. https://www.vdare.com/posts/huma-abedin-and-the-saudi-lobby.

To criticize any of these countries, or to suggest dual loyalty on the part of their supporters in this country, is political death. Of course, that is because such dual loyalty is sufficiently strong that it is dangerous to broach the topic.

Indeed, for some in our Congress, dual loyalty would be a massive improvement.

- Chuck Schumer tells the AIPAC that he is destined to be a "guardian" for the Jewish state,[7] but that he wants to shut down the government if President Trump tries to build a wall.[8]

- Luis Gutierrez allies with foreign governments against the United States and brags his "only loyalty" is to the "immigrant community."[9]

- Raul Grijalva, a Congressman from Arizona, is an alumnus of the Mexican secessionist and racialist group MEChA and has spent his entire political career trying to undermine immigration law for the benefit of Latin America and Latin Americans.[10]

The only reason we can't call men like these traitors is because there's no evidence they ever considered themselves Americans in any meaningful way. What could be more ridiculous than considering Chuck Schumer "a fellow American," on the basis of some imaginary "common interest" he supposedly shares with me?

Or take certain Main Stream Media figures. Bill Maher wants

7   Rosenberg, MJ. "Schumer: I'm on a Mission From God (to Be Israel's Guardian in Senate)." *The Huffington Post*. May 25, 2011. Accessed May 19, 2018. https://www.huffingtonpost.com/mj-rosenberg/schumer-im-on-a-mission-f_b_560091.html.

8   Rodack, Jeffrey. "Schumer: Trump Should Not Risk Shutdown Over Border Wall." *Newsmax*. August 23, 2017. Accessed May 19, 2018. https://www.newsmax.com/Politics/chuck-schumer-donald-trump-risk-shutdown/2017/08/23/id/809313/.

9   Campo-Flores, Arian. "Pushing Obama on Immigration Reform." *Newsweek*. November 27, 2010. Accessed May 19, 2018. http://www.newsweek.com/pushing-obama-immigration-reform-70093.

10 Kammer, Jerry. "Raul Grijalva: From Chicano Radical to Congressman." CIS. October 17, 2009. Accessed May 19, 2018. https://cis.org/Raul-Grijalva-Chicano-Radical-Congressman.

Democrats to ask if you are with "us or the Russians."[11] Maher naturally delights in open borders for America and the replacement of our own population, but has spoken in the past about how "Israel faces the problem of becoming a minority Jewish state within their own country."[12]

It's not double loyalty; that would be giving Maher too much credit. And it's not treason, because Maher just isn't part of my people, by his own standards. When Bill Maher refers to "us," I know that doesn't include me or my readers, and I know "the Russians" hate me a lot less than he does.

I'm with the Russians.

After all, "treason" requires not just providing "aid and comfort" to a foreign nation, but to an enemy. Why exactly is Russia an enemy of the United States?

It's not Russia that makes claims on our territory. It's not Russia that funds extremist networks. It's not Russia that is deliberately sending terrorists into the West.

Of course, there is a Trump associate who has disturbing ties with a country doing just that. The main focus of the investigation into "Russian collusion" is focusing on former National Security Advisor Michael Flynn. But Flynn's strongest ties to a foreign power seem to be increasingly extreme and anti-European Turkey of the autocrat Recep Tayyip Erdoğan. Incredibly, Flynn even wrote an editorial demanding more support for Turkey *on election day itself.*[13]

As Turkey is quite openly facilitating the migrant invasion of Europe and helping ISIS, there's a far better case to claim that our NATO "ally" is a

11 Hanchett, Ian. "Maher: I Want Democrats to Say 'You're Either With Us or With the Russians.'" *Breitbart.* May 13, 2017. Accessed May 19, 2018. http://www.breitbart.com/video/2017/05/12/maher-i-want-democrats-to-say-youre-either-with-us-or-with-the-russians/.

12 Berrin, Danielle. "Bill Maher on Israel, Uncut and Uncensored." *Jewish Journal.* November 29, 2012. Accessed May 19, 2018. https://jewishjournal.com/hollywood/110764/bill-maher-on-israel-uncut-and-uncensored/.

13 Flynn, Michael T. "Our Ally Turkey Is in Crisis and Needs Our Support." *The Hill.* November 08, 2016. Accessed May 19, 2018. http://thehill.com/blogs/pundits-blog/foreign-policy/305021-our-ally-turkey-is-in-crisis-and-needs-our-support.

threat than Russia. And yet Flynn's ties to Turkey go all but unmentioned outside evangelical Christian websites. The MSM is utterly indifferent to Flynn's ties to Erdoğan, even when they seem to be utterly dedicated to destroying General Flynn personally.

Part of it simply could be that the defense industry and the "Deep State" need an enemy with a powerful conventional military to justify their wealth and power. As it can't be China (that would be racist), Russia will do.

But the real reason why Russia is hated is because it is a *media threat*. Russia is funding, or at least is tied to, several alternative media sources: RT, possibly WikiLeaks, Sputnik, etc. Contrary to MSM claims, RT is hardly friendly to the Alt Right, instead promoting progressive hosts such as Thom Hartmann. But theirs is at least a slightly different point of view than the monolithic narrative promoted on every late-night comedy show, network news broadcast, cable news broadcast, newspaper headline, and establishment website.

There is also an undeniable, and openly articulated, sense of racial hatred expressed against Russians by Jewish members of the media.[14] Russians are hated both as a specific *ethnos* and as a white nation which does not seem to be fully committed to "our values," which, as defined by Weimerica's journalist class, consists of various forms of degeneracy. John Winthrop's "City upon a Hill" we are not.

It's not just idiotic but obscene that the same journalists gleefully involved in deconstructing the American identity now demand that Middle America rally round the flag out of some misplaced Cold War nostalgia. Needless to say, these same journalists loved Russia back when it was Communist and killing millions of Orthodox Christians.

For immigration patriots, it is especially obnoxious because the eradication of the American identity is a result of mass immigration. And immigration is more important than every other issue for two reasons.

First, it affects everything else. You simply can't discuss education,

---

14 Kirkpatrick, James. "Ethnic Hatred Of Russians Celebrated In American Media." *VDARE*. December 15, 2016. Accessed May 24, 2018. https://www.vdare.com/posts/ethnic-hatred-of-russians-celebrated-in-american-media.

healthcare, counter-terrorism, environmentalism, the class divide or any other topic without confronting immigration. Ignoring immigration ensures that no problem can ever be solved; indeed that every problem consistently gets worse. To take just one example, Americans are sent all over the world to die because "we have to fight them there so they don't come here," and then our government goes out of its way to bring terrorists here. And of course, as more problems are imported, the managerial class obtains more power to govern social relations and its own power grows. This is why it is hard to believe those who support open borders are actually working to defend the national interest in good faith.

But the second reason is even more important: immigration cuts to the heart of what a country is, of who you mean when you say, "my people." Are Americans still one people? Indeed, it's hard to claim America is even a geographic expression: referring to the United States using the shorthand "America" is now designated as offensive. The replacement of existing American citizens is celebrated by the media and funded by our own government.

And even citizenship means nothing, The MSM constantly promotes illegal immigrant Jose Antonio Vargas and his illegal friends or the protesters who parade under foreign flags not just as "Americans" but as people somehow more American than us.

It's a strange definition of patriotism by which wanting peaceful relations with Russia is "treason" but banning the American flag in public schools because it might offend Mexicans is government policy.[15]

Naturally, Leftist intellectuals and the reporters who parrot their ideas do have some vague idea of "American" identity — that of a "proposition" or "universal" nation which exists only to fight a global struggle for equality. But can you betray a "proposition nation"? How exactly does someone turn against a "universal nation"?

15 Kirkpatrick, James. "Anti-White Hecklers Veto Endorsed by the Supreme Court; American Flag Stays Banned." *VDARE*. March 31, 2015. Accessed May 19, 2018. https://www.vdare.com/posts/anti-white-hecklers-veto-endorsed-by-the-supreme-court-american-flag-stays-banned.

Actually, you can. If you are part of the historic American nation, one of those European-Americans who actually think of this country as a real nation with a real culture, you are in a strange way the only people excluded from what it means to be a modern "American." To consider America a particular place with a specific culture and history that not everyone in the world can join simply by existing is treason to a "universal nation." Everyone in the world can be an "American" — except, you know, actual Americans.

This is why the MSM is insistent that the governing philosophy of "America First," which should simply be a truism for any rational American government, is instead something subversive and dangerous.

The hard truth is that "our" rulers aren't the guardians of our sovereignty, but the greatest threat to our independence.

And this isn't an unprecedented circumstance in history. During the Napoleonic occupation of Prussia, Carl von Clausewitz violated his king's orders to join the invasion of Russia and instead joined the Tsar's forces in the hope of someday liberating his own country. After all, it wasn't Tsar Alexander that was occupying Prussia; it was Napoleon. And in the end, he won; Prussia was restored, and eventually it was Prussia that would unite all of Germany.

The same situation applies today. Today, those actively pursuing the destruction of my people, culture and civilization aren't in Moscow. I don't even concede that those are enemies at all.

Our enemies are in New York, Washington, and Los Angeles, in "our" own media companies, government bureaucracies, and intelligence agencies. The real America is under occupation — and resistance to collaborators is patriotism to our country. We elected Donald Trump because we thought he could help disrupt and perhaps even end that occupation, so we could have a country once again.

The attempt to destroy the President has ripped the mask off the forces behind this occupation. And we owe no loyalty to the collaborators who are trying to destroy his administration, dispossess our people, and destroy our country.

Because in the end, "treason" to the occupation is loyalty to America.

CHAPTER SEVEN

"*DIE!*"

The Unlimited Radicalism of Antifa — Enforcer for Democrats (and, Tacitly, Conservatism Inc.)

Antifa: What Americans Need To Know About The Alt-Left, WND, 2017, 99pp., $2.99

In the alien invasion movie *Independence Day* (1996), the beleaguered President of the United States, hoping he can forge some kind of a peace that would at least allow the survival of the human race, pleads, "What is it you want us to do?" The alien's response is simple. "Die."

The mind of a rational person rebels at the suggestion of such an unlimited, existential conflict. After all, reasonable people should always be able to come to a compromise, some settlement which will avoid violence and chaos. But there are some people who cannot be reasoned with, whose objectives are so unlimited and irrational that not only compromise, but even co-*existence* with them, is impossible.

Americans face such an existential threat in the form of the Leftist vigilante group that calls itself "Antifa." And now Americans have the first examination of the so-called "anti-fascists" from a patriot perspective in a new book: *Antifa: What Americans Need To Know About The Alt-Left*.

Antifa have been plaguing immigration patriots for many years. But it's only recently that the average American has become aware of their existence. The attacks on Trump supporters during and after the presidential campaign have made Americans aware of what the president eventually termed the "Alt Left." Of course, most establishment conservatives were using the term "Alt" simply as a synonym for "bad." And their typical criticism of the black-clad thugs was that they were "the real fascists." The huckster Dinesh D'Souza has built an entire career in presenting this alternate history to the gullible and well-meaning.[16]

Structured as a "Special Report," *Antifa* rejects this Conservatism Inc. cliché and provides an accurate history of the rise of fascism as well as anti-fascism. It argues that the entire debate about fascism and "anti-fascism" is essentially backwards: Fascism arose as a reaction to the Communist revolution in Russia and the attempted Communist revolutions in Hungary, Slovakia and parts of Germany: "Without communist revolution and without the vanguard leftist parties that launched those revolutions, there would have been no reason for fascism ever to exist," the anonymous author writes. "Essentially, the communist revolutionaries and their 'direct action' tactics had created their own nemesis capable of defeating them in the streets and willing to compete with them for the loyalty of the workers."

Similarly, instead of arising as a response to fascism, the modern Antifa movement was "just a brand for already existing communist and anarchist activists" — yet another "front group" in the long line of "front groups" the Reds have cobbled together throughout their bloody history. In some ways, the brand hasn't even developed since the 1930s, as contemporary Antifa still use the "flags within flags" and "three arrows" logos first created by the German Communists (KPD) and Socialist (SPD) parties.

"Anti-fascism," as the author details, has been a remarkably consistent slogan of the Totalitarian Left in all its manifestations. From the Berlin Wall (the "Anti Fascist Protection Rampart") to the British "Anti Nazi League" (a creation of the Socialist Workers Party), this Left (including left-anarchists such as the "autonomists") always frames itself as the only defense against "fascism." Of course, by "fascists," it means everyone else in the world.

16 Hood, Gregory. "America: Imagine a World Without Her." *Counter-Currents*. July 17, 2014. Accessed May 19, 2018. https://www.counter-currents.com/2014/07/america-imagine-a-world-without-her/.

Given current events, it's worth noting that most of Orwell's *Homage to Catalonia* is about the vicious infighting between various Spanish Leftist factions, all ostensibly at war with Francisco Franco. And, as the author of *Antifa: What Americans Need to Know about the Alt-Left* points out, Spanish Republican heroine Dolores Ibárruri, who famously utilized the Antifa *No Pasarán!* ("They shall not pass") slogan during the Battle for Madrid, was a Stalinist who thoroughly approved of the bloody purges against Trotskyists and anarchists because she claimed they were "fascists."[17]

Indeed, *Antifa: What Americans Need to Know about the Alt-Left* is a critical warning to every American, not just conservatives, that they are all being targeted by Antifa. Just as every Communist regime has always violently targeted "wreckers" to explain policy failures, so must Antifa target an ever increasing number of "fascists" as the impossible (and undesirable) goal of "equality" remains forever over the horizon.

No one can even define "racism" anymore; being "colorblind" has gone from the definition of anti-racism to proof of white supremacy within only a few years. As *Antifa*'s author notes:

[T]he process of continuous social revolution has no limits. Average citizens may say they are opposed to "racism" but … that word is being continuously redefined so that almost everyone who is not actually Antifa is a "racist," and therefore a target. Words such as "ableism," "heteronormativity," or "transphobia" would have drawn confused stares from the vast majority of the population even a few years ago. Today, they are seen as grounds to get someone fired from his or her job or attack him or her in the street.

As "anti-fascism" quite explicitly defines itself as anti-liberal (in the classical sense of liberalism), repudiates the right to free speech and takes upon itself the responsibility to enforce, through violence, a remarkably narrow definition of what people can and cannot say, it is of course quintessentially totalitarian. And, not surprisingly, it is the Main Stream Media

---

17 Ibárruri, Dolores. "Reply to the Enemies, Slanderers and Wavering Elements." *Communist International*, November 1937, 808-13. Accessed May 24, 2018. https://www.marxists.org/archive/ibarruri/1937/08/10.htm.

journalists, who themselves now operate almost entirely as commissars, to enable these terrorists by consistently providing them adoring coverage and spearheading their attack campaigns. Indeed, reporters keep running interference for Antifa even as Antifa itself keeps physically attacking them.[18]

Of course, many "conservatives" don't particularly want to hear this either. After all, Conservatism Inc. has a long history of tacitly working with Antifa to police "the movement." Thus, *National Review* was silent when Antifa began closing down American Renaissance conferences, even suppressing a diary item by John Derbyshire about the matter in 2011[19] — because American Renaissance had made devastating criticisms of *National Review*'s cuckservatism and its betrayal of immigration patriotism that the *NR* girly-boys could not answer, especially while pursuing their real careers as MSM token Rightists.[20]

And the Beltway Right is hardly interested in a serious discussion of political history anyway. It's quite content to voice the aforementioned platitudes about progressives being "the real fascists."

But *Antifa* demonstrates that "anti-fascism" is not merely Left Totalitarianism, but now deeply anti-white. All efforts by well-meaning grassroots conservatives to try to prove they are not "fascist" or "racist" are doomed to failure: "By definition, Antifa *must* have enemies that can be dehumanized as evil and dangerous; otherwise they lose their entire reason for existence."

Indeed, many European-Americans are starting to understand that

---

18 Nolte, John. "Physical Assault on Journalists' Rap Sheet: Antifa: 10 – Trump Supporters: 0." *Breitbart*. August 31, 2017. Accessed May 19, 2018. http://www. breitbart.com/big-journalism/2017/08/31/physical-assault-journalists-rap-sheet-antifa-10-trump-supporters-0/.

19 Derbyshire, John. "*National Review* Online Diary." John Derbyshire. February 2011. Accessed May 19, 2018. http://www.johnderbyshire.com/Opinions/Diaries/2011-02. html#15.

20 Lubinskas, James P. "The Decline of *National Review*." *American Renaissance* 11:9 (September 2000): 1; 3-6. Accessed May 24, 2018. https://www.amren.com/ news/2012/04/the-decline-of-national-review/.

the demands for "equality" were *never* about equality. The goalposts will always be moved; the demands for more concessions and redistribution of wealth always increased. No matter how much conservatives (and whites in general) give, the establishment Left, following in the train of its Antifa vanguard, will always demand more.

Immigration patriots also should pay careful attention to *Antifa*. Many grassroots Americans continue to show a baffling naïveté when it comes to the immigration debate. It's not uncommon to hear conservatives, or even Trump supporters, say they want to "be fair" to DACA recipients or welcome legal, as opposed to illegal, immigrants. But claims that illegals are "new Americans" are just as dishonest as claims that Antifa are simply "opposed to fascism." In both cases, friendly-sounding propaganda is used to conceal a far more radical agenda.

In his weird way, and perhaps despite himself, Donald Trump has forced many Republicans into recognizing the Antifa threat at last. *Antifa: What Americans Need to Know about the Alt-Left* is an indication that mainstream conservatives are finally waking up to the terrifying reality of the American Left's paramilitaries.

And perhaps it is a sign average Americans will no longer allow their declared enemies to tell them what they are allowed to think, say, and hear.

CHAPTER EIGHT

Katie Hopkins and Katie McHugh

FIRED BY MEDIA FOR TELLING TRUTH ABOUT ISLAM

On the 73rd anniversary of D-Day, it appears only a cynic could say that France and the United Kingdom "won" World War II. As this is written, news comes of a self-described "soldier of the caliphate" attacking police in Paris, trapping thousands inside the Notre Dame Cathedral. This comes only days after the London Bridge terrorist attack, which itself came only days after the recent attack at an Ariana Grande concert in Manchester. Terrorism is, as the Prime Minister of France so memorably put it not long ago, something we are "going to have to live with" now.[1] And while he was speaking for the French, he may as well have spoken for all of Western Europe.

The response of those who rule the West and their Main Stream Media lackeys (it would be obscene to call them "elites") is to deny that a problem even exists and to attempt to destroy those who point it out.

There is now a distinct pattern of the Left claiming a scalp after each new terrorist attack. It remains to be seen who will be the victim after Paris, but two Katies were the casualties after the attacks in England: Katie Hopkins, formerly of the UK's Liberty Broadcast Channel broadcast channel; and Katie McHugh, formerly of *Breitbart*.

In both cases, the ostensible justification was a tweet made in anger immediately after the terrorist attacks. Katie Hopkins (who retains her column at the *Daily Mail*) called for a "final solution" to terrorism after the attack in Manchester. Presumably recognizing the unfortunate parallel of

---

1   Friedman, Uri. "Learning to Live With Terrorism." *The Atlantic*. August 15, 2016. Accessed May 19, 2018. https://www.theatlantic.com/international/archive/2016/08/terrorism-resilience-isis/493433/.

the phrasing, she quickly deleted the tweet, but continued to rage against how Muslim terrorism has become an accepted part of life in Britain. Needless to say, in the plain literal meaning of her statement, there was nothing untoward about it.

But in the birthplace of the English-speaking world's liberties, this led to police reports against Hopkins. She was soon afterward fired from LBC, a decision which we are told led to "cheers and applause" from the staff and was greeted by the Leftist press as some kind of a great national triumph.[2]

After the London Bridge attack, Katie McHugh of *Breitbart* also expressed a healthy sense of outrage and tweeted the obvious point, "There would be no deadly terror attacks in the U.K. if Muslims didn't live there. #LondonBridge."[3]

The Left seized on her tweet, among other things mocking the young woman for supposedly ignoring the Irish Republican Army. Of course, as even the fanatically anti-Trump John Schindler noted, there is no comparison: the sheer number of jihadists in the United Kingdom, the Islamists' eagerness to use indiscriminate violence, and the apocalyptic motives of the caliphate's Western servants make both compromise and containment impossible. Schindler even referenced the great Enoch Powell and warned, "[I]t's difficult to say Powell was wrong in his essential point."[4]

Nonetheless, McHugh was fired from *Breitbart*. This was especially stunning given that at the very moment *Breitbart* issued McHugh's pink

2   "Media Mole." "YOU'RE FIRED at Last! Katie Hopkins Is Sacked by LBC after 'final Solution' Tweet." *New Statesman*. May 26, 2017. Accessed May 19, 2018. https://www. newstatesman.com/politics/media/2017/05/you-re-fired-last-katie-hopkins-sacked-lbc-after-final-solution-tweet.

3   Morgan, A. W. "*Breitbart* Cans Writer Katie McHugh For Telling Truth About London Attack." *VDARE*. June 5, 2017. Accessed May 19, 2018. https://www.vdare. com/posts/breitbart-cans-writer-katie-mchugh-for-telling-truth-about-london-attack.

4   Schindler, John R. "There Is No Intelligence Solution to Britain's Rivers of Blood." *Observer*. June 04, 2017. Accessed May 19, 2018. https://observer.com/2017/06/london-bridge-isis-attack-british-m15/.

slip, Donald Trump was engaging in a campaign-style tweetstorm defending his travel ban from certain Muslim countries: "That's right, we need a TRAVEL BAN for certain DANGEROUS countries, not some politically correct term that won't help us protect our people!"[5] Simultaneously, *Breitbart* icon Nigel Farage, hero of Brexit and former leader of UKIP, was broaching the idea of internment camps.[6]

Breitbart's shameful conduct was especially concerning given the site's publishing history and associations, which in the past included defiance of political correctness, frank reporting of racial realities in crime, and championing of European nationalist movements. McHugh's tweet was not only true, but it also could barely even be considered edgy by *Breitbart* standards, or even *National Review* standards. Furthermore, it was a *tweet*.

Right-media watcher Will Sommer argues *Breitbart* is collapsing as it pursues respectability, advertisers, permanent congressional press passes, etc. He predicts that any employee who gets in the way of that quest can expect to be fired, observing accurately that McHugh would still have had her job a year or two ago "when *Breitbart* still had a 'black crime' section and employed Milo Yiannopoulos."[7] Charles Johnson of GotNews similarly charges that *Breitbart* is losing hits, as well as its brand, because it is dependent on advertisers and donors, not readers.[8]

Some years ago, Jonah Goldberg called *VDARE* founder Peter

---

5   realDonaldTrump. (2017, June 5). That's right, we need a TRAVEL BAN for certain DANGEROUS countries, not some politically correct term that won't help us protect our people! [Tweet] https://twitter.com/realDonaldTrump/status/871899511525961728.

6   "Farage Says Calls for Internment Camps for Terrorist Suspects Could Grow in Britain." RT. June 5, 2017. Accessed May 19, 2018. https://www.rt.com/uk/390990-nigel-farage-internment-terrorism/.

7   Sommer, Will. "Right Richter: Between *Breitbart* and a Hard Place." *Tiny Letter.* June 6, 2017. Accessed May 19, 2018. https://tinyletter.com/rightrichter/letters/right-richter-between-breitbart-and-a-hard-place.

8   *What Happened to Breitbart News and Katie McHugh.* Performed by Charles Johnson. Facebook. June 5, 2017. Accessed May 24, 2018. https://www.facebook.com/charles.c.johnson/videos/10209187147295931/?pnref=story.

Brimelow a "once-respected conservative voice," to which Brimelow countered that *National Review* had become a "once-conservative, now respected, magazine."[9] *Breitbart*, of course, will be neither. The Left is committed to branding the site irrevocably as a "white nationalist" publication.

And significantly, the Left is assisted in this task by former writers from Beltway Right magazines such as Betsy Woodruff of *The Daily Beast*, formerly of *National Review* and Red Alert Politics. Similarly, the journalist responsible for leading the point and sputter campaign that cowed *Breitbart* was Oliver Darcy, once managing editor of Glenn Beck's *TheBlaze*. The conservative Leadership Institute, where Darcy worked before *TheBlaze*, once bragged he wasn't a "typical liberal journalist."[10] But from his new perch at CNN, Darcy waged a sadly typical campaign to drive out McHugh, enabled naturally by traitorous Breitbart colleagues eager to leak denunciations of her to the very network President Trump habitually labels "fake news."[11] (In passing, it should be noted that activists who migrated from the Left to the Right include such titans as James Burnham and Whittaker Chambers. Can anyone imagine reading Betsy Woodruff or Oliver Darcy after their deaths?)

Breitbart donors wondering why their investment's value is plummeting should be demanding to know why the leakers weren't the ones fired, rather than McHugh.

The urge to control speech after a terrorist attack by cracking down

---

9   Brimelow, Peter. "Peter Brimelow ('a Once-respected Conservative Voice') on Goldberg of *National Review* (a Once-conservative, Now Respected, Magazine)." *VDARE*. March 1, 2002. Accessed May 19, 2018. https://www.vdare.com/articles/peter-brimelow-a-once-respected-conservative-voice-on-goldberg-of-national-review-a-once-co.

10 Wehe, Carol, and Carmela Martinez. "The 'Viral Genius' Journalist." Leadership Institute. October 2, 2014. Accessed May 19, 2018. https://www.leadershipinstitute.org/News/?NR=10817.

11 Darcy, Oliver. "*Breitbart* Employees Infuriated by Colleague's 'appalling' Comments after London Terror Attack." CNN. June 4, 2017. Accessed May 19, 2018. http://money.cnn.com/2017/06/04/media/breitbart-reaction-london-tweets/index.html.

on victims is now typical of the so-called "center-right." Theresa May's solution to the problem of Muslim terrorism in the UK is to *censor the internet*, which of course will take the form of an anarchico-tyrannical policy of cracking down on British nationalists while doing nothing to stop jihadists.[12] The only way you could use censorship to stop jihadists is if you took a page from Geert Wilders's book and banned the Koran.

From *Breitbart* to May, from CNN to Ariana Grande, the West is living in denial. Hopkins and McHugh have been targeted because they suggest actually doing something to solve the problem, namely: 1) getting Muslims out of Europe and 2) stopping more from coming.

It's not that Europeans and European-Americans don't know that this would solve the problem. Nor does anyone deny Europe is headed to submission if Muslim immigration continues. But to identify the obvious problem, the obvious solution, and the obvious consequences if the solution is not carried out is to impose a moral burden most Westerners do not want to accept.

Hence, Hopkins, McHugh and others like them become the targets of hatred, and their defenestration a cause for rejoicing, because to even allow them to speak would condemn those who remain imprisoned by their own cowardice.

At a certain point, the refusal to understand becomes a moral failing. The cuck who won't dump his cheating girlfriend, the heroin addict who tells himself he doesn't have a problem, the obese woman who insists she is healthy while destroying herself—all can be figures of sympathy, but only to a point. Those who present harsh truths to these unfortunates are often condemned for their trouble, while those who offer comforting lies are praised by them. But given sufficient knowledge of both problem and solution, victimhood becomes collaboration.

We have reached this point in the West. Katie Hopkins and Katie McHugh are suffering for the sins of our supposed leaders, both in Con-

12 Shackford, Scott. "Theresa May's Call for Internet Censorship Isn't Limited to Fighting Terrorism." *Reason*. June 05, 2017. Accessed May 19, 2018. https://reason.com/blog/2017/06/05/theresa-mays-call-for-internet-censorshi.

servatism Inc. and in the high councils of state. To refuse to defend them is to join their tormentors and become complicit in our own destruction. And to remain silent is acquiesce not just to their condemnation, but the condemnation of our entire civilization.

CHAPTER NINE

Kevin Williamson Firing
Shows Conservatism Inc. Has
Triangulated Itself Into Irrelevance

The flagship organ of Conservatism Inc. is suddenly worried about intellectual diversity after *The Atlantic* fired former *National Review* contributor Kevin Williamson. David French thinks it is "cowardly."[1] Jonah Goldberg thinks it is a victory for mob rule.[2] Michael Brendan Dougherty denounces "the sudden onset of illiteracy and bad faith of people writing about my former colleague, Kevin Williamson."[3] The phrase which comes to mind, six years after John Derbyshire was purged from *National Review* for speaking truthfully about race, is "self-discrediting." And Conservatism Inc. has put itself in this position by triangulating and "purging" itself into irrelevance.

The comments which terminated Williamson's brief *Atlantic* career were his supposedly ironic musings about whether women who had abortions should be given the death penalty. Goldberg is particularly outraged by this because Williamson never made this sardonic

1   French, David. "On the Cowardly Firing of Kevin Williamson." *National Review*. April 05, 2018. Accessed May 19, 2018. https://www.nationalreview.com/corner/kevin-williamson-firing-by-the-atlantic-cowardly/.

2   Goldberg, Jonah. "Kevin Williamson, Thought Criminal." *National Review*. April 6, 2018. Accessed May 19, 2018. https://www.nationalreview.com/g-file/kevin-williamson-thought-criminal/.

3   Dougherty, Michael Brendan. "Imagine a Genocide." *National Review*. April 06, 2018. Accessed May 19, 2018. https://www.nationalreview.com/corner/imagine-a-genocide/.

argument in the pages of *National Review*, let alone *The Atlantic*. "Kevin *was fired for what he thinks*," intones Goldberg, with the italics in the original.[4]

Of course, John Derbyshire's version of "The Talk," which advised people to avoid African-Americans in certain circumstances for their own safety, was similarly not published in *National Review*, but in Takimag.[5] Yet this did not save Derbyshire from being denounced by his former colleagues at *National Review* when said magazine "parted ways" with him.[6] This is especially odd considering Derbyshire's advice wasn't about hanging or hurting people, but keeping them alive. Indeed, many naïve white people would still be alive had Derb's advice been followed.

To take another example, Robert Weissberg was also fired from *National Review* for actions unrelated to his job there. His sin: appearing at an American Renaissance conference — even though his speech there actually denounced "white nationalism" as impossible. *NR* editor Rich Lowry actually thanked the Antifa-cum-hall monitors who alerted him.[7] Among those publications rejoicing at Weissberg's fate: naturally, *The Atlantic*.[8]

In short, Jonah Goldberg isn't defending a principle. He, like Ben Shapiro, is simply angry because *The Atlantic* is getting to act as the censor — rather than himself. Consider this sample tweet (one of many) of

---

4   Goldberg, Jonah. "Kevin Williamson, Thought Criminal." *National Review*. April 6, 2018. Accessed May 19, 2018. https://www.nationalreview.com/g-file/kevin-williamson-thought-criminal/.

5   Derbyshire, John. "The Talk: Nonblack Version." *Taki's Magazine*. April 5, 2012. Accessed May 19, 2018. http://takimag.com/article/the_talk_nonblack_version_john_derbyshire/print#axzz5FzcsCaSr.

6   Lowry, Rich. "Parting Ways." *National Review*. April 7, 2012. Accessed May 19, 2018. https://www.nationalreview.com/corner/parting-ways-rich-lowry/.

7   Lowry, Rich. "Regarding Robert Weissberg." *National Review*. April 11, 2012. Accessed May 19, 2018. https://www.nationalreview.com/phi-beta-cons/regarding-robert-weissberg-rich-lowry/.

8   Reeve, Elspeth. "Racist Writers Are Right to Feel Threatened." *The Atlantic*. April 11, 2012. Accessed May 19, 2018. https://www.theatlantic.com/politics/archive/2012/04/racist-writers-are-right-feel-threatened/329438/.

Goldberg's from 2012: "For the record, I find my colleague John Derbyshire's piece fundamentally indefensible and offensive. I wish he hadn't
written it."[9]

Still, while *tu quoque* is satisfying rhetorically, the Williamson episode
does show that the limits of permissible opinion are narrowing rapidly — despite (or perhaps because of) Donald Trump's election. It was *The
Atlantic* that hosted a serious discussion on *The Camp of the Saints* in
1994.[10] Back in 1971, the magazine was discussing racial realism; today,
it's mad there aren't enough black riots.[11]

As Ben Domenech notes darkly:

> This story is a predictable continuation of the Left's ownership not just of me-
> dia but indeed of all institutions. ... If you have wrongthink, you will not be
> allowed for long to make your living within any space the Left has determined
> they own — first the academy, then the media, then corporate America, and
> now the public square.[12]

This is true. But Domenech is not exactly a model of intellectual toler-
ance himself: he has denounced his critics on the Right, such as the late
Lawrence Auster, as "Evilcons."[13] Domenech, who appropriately is now
Meghan McCain's husband, has also attacked Donald Trump and those

9   JonahNRO. (2012, April 6). For the record, I find my colleague John Derbyshire's
    piece fundamentally indefensible and offensive. I wish he hadn't written it. [Tweet]
    https://twitter.com/JonahNRO/status/188399150042320896.

10 Connelly, Matthew, and Paul Kennedy. "Must It Be the Rest Against the West?" *The
    Atlantic*, December 1994, 61-84. Accessed May 19, 1994. https://www.theatlantic.
    com/past/docs/politics/immigrat/kennf.htm.

11 Sailer, Steve. "The Atlantic 1971 vs. The Atlantic 2018." *VDARE*. April 6, 2018.
    Accessed May 19, 2018. https://www.vdare.com/posts/the-atlantic-1971-vs-the-
    atlantic-2018.

12 Domenech, Ben. "Firing Kevin Williamson Is Just the Beginning." *The Federalist*.
    April 06, 2018. Accessed May 19, 2018. http://thefederalist.com/2018/04/06/firing-
    kevin-williamson-is-just-the-beginning/.

13 Domenech, Ben. "EvilCons." The Ben Files. July 31, 2003. Accessed May 19, 2018.
    https://web.archive.org/web/20030816153130/http://bendomenech.com/blog/
    archives/001069.html.

on the authentic American Right for pursuing "identity politics" instead of "limited government."[14] On top of that, he is notorious for plagiarism,[15] but this isn't exactly an example — even though you feel like you've heard this same argument a million times before.

But given that Williamson is being punished by the "free market," and not "the state," what is Domenech even complaining about? Here's your limited government, good and hard. After all, as long as it's not a government bureaucrat giving the order, that's "freedom," right?

Indeed, in one of those little moments which makes one believe in divine justice, Williamson's first (and last) *Atlantic* column was precisely on this theme, bemoaning the fall of "classical liberalism" and blasting Victor Davis Hanson for advocating regulation of tech companies, "perhaps on the public utility model."[16] Just hours before the news of Williamson's termination, Hanson responded in *National Review*:

> In light of what is revealed near daily about Silicon Valley, Facebook, I do not think I was in error in worrying about either its agendas or methods, or the paradox of the tech sector thus far receiving a pass from the usual muck-raking Left. … Sadly, I think Kevin Williamson will soon find that *National Review* was far more tolerant of his controversial views than will be true at *The Atlantic*.[17]

And so indeed Williamson did.

Not to belabor the point, but on Saturday, Twitter CEO Jack

14 Domenech, Ben. "Are Republicans For Freedom or White Identity Politics?" *The Federalist*. August 31, 2015. Accessed May 18, 2018. http://thefederalist.com/2015/08/21/are-republicans-for-freedom-or-white-identity-politics/.

15 Bailey, Jonathan. "The Ben Domenech Scandal." *Plagiarism Today*. March 26, 2006. Accessed May 19, 2018. https://www.plagiarismtoday.com/2006/03/24/the-ben-domenech-scandal/.

16 Williamson, Kevin D. "The Passing of the Libertarian Moment." *The Atlantic*. April 02, 2018. Accessed May 20, 2018. https://www.theatlantic.com/politics/archive/2018/04/defused/556934/.

17 Hanson, Victor Davis. "A Response to Kevin Williamson." *National Review*. April 05, 2018. Accessed May 20, 2018. https://www.nationalreview.com/corner/kevin-williamson-national-review-response-atlantic-piece/.

Dorsey approvingly cited[18] a story interpreting current American politics as a "civil war" in which conservatives must be driven completely out of institutional power, as they have been in California.[19]

Ensuring that those who want to destroy us have more money and power to do it isn't much of a program. Yet that's Williamson's conservatism.

Indeed, rendering conservatism toothless is something of a specialty for Williamson. "He loves to take arguments to the breaking point in hopes of shocking readers with his cold, unbound logic," writes Jack Shafer in *Politico*, calling him a "conservative fire-breather."[20]

But it's not really true. Williamson finds a problem with the Left, deconstructs it with colorful prose, and then forces it into a normal Conservative Inc. frame which is guaranteed to fail. Positioning the likes of Kevin Williamson as a "fire-breather" is just another way Main Stream Media journalist/activists are trying to move the Overton Window ever leftward.

This isn't to say Williamson is stupid. He may be something worse. He probably knows more than he is letting on. For example, he has favorably cited Sam Francis when discussing the concept of "anarcho-tyranny."[21] He also has some measure of skill in crafting amusing *ad hominem* attacks. (I've referred to him as an obese version of Anton LaVey: game recognize game.)[22] Yet Williamson's signature technique is not to take ideas to their

---

18 jack. (2018, April 5). Great read https://twitter.com/ev/status/9809… [Tweet]. https://twitter.com/jack/status/982096889930657792.

19 Leyden, Peter, and Ruy Teixeira. "The Great Lesson of California in America's New Civil War." *Medium*. January 19, 2018. Accessed May 20, 2018. https://medium.com/s/state-of-the-future/the-great-lesson-of-california-in-americas-new-civil-war-e52e2861f30.

20 Shafer, Jack. "Congrats, Jeff Goldberg. You Just Martyred Kevin Williamson." *Politico*. April 06, 2018. Accessed May 20, 2018. https://www.politico.com/magazine/story/2018/04/06/kevin-williamson-atlantic-jeffrey-goldberg-217831.

21 Williamson, Kevin D. "Meet the New Serfs: You." *National Review*. October 23, 2014. Accessed May 20, 2018. https://www.nationalreview.com/2014/10/meet-new-serfs-you-kevin-d-williamson/.

22 Kirkpatrick, James. "'The Little Cucks' — *NATIONAL REVIEW*, Kevin D. Williamson And The Pointless Persuasion." *VDARE*. August 29, 2017. Accessed May 20, 2018.

logical conclusion, but to take idiotic Beltway Right premises to their logical conclusion. Thus, we get all-or-nothing, eliminationist rhetoric about abstract ideological stances and a refusal to recognize demographic realities.

For example, writing about Detroit, Williamson pins the city's woes on "progressivism in its final stages of decadence" and blames it for "the death of its children."[23] Yet Portland is so progressive that Republicans who want to march in a parade get threatened with death.[24] However, (as long as you are quiet about your politics) Portland is consistently ranked one of the best places to live in America, and, not coincidentally, one of the whitest.

Speaking of Portland, the Leftists there are renaming schools once dedicated to Thomas Jefferson because he was a slaveholder. Nationally, the Democrats' traditional Jefferson-Jackson dinners are also being renamed because of concerns about "racism." This defies Williamson's 2015 column declaring this would never happen.[25]

People are not driven by party labels, but more primal forces such as identity and power. The truth is that we are not at "peak Leftism," and the Left won't stop until it is forced to. Leftists have no reason to pay attention to Conservatism Inc. complaints. Not only do conservatives have no institutional power, their intellectual leaders are constantly lecturing them that it is immoral to pursue power.

---

https://www.vdare.com/articles/the-little-cucks-national-review-kevin-d-williamson-and-the-pointless-persuasion.

23 Williamson, Kevin D. "Progressivism Kills." *National Review*. February 01, 2014. Accessed May 20, 2018. https://www.nationalreview.com/2014/02/progressivism-kills-kevin-d-williamson/.

24 Hoft, Jim. "Portland Cancels Annual Avenue of Roses Parade After Antifa Terrorists Promise to Rush Parade and Beat Republicans." *The Gateway Pundit*. April 26, 2017. Accessed May 24, 2018. http://www.thegatewaypundit.com/2017/04/portland-cancels-annual-avenue-roses-parade-antifa-terrorists-promise-rush-parade-beat-republicans/.

25 Kirkpatrick, James. "It's About Race, Not Party — Democrats Ban Jefferson-Jackson Dinner." *VDARE*. July 23, 2015. Accessed May 19, 2018. https://www.vdare.com/posts/its-about-race-not-party-democrats-ban-jefferson-jackson-dinner.

If there was a serious American Right, we'd be having discussions about nationalizing social networking sites or at least guaranteeing free speech online. Instead, after a desperate struggle during the 2016 campaign, the only meaningful accomplishment of the united Republican government is a tax cut for the people who are openly vowing to destroy us.

It's not surprising we get such stupid, self-destructive ideas because "the conservative movement" has systematically expelled and disavowed anyone who had anything interesting or creative to say.

Now, after decades of internal purges and appeasement, the cuckservatives of Conservatism Inc. are complaining that Leftists won't give them a platform. But why should they? The cucks have performed their function. They neutered the Beltway Right. Leftists don't need them anymore.

Luckily, neither do American patriots.

CHAPTER TEN

"If You Fight Your Enemies, They Win"

WHY CONSERVATISM INC. WON'T DEFEND FREE SPEECH

In early 2016, Canadian Prime Minister Justin Trudeau announced his country would no longer bomb the Islamic State. Defending this decision, the prime minister stated: "Call us old-fashioned, but we think that we ought to avoid doing precisely what our enemies want us to do. They want us to elevate, to give in to fear, to indulge in hatred, to eye one another with suspicion, and to take leave of our faculties."[1] This was famously paraphrased by Gavin McInnes, among others, as, "If you kill your enemies, they win."[2] Though Justin Trudeau never actually said this, it encapsulated his worldview so precisely that many people assumed it was a quotation.

Unfortunately, most Conservatism Inc. operatives say the same kinds of things about technology oligopolies. The Beltway Right acknowledges censorship, demonization, and marginalization by tech mega companies such as Google, Facebook, and Twitter, but doesn't want to do anything about it. Thus, even though the Republican Party controls both Congress and the White House, the conservative and nationalist online activists who won Donald Trump the presidency in an unprecedented upset are being systematically suppressed and "the conservative movement" is saying nothing.

---

1 "Canada IS Airstrikes: Trudeau Announces 22 February End Date." BBC News. February 08, 2016. Accessed May 21, 2018. http://www.bbc.com/news/world-us-canada-35526255.

2 McInnes, Gavin. "'If You Kill Your Enemies, They Win': Justin Trudeau's Greatest Quotes!" *The Rebel.* March 15, 2016. Accessed May 21, 2018. https://www.therebel.media/justin_trudeau_s_greatest_quotes.

For example, in a recent interview with *Breitbart,* Klon Kitchen, the Heritage Foundation's senior research fellow for technology, said that Facebook has the right to censor whomever it wants. "I think Facebook is a private company," he said. "[T]he Heritage Foundation is going to be very clear about a private company's right to organize and conduct its business as it sees fit."[3]

In a separate piece, *Breitbart*'s Bokhari denounced both Heritage and the libertarian think tank "TechFreedom," another group opposing regulation of Facebook and other social networking giants. Bokhari argued establishment conservatives are failing to understand the core issue:

> None of these free market geniuses have grasped that Google and Facebook aren't just monopolies (any first-grade economics teacher can tell you that a market dominated by monopolies is not "free"), they are unique in the vast power they have over the flow of information. No other organization in history has had the power to shape opinion, control public discourse, and influence democratic voters.[4]

As the last Radio *VDARE* argued, the power of these mega-companies creates the potential for a "managed democracy" such as Vladimir Putin's Russia is alleged to be.[5] Indeed, the situation in America is more tyrannical and more dangerous. In Russia, the people at least know whom to hold responsible if the system fails them. In America, because the actors controlling the flow of information are not technically part of the government, there is an illusion of a "marketplace of ideas," when there is actually

3   Bokhari, Allum. "Heritage Foundation Defends Facebook's 'Right' to Censor, Will Oppose Regulation." *Breitbart.* May 03, 2018. Accessed May 21, 2018. http://www.breitbart.com/tech/2018/05/03/heritage-foundation-defends-facebooks-right-to-censor-will-oppose-regulation/.

4   Bokhari, Allum. "Bokhari: 'Free Market' Defenders of Tech Giants Are Useful Idiots." *Breitbart.* May 06, 2018. Accessed May 21, 2018. http://www.breitbart.com/tech/2018/05/06/free-market-defenders-of-tech-giants-are-wrong/.

5   Dare, Virginia. "*VDARE* Radio: Mark Zuckerberg, Conservatism Inc. And America's Managed Democracy." *VDARE.* May 03, 2018. Accessed May 21, 2018. https://www.vdare.com/radio_vdare/vdare-radio-mark-zuckerberg-conservatism-inc-and-america-s-managed-democracy.

just one narrative being promoted. Only a cynic can speak of "democracy" when the public's access to information, and therefore the public's view of reality, can be determined by the push of a button.

As even Main Stream Media journalists now concede, Facebook (and its algorithm) now has the power to direct massive amounts of traffic to whatever companies it wants. Because no one actually knows what the algorithm is and because it continually changes, Facebook essentially has the power to destroy any company it desires.[6] Given the company's Leftist views, this means every conservative website is on the endangered list.[7]

Even before Trump's election, a study found Google's search results have a liberal bias.[8] Now, Google is using the Southern Poverty Law Center to police content on YouTube, which Google owns.[9] Google is also censoring its search results to please various pressure groups, such as the Islamic lobby.[10]

Needless to say, modifying search results could have a massive impact

6   Ingram, Mathew. "The Facebook Armageddon." *Columbia Journalism Review*. Winter 2018. Accessed May 21, 2018. https://www.cjr.org/special_report/facebook-media-buzzfeed.php.

7   Hawkins, John. "How Conservatives Are Being Destroyed by Facebook, Twitter and Google Without Even Realizing It." *Townhall*. January 13, 2018. Accessed May 21, 2018. https://townhall.com/columnists/johnhawkins/2018/01/13/how-conservatives-are-being-destroyed-by-facebook-twitter-and-google-without-even-realizing-it-n2433962.

8   Nicas, Jack. "Google Search Results Can Lean Liberal, Study Finds." *The Wall Street Journal*. November 21, 2016. Accessed May 21, 2018. https://www.wsj.com/articles/google-search-results-can-lean-liberal-study-finds-1479760691.

9   Hasson, Peter. "EXCLUSIVE: YouTube Secretly Using SPLC To Police Videos." *The Daily Caller*. February 27, 2018. Accessed May 21, 2018. http://dailycaller.com/2018/02/27/google-youtube-southern-poverty-law-center-censorship/.

10 Spencer, Robert. "Google Changes Search Results to Conceal Criticism of Islam and Jihad." *LifeSiteNews*. August 2, 2017. Accessed May 21, 2018. https://www.lifesitenews.com/opinion/google-changes-search-results-to-conceal-criticism-of-islam-and-jihad.

on the upcoming midterm elections.[11] Michael Brendan Dougherty, writing at *National Review*, quotes Niall Ferguson's post-election prediction that "2016 will never happen again" because tech oligarchs won't let it. Dougherty suggests the tech oligopolies are currently trying to swing an upcoming referendum in Ireland on abortion by restricting online ads on the issue. Because the pro-abortion side of the referendum enjoys the all-but-universal support of traditional broadcast and print media, the tech oligarchs are effectively preventing the less-well-funded pro-lifers from combating media bias. Dougherty calls the situation "extremely serious" and asks: "If they [tech companies] feel the need to appease center-left critics by preemptively disarming Irish pro-lifers, whom will they seek to silence, and throttle, next?"[12]

The answer is obvious — us. The war has already begun. Joseph Farah, the head of one of the oldest conservative websites, *WND*, argues that Google and Facebook are conducting a "scorched earth campaign" against independent media — and that our government's regulatory agencies do not understand the new online environment:

> The U.S. government has long recognized its responsibility in preserving a free and open environment of debate ever since the dawn of radio and television, by ensuring that the *means of distribution* of such content did not fall into the hands of monopoly control. The Federal Communications Commission has prevented media consolidation in individual markets. But, with the advent of the internet, local media consolidation poses less of a threat than national and international media consolidation.[13]

11 Bondi-Camacho, Haelena. "Beyond Cambridge Analytica: How Tech Giants Can Impact Elections." Capital Research Center. April 19, 2018. Accessed May 21, 2018. https://capitalresearch.org/article/beyond-cambridge-analytica-how-tech-giants-can-impact-elections/.

12 Dougherty, Michael Brendan. "Silicon Valley Deletes the Pro-Life Campaign in Ireland." *National Review*. May 09, 2018. Accessed May 21, 2018. https://www.nationalreview.com/2018/05/silicon-valley-deletes-the-pro-life-campaign-in-ireland/.

13 Farah, Joseph. "Google-Facebook Control of Speech Is Threat to Nation." *WND*. April 01, 2018. Accessed May 21, 2018. http://www.wnd.com/2018/04/google-facebook-control-of-speech-is-threat-to-nation/.

The good news is that at least some conservatives seem to be awakening to this reality. Thus, Senator Ted Cruz, in a recent op-ed for Fox News, argued that Facebook should be considered a "neutral public forum" that cannot engage in political censorship. It must be "neutral" in order to enjoy the protection of Section 230 of the Communications Decency Act (CDA), which prevents social networks from being held liable for illegal threats made on their platform. Needless to say, Facebook could not function without such protection. But with this legal privilege comes the responsibility to protect freedom of speech. As Ted Cruz put it:

> [I]f Facebook is busy censoring legal, protected speech for political reasons, the company should be held accountable for the posts it lets through. And it should not enjoy any special congressional immunity from liability for its actions.[14]

Why isn't Heritage taking up Senator Cruz's call? A possible answer: as noted, is that Facebook is seeking to counter accusations of bias by recruiting outside forces to determine what is "biased" and what is not. Instead of an objective standard or the general protection of free speech, Facebook will meet with "advisors" — including, not surprisingly, Klon Kitchen of Heritage. The point man for the effort is the useless former GOP senator from Arizona, John Kyl.[15]

The endgame is obvious. Heritage is in a position of huge power because of this decision. As it is, after all, the organization that fired Jason Richwine for realistically discussing immigration policy, it certainly won't

14 Cruz, Ted. "Facebook Has Been Censoring or Suppressing Conservative Speech for Years." Fox News. April 11, 2018. Accessed May 21, 2018. http://www.foxnews.com/opinion/2018/04/11/sen-ted-cruz-facebook-has-been-censoring-or-suppressing-conservative-speech-for-years.html.

15 Guynn, Jessica. "Is Facebook Too Liberal? It Pledges to Investigate Charges It's Biased against Conservatives." USA Today. May 03, 2018. Accessed May 21, 2018. https://www.usatoday.com/story/tech/news/2018/05/03/facebook-pledges-investigate-charges-bias-against-conservatives/574505002/.

protect free speech as such.[16] Instead, it will seek protection for Conservatism Inc. by telling Facebook to purge, censor, and deplatform nationalists and populists, thus continuing the defining tradition of the useless Beltway Right. Conservatism Inc. is just as much of an enemy of free speech as are Google and Facebook.

The answer: government or judicial action to protect freedom of debate online. All legal speech needs protection, and as the late Christopher Hitchens famously argued (paraphrasing John Stuart Mill), those who speak differently don't just deserve the right to speak, but "That person's right to speak must be given extra protection."[17]

But the fact that the Heritage Foundation isn't championing a principled view of freedom of speech suggests that it is more interested in increasing its own power, not in protecting Americans' fundamental liberties or, for that matter, any chance of Republicans winning another election.

As demographics continue to change because of mass immigration, the white cultural norm of freedom of speech will come under increasing pressure. If it is to be preserved, there must be action now. If there is not action, America will no longer be a free country but just another autocracy — one with a ruling caste far more unaccountable and hostile to the host population than anything that exists in Moscow.

16 Kirkpatrick, James. "No Way Out But Through-Jason Richwine And The Future of Conservatism." *VDARE.* May 15, 2013. Accessed May 24, 2018. https://www.vdare.com/articles/no-way-out-but-through-jason-richwine-and-the-future-of-conservatism-inc.

17 The Editors. "Christopher Hitchens: 'Freedom of Speech Means Freedom to Hate.'" *The Skeptical Libertarian.* September 30, 2014. Accessed May 21, 2018. http://blog.skepticallibertarian.com/2014/09/30/christopher-hitchens-freedom-of-speech-means-freedom-to-hate/.

CHAPTER ELEVEN

RYANISM IS DEAD
But Has It Killed Trumpism?

"It was all a game, or a way of making a living," said Joe Sobran about the conservative movement.[1] And what a living it is. Paul Ryan, Republican Speaker of the House, is cashing out and will not run for re-election. Like his fellow former "young gun" Eric Cantor, who moved on to making millions on Wall Street as an investment banker,[2] Ryan is now poised for a lucrative post-political career.[3]

Ryan seems to think he can hold his position for the remainder of this Congress, but the fact is that he has selfishly abandoned a party terrified of what may be a historic defeat in the upcoming midterm elections, with one Republican incumbent after another trying to duck out. And all the Republicans running for the exits are getting ready to pin the blame on President Donald Trump.[4]

1   Sobran, Joe. "How I Got Fired by Bill Buckley." Burlingame, CA: Center for Libertarian Studies, 1994. Accessed May 22, 2018. https://web.archive.org/web/20080602094748/ http://www.mecfilms.com/universe/articles/fired.htm.

2   Caldwell, Patrick. "Surprise! Former GOP Leader Eric Cantor Lands $3.4 Million Finance Job." *Mother Jones*. September 2, 2014. Accessed May 21, 2018. https://www.motherjones.com/politics/2014/09/eric-cantor-cashes-34-million-wall-street/.

3   Green, Jeff, John McCormick, and Bill Allison. "Ryan Poised to Earn Millions Even If He Sheds 'Weekend Dad' Role." *Bloomberg*. April 12, 2018. Accessed May 21, 2018. https://www.bloomberg.com/news/articles/2018-04-12/ryan-poised-to-earn-millions-even-if-he-sheds-weekend-dad-role.

4   Kamisar, Ben. "Loss of Ryan Hits Hard for House Republicans." *The Hill*. April 12, 2018. Accessed May 21, 2018. http://thehill.com/homenews/campaign/382773-loss-of-ryan-hits-hard-for-house-republicans.

Even by his own wonkish standard of limiting government spending and preventing the fiscal crisis of soaring entitlement costs, Paul Ryan is a failure. Indeed, Ryan somehow managed the impressive task of funding the Left's priorities while not funding those of his president in the latest Omnibus spending bill.[5]

Yet this presupposes that Paul Ryan's job was to achieve political victories. It wasn't. It's like saying "political consultants" Rick Wilson or Ana Navarro have the job of winning elections. In fact, their job is to get money from the gullible and denounce the Republican base on Left-dominated Main Stream Media. They are good at their job — once you understand what it is. Similarly, Paul Ryan was good at his job. He delivered for his donors with the tax cut and he is now moving on to his reward.

Still, that leaves other Republicans in Congress who are fiercely opposed to the president personally but who want to stay in office until they too can arrange their payoffs. Obviously, what they intend to do is to make sure any upcoming political defeat is blamed entirely on President Trump, not on the GOP generally.

Conservative pundit Erick Erickson, a longtime opponent of President Trump, recently claimed that a Republican Congressman told him he hates the president, is eager to impeach Trump, and only defends the nominal leader of the GOP publicly because he has to for political reasons.[6] Naturally, this Republican lawmaker also blames the supposedly forthcoming "Blue Wave" on President Trump himself. There are many reasons to question Erickson's own political judgement, but he does not have the reputation of a liar. And this tale fits exactly with how the Congressional Republican Party is behaving.

---

5   "Washington Watcher." "GOP Punts On Immigration. They Might Get Away With It — But Will America?" *VDARE.* March 26, 2018. Accessed May 21, 2018. https://www.vdare.com/articles/gop-punts-on-immigration-they-might-get-away-with-it-but-will-america.

6   Erickson, Erick. "A Congressman's Profanity Laced Tirade in a Safeway Grocery Store." *The Resurgent.* April 11, 2018. Accessed May 21, 2018. https://web.archive.org/web/20180411205258/https://www.themaven.net/theresurgent/erick-erickson/a-congressman-s-profanity-laced-tirade-in-a-safeway-grocery-store-SeHI2l5bIECGQn4gmnzGaw/?mc_cid=10d8170a1d&mc_eid=3cc50e048e&full=1.

The endgame is equally clear. The Democrats retake Congress, move to impeach, and Congressional Republicans pretend to be "shocked, shocked" at whatever the unlimited investigation digs up. Vice President Mike Pence takes over (one reason so many of us opposed his selection) and the Republicans try to go back to being the polite losers of the Barack Obama years.

The irony, of course, is that President Trump set himself up for betrayal by adopting Speaker Ryan's agenda in the critical first days of his administration. In Trump's book *The Art of the Comeback*, he wrote: "Some of the people who forgot to lift a finger when I needed them, when I was down, they need my help now, and I'm screwing them against the wall."[7] But he didn't do this after the election.

Even though many Republicans, including Paul Ryan, did their best to throw the 2016 contest, President Trump reacted not with vengeance but with mercy. Indeed, in what Steve Bannon called the "original sin" of the administration, the President turned to old GOP hands to fill his staff and push standard GOP policies such as tax cuts, deregulation, and a repeal of Obamacare.[8]

Needless to say, the MSM, has got this completely backwards (e.g., "Paul Ryan Personifies the Devil's Bargain the GOP Struck With Trump"[9]) — no doubt because of the need to galvanize the Left by caricaturing Trump as extreme.

On one level, President Trump's "original sin" — or "Devil's

---

7   Glover, Scott, Maeve Reston, and Brenna Williams. "How Donald Trump Sees Himself." CNN. April 01, 2016. Accessed May 21, 2018. https://www.cnn.com/2016/04/01/politics/how-donald-trump-sees-himself/index.html.

8   Shepherd, Todd, and Evan Vucci. "Steve Bannon: Trump Administration's 'original Sin' Was Embracing the Establishment." *Washington Examiner*. September 10, 2017. Accessed May 21, 2018. https://www.washingtonexaminer.com/steve-bannon-trump-administrations-original-sin-was-embracing-the-establishment/article/2633966.

9   Brownstein, Ronald. "Paul Ryan Personifies the Devil's Bargain the GOP Struck With Trump." *The Atlantic*. April 11, 2018. Accessed May 21, 2018. https://www.theatlantic.com/politics/archive/2018/04/paul-ryan-personifies-the-devils-bargain-the-gop-struck-with-trump/557783/.

Bargain" — hurt him because his administration has been plagued with leaks from disloyal staffers from day one. Yet it was on policy grounds that Trump's gesture of unity failed most spectacularly.

President Trump committed himself to repealing and replacing Obamacare only to find that, after years of campaigning against it, the conservative movement and the Republican Party didn't have a plan for what they wanted to replace it with. This failure is now looming over the midterms, as health care is consistently identified as the top issue for most voters. Traditional conservatives are furious that Obamacare was not repealed while swing voters will blame the incumbent party for rising premiums.[10]

Republican voters specifically identify immigration as the most important issue in midterm elections.[11] Indeed, Paul Ryan's departure is being mourned by the open-borders lobby.[12] With Ryan out, the chattering classes are also denouncing Trump's GOP, which is described by Chuck Todd and others as the "opposite" of Ryan's GOP on immigration.[13]

Yet the post-election "Trump Effect" appears to be over — illegal immigration is rebounding and American workers are once again being displaced by foreigners.[14] As Ann Coulter reminds us every day, there is also

---

10 Burns, Caitlin Huey. "Could Health Care Come Back to Hurt GOP in Midterms?" RealClearPolitics. March 30, 2018. Accessed May 21, 2018. https://www.realclearpolitics.com/articles/2018/03/30/could_health_care_come_back_to_hurt_gop_in_midterms_136669.html.

11 Binder, John. "Republican Voters: Immigration Most Important Issue in Midterm Elections." *Breitbart*. March 21, 2018. Accessed May 21, 2018. http://www.breitbart.com/big-government/2018/03/21/republican-voters-immigration-most-important-issue-in-midterm-elections/.

12 Munro, Neil. "Amnesty Advocates Mourn Ryan's Exit." *Breitbart*. April 12, 2018. Accessed May 21, 2018. http://www.breitbart.com/immigration/2018/04/11/amnesty-advocates-mourn-paul-ryan-exit/.

13 Todd, Chuck, Mark Murray, and Carrie Dann. "With Paul Ryan's Exit, Trump's Hold on the GOP Is Now Complete." NBC News. April 12, 2018. Accessed May 21, 2018. https://www.nbcnews.com/politics/first-read/paul-ryan-s-exit-trump-s-hold-gop-now-complete-n865346.

14 Rubenstein, Edwin S. "National Data | March Jobs — Trump Effect OVER,

no border wall. And, for some unknown reason, President Trump refuses to mention a remittance tax, which would not only fund the wall but
make Mexico pay for it. Immigration patriots, in short, are not energized
to turn out for Trump.

President Trump is also reportedly wobbling on trade, the other key
issue besides immigration that allowed him to win the Rust Belt. Senator
Ben Sasse, one of the Republicans who hates President Trump most, is
gleefully reporting that America may rejoin the Trans-Pacific Partnership.[15] Why President Trump is siding with Ben Sasse, who didn't support
him during the election, instead of with his voters, is mystifying.

President Trump didn't win as a normal Republican. It's doubtful
a normal Republican could have won in 2016 or, maybe, can ever win
again — Ryanism is dead electorally, even if Washington, D.C. hasn't no-
ticed yet. President Trump won because he ran as a "national conservative" — on a platform of immigration restriction, a nationalist trade agenda, a restrained foreign policy, and populist economic policies.

Trump could have functioned as a kind of Third Party unto himself, working with Democrats on issues like infrastructure and trade and
driving wedges into that party's coalition. Instead, President Trump has
trusted the very Republicans whom he spent the whole primary fighting — especially Speaker Ryan. He put his MAGA movement, his personal
appeal, and his populist credentials at the service of Ryan's Chamber of
Commerce Republicanism.

The result has been the worst of both worlds: hatred of President
Trump energized the Left while GOP establishment policies did nothing
to expand President Trump's coalition on the Right.

Displacement/Foreign-Born Population Surge To New Highs. Legislation Needed
NOW." *VDARE*. April 09, 2018. Accessed May 24, 2018. https://www.vdare.com/
articles/national-data-march-jobs-trump-effect-over-displacement-foreign-born-
population-surge-to-new-highs-legislation-needed-now.

15 Spiering, Charlie. "Ben Sasse: Donald Trump Ready to Rejoin TPP and Help
American Farmers." *Breitbart*. April 12, 2018. Accessed May 21, 2018. http://www.
breitbart.com/big-government/2018/04/12/ben-sasse-donald-trump-ready-rejoin-
tpp/.

Now, Speaker Ryan is getting out to enjoy his reward, leaving President Trump to take the fall.

Maybe Trump's luck, always amazing, will continue. In a savage *New York Times* column entitled "Good Riddance, Mr. Speaker" American Greatness editor Christopher Buskirk writes "For his entire career, Mr. Ryan has been the wunderkind who couldn't deliver," and concludes, entirely correctly, that:

> Republicans need a leader who is in step with the president and his agenda, one who emphasizes pro-citizen immigration policies, pro-worker economic policies and an America First national security policy that is circumspect about foreign military intervention.[16]

Maybe one will emerge. Maybe. But the bottom line is that Donald Trump has now only a few months to turn things around. Candidate Trump, populist wrecking ball, could overcome this situation. But it's uncertain whether President Trump, leader of the Republican Party, still can.

---

16 Buskirk, Christopher. "Good Riddance, Mr. Speaker." *The New York Times*. April 12, 2018. Accessed May 21, 2018. https://www.nytimes.com/2018/04/11/opinion/paul-ryan-retiring-speaker.html.

POSTSCRIPT

National Conservatism
AFTER TRUMP

Political reporters and conservative "intellectuals" like to pretend Donald Trump came out of nowhere. Nothing could be further from the truth. For those who were paying attention, there had been a new movement taking shape within the Republican Party in recent years. Over the last decade, the conservative grassroots was able to repeatedly defeat top-down-driven efforts by the GOP leadership, the mass media, and even GOP presidents like George W. Bush to implement amnesty for illegal aliens. Despite being almost unrepresented in major Beltway Right institutions, immigration restrictionism proved to be the singular issue that allowed a political leader to establish credibility with the Republican base. From John McCain to Marco Rubio, one prospective GOP "leader" after another foundered on the rocks of "comprehensive immigration reform," as the Republican base made it clear again and again that it was unwilling to follow its self-appointed spokesmen. This was especially striking because the push for immigration liberalization was not just coming from groups like the Chamber of Commerce, but even from supposedly "authentic" conservatives. After all, year after year the organizers of the Conservative Political Action Conference (CPAC) would stack panels on immigration with amnesty supporters.

Perhaps even more important was the conservative rebellion on trade. Despite the long Republican tradition of protectionism, "free trade" has become a pillar, not just of conventional Republicanism, but of the "true conservative" creed. From *National Review* to Ben Shapiro, from Speaker of the House Paul Ryan to 2012 standard-bearer Mitt Romney, both conservative opinion makers and Republican politicians seemed unanimously in support of economic globalization. Until recently, the only figures recognizable to the average conservative that would consistently oppose "free trade" were Pat Buchanan and the late Phyllis Schlafly,[1] neither of whom are popular among the Beltway Right. And yet the Trans-Pacific Partnership experienced huge opposition from grassroots conservatives.

There was one, and only one established political leader credibly taking the lead on both these positions. That was Alabama Senator Jeff Sessions (with an assist from his policy aide Stephen Miller). Since Congressman Tom Tancredo's unfortunate retirement,[2] Senator Sessions had been the leading immigration patriot in Congress. And in the run up to the 2016 election, Senator Sessions was also helping to rally opposition to globalist trade deals, using *Breitbart* as his megaphone to the outside world. Critically, Senator Sessions (presumably with Miller's help) made the economic case on both of these issues, repeatedly pointing out that mass immigration and "free trade" were a direct attack on American workers. The only people who benefited from this were those Senator Miller characterized as plutocratic "masters of the universe" who had no loyalty to this country.[3]

It is often said that Donald Trump has no long-standing political principles, but this isn't true when it comes to free trade. He's been critical of such agreements since the 1980s. However, despite his campaign boasts about "building the wall" and deporting illegals, many conservatives during the primaries were concerned that they could not trust Trump

---

1 Schlafly, Phyllis. "Free Trade Cheats Americans." January 22, 2013. Accessed March 28, 2019. https://www.creators.com/read/phyllis-schlafly/01/13/free-trade-cheats-americans.

2 Associated Press. "Tancredo retires." *Politico*. August 12, 2008. Accessed March 28, 2019. https://www.politico.com/story/2008/12/tancredo-retires-016296.

3 Key, Pam. "Sessions: America Not an Oligarchy Where Masters of the Universe Decide Immigration Law." *Breitbart*. September 18, 2014. Accessed January 10, 2019. https://www.breitbart.com/video/2014/09/18/sessions-america-is-not-an-oligarchy-where-the-masters-of-the-universe-decide-immigration-law/.

on immigration. It was this concern over whether Trump was for real that pushed so many conservatives behind Ted Cruz. During the early stage of the Republican primaries, Donald Trump was in desperate need of someone to give him a stamp of authenticity, for someone with a real connection with the conservative grassroots to anoint him as the chosen standard-bearer for the new populism.

More than that, because Ted Cruz so completely personified what it meant to be a "true conservative," Donald Trump needed a subtly different brand. Trump wasn't a "true conservative," but a "conservative of the heart," as Pat Buchanan put it during his own campaigns. Trump would exemplify the hopes and aspirations of the betrayed American working class, gutted by both outsourcing and mass immigration. Yet for the reality TV star to be taken seriously, he needed someone to vouch for him.

The only person who could give Donald Trump that standing was Senator Jeff Sessions. And when Jeff Sessions put on that red MAGA hat in Alabama, it seemed like the beginning of a new age. Donald Trump promised that if he were nominated, the GOP would be a "workers' party." Nationalist trade policies, nonintervention (as exemplified by Trump's scorn for the Bushes and their Iraq war), and immigration restriction would be the new pillars of the GOP. The issues of the heart Pat Buchanan talked about many years ago[4] would become the main policy priorities, rather than the entitlement cuts Paul Ryan and his cohorts so lusted for. The GOP would become a nationalist party rather than a thinly veiled corporate lobbying conglomeration.

Now, at the midpoint of the Trump Administration, many of these hopes are dashed. To be fair, President Trump has done more on immigration than perhaps any other president of the last few decades, and Jeff Sessions has repealed many of the Obama Administration's more egregious administrative policies. Yet the fact remains that there is no wall, no mandatory E-Verify, and no major immigration restrictionist legislation.

4   Alberta, Tim. "'The Ideas Made It, But I Didn't.'" *Politico*. May/June 2017. Accessed March 28, 2019. https://www.politico.com/magazine/story/2017/04/22/pat-buchanan-trump-president-history-profile-215042.

Both the president and his Attorney General have the reputation of being hardliners on the immigration issue, yet little of substance has been accomplished and what they have done will just be reversed by the next administration.

More importantly, President Trump's relationship with Jeff Sessions has been completely destroyed by the Russian "meddling" investigation.[5] Even as this is being written, President Donald Trump is once again taking to Twitter to slam his Attorney General for not doing enough to protect him. Of course, ultimately, it is Donald Trump who handed his enemies a sword to attack him, particularly by not firing James Comey on his first day in office. Though Jeff Sessions could have done more to squelch the ridiculous and subversive Mueller investigation, even the best Attorney General may well have been thwarted by President Trump's self-destructive tendencies. However, because of President Trump's strong personal bond with his core supporters, "Sleepy" Jeff Sessions has become a figure of hatred and scorn among many right-wingers. This is a tragedy not just for the president, but for the whole national conservative movement that once seemed so promising. Considering the scope of the disaster, it's perhaps fitting that the Republicans even managed to lose Jeff Sessions's Alabama Senate seat to the Democrats.[6]

The conservatism that Jeff Sessions was creating was something akin to National Conservatism, an ideology far more recognizable in Europe than in the United States. National Conservatism puts the culture, identity and sovereignty of the nation-state first, rather than prizing an abstract dedication to "limited government" or "free markets." Though the term is rarely used, it is clearly what is invoked with campaign slogans such as

---

5 "Attorney General Jess Session Resigns at Trump's Request." *Washington Post.* November 07, 2018. Accessed March 28, 2019. https://www.washingtonpost.com/world/national-security/attorney-general-jeff-sessions-resigns-at-trumps-request/2018/11/07/d1b7a214-e144-11e8-ab2c-b31dcd53ca6b_story.html.

6 Brimelow, Peter. "'Blessed Are Ye, When Men Shall Revile You'—Roy Moore vs. Christophobia And The Homosexual Lobby." *VDARE.* December 07, 2017. Accessed March 28, 2019. https://vdare.com/articles/blessed-are-ye-when-men-shall-revile-you-roy-moore-vs-christophobia-and-the-homosexual-lobby.

Make America Great Again and proposals to revitalize the space program, prohibit flag burning, and protect American industry from unfair competition. As President Trump's election victory proved, there is a vast constituency for this kind of program, especially white working class voters in the Rust Belt who gave the Republicans victory in the Electoral College. However, because of the nature of the conservative movement, National Conservatism remains inchoate, incoherent, and undefined. "Nationalism" is even something of a dirty word to the Beltway Right.

National Conservatism is a ghost, an impulse, a will-o'-the-wisp fluttering in and out of the Beltway Right. Conservatism can't win on its stated policy preferences of entitlement cuts, foreign interventionism, and upper-class tax breaks. It must appeal to nationalist symbols and anti-leftist sentiment to generate populist energy. However, the actual policy agenda that would create a truly populist, nationalist movement is a non-starter within Conservatism Inc. The American Right is thus doomed to a phony populism, with enough nationalist dog whistles to infuriate and energize leftists but not enough substance to win over a loyal constituency.

The way out, of course, is to overcome Conservatism Inc. Senator Jeff Sessions started that process and Donald Trump could have completed it. But President Trump's has largely governed like a typical "movement conservative" — like Mike Pence, as Ben Shapiro bragged.[7] "Never Trump" conservatives, despite opposing the GOP nominee throughout the primaries, also received most of the administration jobs. Thus, at the very moment of victory, the National Conservatives who could have lain out a policy agenda and built a new winning Republican coalition have been excluded from power. As always, the true right is never defeated — only betrayed. The result is the worst of both worlds — an administration that is condemned as "nationalist" and "far-right" when it is the same old

---

7   Benson, Guy. "'Never Trump' Conservative Ben Shapiro Explains Why He's Now 'More Apt' to Support Trump in 2020, Warns Against GOP Primary Challenge." *Townhall.* August 08, 2018. Accessed January 10, 2019. https://townhall.com/tipsheet/guybenson/2018/08/08/listen-never-trump-conservative-ben-shapiro-makes-the-case-for-trump-2020-warns-against-a-gop-primary-challenge-n2507814.

Conservatism Inc. What's more, Jeff Sessions's future has been ruined by his entry into the administration and the resulting tensions with Trump.

And yet Donald Trump, despite his many failures, may still hold the key to building a new National Conservative GOP, even if his administration fails. The Republican base still largely supports him, and candidates such as Kris Kobach, Lou Barletta, and Corey Stewart continue to win Republican primaries. All it would take is one Republican politician with a bit more polish than Trump to step forward and claim his legacy. Senator Tom Cotton of Arkansas is one strong possibility. Though the conservative movement itself has learned nothing, the Republican base has, and it is doubtful someone like Mitt Romney could ever again win a majority of GOP voters. Indeed, if Trump fails, the resulting Democratic government will likely be so extreme and so overtly anti-right that the next Republican leader will make Trump himself look like Gerald Ford.

Since the catastrophe of the first Unite the Right rally in Charlottesville, Virginia, the Alt Right has lost whatever foothold it had in the Republican party. Yet there remains a constituency hungry for populist economic policies, civic nationalism, and opposition to political correctness. President Trump was not the God-Emperor we hoped for, nor a sufficiently canny politician to reorient the Republican Party in a National Conservative direction. However, he has eased the path for a future Republican to do so. The 2016 primaries proved Conservatism Inc. doesn't have much of a constituency outside the Beltway, and it is unlikely to gain strength in the future, regardless of what President Trump does or doesn't do. The winning nationalist coalition is still there, waiting for a politician ambitious enough to claim it. The only danger is that mass immigration will extinguish the American nation itself before a leader can step forward.

AFTERWORD

John Derbyshire

The essays by my colleague James Kirkpatrick in this book cover the years 2013-2018 — in terms of U.S. politics, the two and a half cycles from the 2012 presidential election to the 2018 midterms.

That six-year span was not sensationally eventful. There were no new major wars, no devastating economic crises, no genocides or nation-shaking terrorist atrocities (although James gives fair coverage to "The Lesson of *Charlie Hebdo*"), no annexations or re-arrangements of national borders, no great plagues or natural disasters. These were, by historical standards, a quiet six years.

To Americans, however, they didn't *seem* quiet. The riots in Ferguson, Mo. and Baltimore; the rise of Black Lives Matter and Antifa; Donald Trump's dramatic victory in November 2016; the Unite the Right rally in Charlottesville, Va. the following August; anti-Trump hysteria on the political left; disorientation and paralysis in the Republican Party... We have been getting a strong impression of familiar patterns shifting and altering, of molds being broken, of old things lame and helpless in senility while new things struggle to be born.

When we look across to the European homelands we see the same. The globalist-managerialist hegemony personified by the European Union is beginning to crack and split. Britain's June 2016 vote to leave the EU opened the most visible fissure; but there are now significant nationalist parties in all the main European countries. In their efforts to thwart these parties, the established political powers in those countries are abandoning ancient liberties and borrowing techniques of news manipulation and information suppression from the mid-20th-century totalitarian regimes.

Lurking behind all the storm and fury is the implacable arithmetic of demography. Of the forty-seven European nations and territories listed in the *CIA World Factbook*, only the Faroe Islands, pop. 51,000, has a Total Fertility Rate above 2.09 children per woman; while Portugal, Poland, Romania, and Bosnia are all below 1.4. Of the fifty-six African nations and territories listed, only four, with total population eight million, have a TFR *less* than 2.09; while Mali, Chad, Burundi, Angola, and Niger are all 5.9 or higher.

North America does not face quite such dramatic contrasts. The highest TFR in our neighborhood is Guatemala's at 2.87. Mexico's is a mere 2.22. However, all the nations to our immediate south are ill-governed, with massive social inequality and great numbers of desperately poor inhabitants. The smaller Central American nations are little more than gangster fiefs whose law enforcement authorities, and some of whose actual governments, are hirelings of the crime bosses. Inhabitants of these places who can afford the people-smugglers' fees are just as keen to escape to orderly, prosperous countries further north as are Africans.

None of this would matter much if First World nations had a robust desire to control immigration in the interests of their own citizens. A few do, including even some of those with the lowest fertility rates: Hungary (1.45), Japan (1.42), Poland (1.36). Most do not. Instead they — we — watch passively while massive migrant inflows depress our workers' wages, strain our welfare systems, establish alien colonies in our towns and cities, and disperse the social capital painstakingly built up over centuries of common ethnicity.

What accounts for that passivity? Some of the motive forces are in plain sight. Big old established political parties in the Western world are financed and supported largely by capitalists, for whom the price of labor can never be too low. Foreigners from poor places are cheaper than our own citizens. Foreigners present *illegally* in one's country who fear deportation will not complain about working conditions.

Social and racial antagonisms are also in play. I use the phrase "Cold Civil War" to cover the purely social aspect, defining it as analogous to the Hot Civil War of the 1860s: "two big groups of white people who can't stand the sight of each other."

In the eyes of one group, the other group is composed of boorish sneering rednecks who drive rusting pickup trucks with a gun rack behind the driver's seat and who spend their Sunday mornings handling snakes and speaking in tongues. The converse stereotype is of effete big-city professionals with untucked shirts and close-trimmed facial hair sipping a seven-dollar cup of designer coffee while fretting about Global Warming and the sufferings of poor people in remote countries.

In the U.S.A. the old specter of race is a factor in complicated ways. The Goodwhite — the start-up data analyst sipping his Toasted White Chocolate Mocha Frappuccino at Starbucks — sees his Badwhite enemy as filled with hatred and resentment towards nonwhites, especially towards blacks and south-of-the-border Amerindians. On the premises of Moral Foundation Theory, this strongly offends the Goodwhite's high score on the care/harm axis.

His fretful universalism slops over into anti-white ethnomasochism, especially in the academy, where freshman students are now put through compulsory courses on the wickedness of "white supremacy" and the injustice of "white privilege." The Goodwhite does not usually hate himself — much more often he takes smug pride in his own high virtue — but he hates those *other* whites, and their ancestors, and the nation they built.

Conversely with the Badwhite, who is correspondingly upset by Goodwhite pet projects like Affirmative Action or sanctuary policies for illegal aliens. These policies offend his preferences for fairness and ingroup loyalty. He is probably also scornful of Goodwhite snobbery and hypocrisy as captured by, for example, Joe Sobran's quip that "The purpose of a college education is to give you the correct view of minorities, and the means to live as far away from them as possible."

These are the main motive forces of the Cold Civil War. Some observers, drawing on evolutionary biology, have speculated that they are epiphenomena of something deeper. Strange psychic aberrations like ethnomasochism are commonest among northwest Europeans, especially

Anglo-Saxons and Scandinavians. These are also, of all the world's peoples, the ones most successful at creating stable, consensual national governments with high levels of trust among their people.

Are these two peculiarities related? Is the first just the dark side of the
second? Do the normal human attachments of family and tribe somehow curdle, in a high-trust society, into binary loathing of co-ethnics and
pathological altruism towards outsiders?

I can't give an opinion, not understanding evolutionary biology very
well and not having given sufficient close attention to the arguments. The
Cold Civil War is a reality, though. Its passions dominate our political life,
and increasingly our cultural life, too.

U.S. immigration policy has been a major theater of the Cold Civil War. To stretch the military analogy somewhat, across the past thir-
ty-some years that theater has resembled the static Western Front of
World War One more than any other actual battle zone.

Ronald Reagan inherited the ill-thought-out lackadaisical immigration policies of the previous four administrations — policies rooted in
mid-20th-century assumptions about demography, Cold War hopes that
U.S. hospitality to Third Worlders would dull the appeal of communism
to them, and sentimental romanticization of pre-World War One "Great
Wave" immigrants by their children and grandchildren.

Those policies had gifted the U.S.A. with a big population of illegal
aliens. Reagan's administration attempted to deal with this in 1986 by legislation awarding amnesty to resident illegal aliens while penalizing employers who hired illegals in the future. The amnesty was duly awarded,
but the penal clauses were scotched by powerful business lobbies.

The third of a century that has elapsed since then has been one of
utter stasis in immigration policy. At the time of writing in early 2019 I
have been engaged in transcribing podcasts I made in the mid-2000s. It
has been very depressing to see that the suggestions, criticisms, and complaints I was offering on immigration policy twelve, thirteen, fourteen
years ago are precisely the same as those I offer today.

In law and policy nothing has been changed, nothing has been done.

Our nation's borders and ports of entry are as wide open as ever. Appeals to Ellis Island romanticism are as loud as ever. Employers are as blithe as ever about employing illegal aliens.

The rules on *legal* immigration still allow businesses to replace American workers with cheaper indentured foreign ones, still permit each generation of immigrants to select the next generation via "chain migration," still offer asylum and refugee status — with full welfare rights — to claimants with unverifiable sob stories, still encourage "obstetric tourism" with birthright citizenship, still award a huge annual tranche of visas by blind lottery, still apparently think it beneficent to strip-mine poor, backward nations of their small supplies of talent and enterprise.

To be sure, battles have been fought. Immigration boosters have tried to replicate their 1986 success with similar legislative packages promising to improve the rules with enhanced enforcement in return for large-scale amnesties — "comprehensive immigration reform." Like the "big push" offensives across No Man's Land in World War One, these efforts have all foundered in the mud as angry citizens jammed congressional switchboards with their objections.

One of the biggest of these offensives was the "Gang of Eight" bipartisan (four Republican senators, four Democrats) amnesty/enforcement bill of 2013, which actually passed the Senate in June of that year but then died in committee. James Kirkpatrick catches the tail end of this battle in an early essay here, "Defining America Down."

With the election of Donald Trump in 2016 it seemed that the long stalemate might at last be broken. A wide bench of establishment Republicans, including one of the Gang of Eight senators, had been driven from the field by Trump in that party's primaries. The candidate's promises to put the interests of his countrymen ahead of the interests of foreigners, to end the futile missionary wars of his predecessors, and above all to end illegal immigration across our southern border by building a wall, had captured the imagination of ordinary patriotic Americans.

What followed was anticlimax. As James Kirkpatrick writes, in what I think is the most eloquent of the essays here:

President Trump himself, while unquestionably the best president of my life-time, was not the revolutionary change we had been hoping for. His main legislative accomplishment has been a tax cut any Republican would have pushed for, and as of this writing, there has still been no wall. There is no sense of urgency to his policies; he governs with the same sense of complacency as George Bush, seemingly forgetting his own rhetoric from the campaign about how mass immigration imposes a time limit on how long Republicans can continue to win elections without changing the demographic equation.

It is now plain, I think, that Donald Trump is a transitional figure. We may hope that somewhere in the U.S.A.'s future is a more attentive, more focused, more politically adept campaigner who will restore our national sovereignty, preserve our constitutional liberties, and restore sanity to our immigration policy.

We may also, of course, reasonably fear — as James implies in the passage just quoted — that it is now too late for hope, that the demographic tipping point has been passed. Our nation's future then will be one of rancor and division, leading perhaps at last to actual physical disunion. This wonderful experiment in continental-scale republican government will then be at an end.

James Kirkpatrick declares himself on the side of hope: "I have faith that the best days of our movement, our country, and our people still lie before us." As the father of two young American adults, I long to believe that is true.

Still I wonder why a nation with such tremendous achievements in its past, that put human beings on the Moon in a mere ten years from a standing start, that all through my English childhood was marveled at as a paragon of liberty and common prosperity, as the "can-do" nation for which nothing was impossible, as the vanquisher of great militaristic empires despite having no very outstanding military tradition herself, as the generator of endlessly imaginative and globally fascinating popular culture — why cannot this nation, after thirty-odd years of wrangling, make no progress whatsoever on such an elementary task as securing her own borders?

Well, there are many futures. May James Kirkpatrick's hopes prevail over my own doubts! In any case I thank him for describing with such clarity and insight, from a National Conservative viewpoint, the contours of our nation's political life—and some other nations', too. He has cast his net wide—over these strange last six years. That talents as large and wide as his are on our side is cause for hope all by itself. Onwards, then: onwards and upwards!

OTHER BOOKS PUBLISHED BY ARKTOS

Sri Dharma Pravartaka Acharya	*The Dharma Manifesto*
Joakim Andersen	*Rising from the Ruins: The Right of the 21st Century*
Winston C. Banks	*Excessive Immigration*
Alain de Benoist	*Beyond Human Rights*
	Carl Schmitt Today
	The Indo-Europeans
	Manifesto for a European Renaissance
	On the Brink of the Abyss
	The Problem of Democracy
	Runes and the Origins of Writing
	View from the Right (vol. 1–3)
Arthur Moeller van den Bruck	*Germany's Third Empire*
Matt Battaglioli	*The Consequences of Equality*
Kerry Bolton	*Revolution from Above*
	Yockey: A Fascist Odyssey
Isac Boman	*Money Power*
Ricardo Duchesne	*Faustian Man in a Multicultural Age*
Alexander Dugin	*Ethnos and Society*
	Ethnosociology
	Eurasian Mission
	The Fourth Political Theory
	Last War of the World-Island
	Political Platonism
	Putin vs Putin
	The Rise of the Fourth Political Theory
Edward Dutton	*Race Differences in Ethnocentrism*
Mark Dyal	*Hated and Proud*
Koenraad Elst	*Return of the Swastika*
Julius Evola	*The Bow and the Club*
	Fascism Viewed from the Right
	A Handbook for Right-Wing Youth

OTHER BOOKS PUBLISHED BY ARKTOS

RICHARD RUDGLEY	*Barbarians*
	Essential Substances
	Wildest Dreams
ERNST VON SALOMON	*It Cannot Be Stormed*
	The Outlaws
SRI SRI RAVI SHANKAR	*Celebrating Silence*
	Know Your Child
	Management Mantras
	Patanjali Yoga Sutras
	Secrets of Relationships
GEORGE T. SHAW (ED.)	*A Fair Hearing*
FENEK SOLÈRE	*Kraal*
OSWALD SPENGLER	*Man and Technics*
RICHARD STOREY	*The Uniqueness of Western Law*
TOMISLAV SUNIC	*Against Democracy and Equality*
	Homo Americanus
	Postmortem Report
	Titans are in Town
HANS-JÜRGEN SYBERBERG	*On the Fortunes and Misfortunes of Art in Post-War Germany*
ABIR TAHA	*Defining Terrorism*
	The Epic of Arya (2nd ed.)
	Nietzsche's Coming God, or the Redemption of the Divine
	Verses of Light
BAL GANGADHAR TILAK	*The Arctic Home in the Vedas*
DOMINIQUE VENNER	*For a Positive Critique*
	The Shock of History
MARKUS WILLINGER	*A Europe of Nations*
	Generation Identity
ALEXANDER WOLFHEZE	*Alba Rosa*

CPSIA information can be obtained
at www.ICGtesting.com
Printed in the USA
FSHW020744041119
63721FS